The Language of Contracts

A Handbook of Drafting Techniques

The Language of Contracts

A Handbook of Drafting Techniques

Ben Staveley
Retired solicitor

Bloomsbury Professional
LONDON • DUBLIN • EDINBURGH • NEW YORK • NEW DELHI • SYDNEY

BLOOMSBURY PROFESSIONAL
Bloomsbury Publishing Plc
50 Bedford Square, London, WC1B 3DP, UK
1385 Broadway, New York, NY 10018, USA
29 Earlsfort Terrace, Dublin 2, Ireland

British Library Cataloguing-in-Publication Data

A catalogue record for this book is available from the British Library.

ISBN:	PB:	978-1-52653-030-1
	ePDF:	978-1-52653-032-5
	ePub:	978-1-52653-031-8

Typeset by Evolution Design & Digital Ltd (Kent)
Printed and bound by CPI Group (UK) Ltd, Croydon, CRO 4YY

To find out more about our authors and books visit www.bloomsburyprofessional.com. Here you will find extracts, author information, details of forthcoming events and the option to sign up for our newsletters

Foreword

Precision of thought and language were drilled into me as a young solicitor in the tax department at Freshfields, some decades ago now. One of my teachers was Ben Staveley, the author of this book and at that time a partner in that firm. He was a brilliant tax lawyer, able to reduce the most complex commercial arrangements to their essentials, to overlay the tax legislation and case law, and then to explain the position in a series of straightforward and succinct propositions. Wow: if only all lawyers could do that!

In this book, I see Ben still beating the drum for precision of thought and language. He draws on his long experience of drafting and negotiating contracts to identify the danger areas. He uses his encyclopaedic knowledge of domestic case law to demonstrate the pitfalls. His point is that a well-crafted, carefully considered and clearly expressed contract can reduce or even remove the risk of a dispute arising between the contractual parties.

Disputes often end up being resolved by judges or arbitrators who will try to make sense of the words, context and intended business purpose. But as the author emphasises, this is not usually a good ending for the parties. If the case goes to litigation, '[T]he parties will have lost control of the contract, and be exposed to an outcome which will disappoint at least one of them, who will be faced with substantial cost' (from Chapter 1.4).

This is a very practical work. It aims to help lawyers who are involved in drafting and negotiating contracts. If that is you, keep the book on your shelf and thumb through it regularly, use it as a cross-check for your work, and etch the book's messages into your long-term memory. If you do that, I am confident that you will enhance your skills as a professional and be able to serve your clients better. You may also avoid the embarrassment of having to answer questions about what your contract means or, worse, the jeopardy of legal action to resolve an ambiguity.

This book also makes a valuable contribution to the wider cause of promoting clarity of expression by lawyers. Tradition is important to the legal profession; indeed, our common law is built on cases of the past. But we should not use the language of the past where it has become inaccessible or outmoded. The way we choose to talk about the law and to engage with non-lawyers should reflect contemporary society and be unashamedly modern.

Lady Justice Philippa Whipple
June 2024

Dedication

For Cathy

Preface

Right from the start, contract law is part of English law academic training. But few academic lawyers are primarily interested in how contracts are *drafted*. If they had been, they wouldn't have become academics in the first place.

Many practising lawyers, however, spend much of their working life preparing contracts – drafting them, adapting precedents, or poring over something put forward by the other side. (And, after the contracts are signed, looking through them to try and work out what they really mean.)

Lawyers receive some training on drafting in their vocational training at the start of their careers. Nonetheless, most lawyers probably learn most of their drafting skills in practice: 'on the job'. As a result, many might feel it counter-intuitive to analyse drafting *as a subject* as carefully as they analyse legal problems.

Does this matter? Evidence that it might takes the form of a seemingly never-abating flood of contract dispute cases reaching the courts every year. Many more cases must be being arbitrated or quietly settled. If drafters are trying to keep their clients away from expensive disputes, something is going awry. That impression is brought home to anyone who reads the cases. What emerges is a depressing pattern of recurrent types of mistake. Most of the cases cited in this work were decided this century, many in the 2020s. That rather proves that, despite all lawyers' harnessing of technical skills to make contract drafting easier and more efficient, something is still missing.

Will AI fill the gap? However AI comes to affect the drafting of contracts, it is hard to see how it can supplant the need for a practising lawyer to be able to scrutinise the draft that AI suggests and ask: does it work? Unless things change even more than anyone currently foresees, clients will still want to rely on a flesh-and-blood human being to tell them that the contract works. It may be that the role of the practising lawyer comes increasingly to resemble that of supervising a tireless junior who may just occasionally have misunderstood instructions. But to do so, the lawyer needs to have the same professional analytical skill as would have been needed to draft the contract from scratch if AI had not been on hand to help.

When English law contracts fall into dispute, lawyers are lucky enough to be able to consult Sir Kim Lewison's magisterial work *The Interpretation of Contracts* (Sweet & Maxwell), now in its eighth edition and running to nearly 1,100 pages. That book's stated aim is to help practising lawyers find 'arguments that will advance their client's cause'. But it is not intended as a practical resource for drafters. Bloomsbury publish such a work: Mark Anderson and Victor

Warner's excellent *Drafting and Negotiating Commercial Contracts*, going strong and into its fifth edition.

As its title suggests, *The Language of Contracts* approaches drafting under English law from a slightly different angle. The meaning of contracts depends on the *language* the drafter has used. What does the drafter need to know about how the English language works – in all its wonderful variety – if the drafter is to produce contracts that are both unambiguous and easily understood? That is a question that deserves systematic examination of how judges think about contractual language.

Since contract interpretation is an objective exercise, it is unusual to ask: what was the *drafter* intending to achieve? A judge does not ask what the drafter intended. Nor does the judge even ask what the drafter's client intended. The judge asks what the contractual language signifies to an objective reader. So what the drafter was intending is, to a judge, beside the point. But this work is meant to be of practical help to drafters. Accordingly, when the work discusses decided cases, it often looks at what the drafter may have been trying to get at. In any of those cases, it may be that the drafter was aiming for exactly the outcome the court decided, so that any criticism of the drafting in these pages is groundless. If so, the author apologises.

The work is divided into numbered paragraphs, and most of their headings contain a drafting recommendation. The author hopes that this will build into a checklist that is useful for drafters at a practical level. Nonetheless, drafting in practice is so heavily context-specific that drafters must view the recommendations critically, and apply their own judgement. The author is an ex-lawyer, not a currently practising one. In any case, the book is not intended as legal advice. It represents only one person's view of the issues discussed: other views are tenable. Attention is drawn to the disclaimer contained on the publisher's imprint page.

The author has tried to take into account cases published up to 31 March 2024.

Ben Staveley
3 June 2024

Contents

Table of Statutes

Table of Cases

B

C

D

E

F

G

M

R

T

U

Chapter 1

Process, architecture and structure

Besides drafting clearly themselves, good drafters must also be able to analyse and question the drafting of others; negotiation is a valuable process. Explicit drafting is best. Errors rob drafting of credibility, and are a regular hazard of adapting standard forms. Drafters have to decide how many documents to use, and where to place their material. Good drafting uses headings and gives prominence to important material, taking care with 'surprising' provisions. Drafting should neither be repetitious nor vary in specificity. Cross-references matter. Drafting should be divided into short, manageable units, with a coherent word order and consistent punctuation.

FUNDAMENTALS

1.1 Drafters review others' drafting as often as they draft

1.2 If in doubt, ask what it means

1.3 Negotiation can lead to improved drafting

1.4 Be explicit: leave nothing to chance

1.5 Any mistake corrodes credibility

1.6 Anticipate how a judge will think

STANDARD FORMS AND PRECEDENTS

1.7 Original drafting is the exception, not the rule

1.8 Be careful: adapting a standard form or other precedent is a risk area

1.9 Nor are standard forms and other precedents infallible

1.10 Consider how far the standard form fits your transaction

1.11 Do not leave a blank in a standard form

1.12 Whose standard form should be used?

BASIC ASPECTS OF STRUCTURE AND STYLE

1.13 What 'structure' and 'style' mean for a drafter

FUNDAMENTALS

Drafters review others' drafting as often as they draft

1.1 Unless the parties contract on the basis of a set of terms put forward by one party on a take-it-or-leave-it basis, the classic process of producing bilateral contracts[1] is for one party's drafter to produce a draft and invite the other

[1] Not all contracts are of course bilateral. More than two parties can contract with one another, and law students learn early on that some contracts (of the type discussed in *Carlill v Carbolic Smoke Ball Co Ltd* [1892] 2 QB 484) are labelled *unilateral*. This is something of a misnomer, as at least two parties are necessarily involved in the contract, even if only one of them can enforce it against the other. For simplicity, this work generally assumes that the contracts under discussion are bilateral.

party and their lawyers to comment on it. The party whose drafter initially wields the pen, or the mouse, is generally thought to have an advantage. The first draft can put forward drafting favourable to the drafter's own clients, leaving the other side[2] to identify all the points which to their mind need to be changed so as to reflect a fair balance of interests.

Lawyers may therefore need to react to an initial draft put forward by the other side as often as they prepare first draft themselves: to return serve as often as to serve. That is a different skill from drafting: the skill of reviewing. To review is as hard as to draft: arguably even harder, rather like returning serve, because the drafter/server has the initiative. To review effectively, one must first analyse the effect of the language in the first draft. The reviewer has to consider two questions simultaneously. One is whether the drafting is as unambiguous as it needs to be: to be invulnerable to dispute. The other is whether, even if the answer to that first question is yes, the drafting is acceptable to the reviewer's own side. If not, the drafter will need to turn drafter and suggest some alternative wording. The game is then properly under way, as draft and counter-draft are exchanged over the net.

If in doubt, ask what it means

1.2 This work is not a manual of working practice. But the review process described above necessarily involves the reviewer being able to understand what the first draft *means* (or is intended to mean). If the drafting is obscure, the reviewer can fairly ask the original drafter to explain how the drafting is meant to work. It can be embarrassing for original drafters to have to deal with this, particularly if the first draft contains standard form language that the drafter has borrowed without fully considering it. One piece of basic advice for a junior lawyer is not to send out a first draft for review without having understood, if any of the drafting is borrowed from a standard form or another precedent, what it is meant to achieve and how it does so. Lawyers who cannot explain to a meeting how their own draft contracts are supposed to work will not impress anyone, including (perhaps especially) their own clients.

Experienced lawyers reviewing the drafting of the other side know the value of asking for an explanation in a meeting where both sides are present. If the original drafter has to explain what the drafting is meant to achieve, the explanation allows the parties on *both* sides to get to grips with drafting that they may otherwise have skimmed over. The party whose drafters produced the first draft may have tacitly assumed that their drafters have captured the intended bargain and protected their interests. The party on the receiving side, faced with the other side's first draft, may be tempted to rely on their

2 'The other side' being how one party's lawyers universally refer to the counterparty and its lawyers.

own lawyers to identify what issues arise for their own side. The drafter's explanation as to what was meant can shine a light into corners that would otherwise have remained dusty and unexamined. Difficult issues can be sorted out before the contract is signed, rather than festering without being considered, only to erupt later.

Negotiation can lead to improved drafting

1.3 The process of negotiation is a crucible in which the drafting is refined. At least two pairs of trained eyes are looking critically at the drafting to evaluate whether it 'works', in the sense that, as well as being acceptable to both sides, it is internally consistent and comprehensive enough to deal with all foreseeable possibilities. That provokes healthy discussion on whether the drafting is indeed clear and reflects the parties' consensus.

But this does not happen with all contracts. Various categories of contractual documents are drafted without them being reviewed by those with competing interests. So it is no accident that many documents of this type, after they have been executed, throw up dispute and uncertainty.

Examples where a lack of negotiation can be inferred include the articles of association of a company set up to be privatised;[3] a pension scheme trust deed;[4] a will;[5] an intra-group reorganisation agreement designed to set a company up for sale;[6] and a notice terminating a lease.[7] None of these is likely to have been refined by any process of negotiation between two sides, each considering the language from its own perspective.

Consumer contracts and other contracts which are put forward on a take-it-or-leave-it basis are also entered into without the considered reflection that the negotiation process allows; and are often deficient as a result.

Two leading cases on the law of contractual interpretation[8] exemplify this phenomenon. In *BCCI v Ali* the document was a standard form of release of claims. In the *Investors Compensation Scheme* case, it was a claim form under which the scheme took over certain claims which investors had against third parties. What the documents had in common was that those invited to sign them were not really expected to comment on them or to take legal advice on what they meant.[9] The person or organisation putting them forward was never challenged to explain what they meant before they had been entered into,

[3] *Attorney General of Belize v Belize Telecom Ltd* [2009] UKPC 10.
[4] *Singapore Airlines Ltd v Buck Consultants Ltd* [2011] EWCA Civ 1542.
[5] *RSPCA v Sharp* [2010] EWCA Civ 1474.
[6] *Square Mile Partnership Ltd v Fitzmaurice McCall Ltd* [2006] EWCA Civ 1690.
[7] *Mannai Investment Company v Eagle Star Life Assurance Co Ltd* [1997] 3 All ER 352.
[8] *Bank of Credit and Commerce International SA (in liquidation) v Ali (no. 1)* [2001] UKHL 8; *Investors Compensation Scheme Ltd v West Bromwich Building Society (no. 1)* [1998] 1 WLR 896.
[9] Or even, perhaps, to read them.

by which time it was too late to change them. An expensive and embarrassing dispute was the predictable result.

Negotiations have their drawbacks too. The drafting needs to be seen to satisfy the parties' competing interests, and is pulled this way and that in an attempt to keep everyone happy. The parties set a deadline for the negotiations to be concluded, and are tempted to carry on negotiating up to the last minute. Last-minute changes are made to the draft by drafters who are dog-tired and unable to check carefully enough whether they achieve what they were meant to.[10] The other side's lawyers are no better placed. Nonetheless, negotiation at least allows for a process of reflection and discussion before either side is committed.

Be explicit: leave nothing to chance

1.4 If a drafter leaves unanswered questions about what the contract requires the parties to do, and when and how they have to do it, the parties risk being left uncertain as to their rights and obligations. This is a recipe for dispute. The best drafting is fully explicit, and leaves no room for doubt as to what duties the parties owe each other.[11]

To be explicit, drafters must not merely deal fully and clearly with the issues addressed by their drafting. They must also make sure they have not left anything out.

In practice, contracting parties tend to underrate the value of drafting being fully explicit. In the honeymoon period leading up to a contract being signed, both sides may believe that the sense of common purpose and give-and-take that animates them in trying to reach agreement will persist after the contract has been concluded. Experience shows that this may be an unrealistically rose-tinted view. A drafter's job may therefore include persuading the parties that they should cater explicitly for all foreseeable circumstances rather than relying on goodwill to sort out potentially contentious issues.

If the drafting does not cater for an event which happens, the parties may take different views as to how the gap should be filled. One party or the other may well be driven to arguing that the gap should be filled by an implied term. Whatever the outcome, it is not the parties who will have supplied any implied term, but a judge. The parties will have lost control of the contract, and be exposed to an outcome which will disappoint at least one of them, who will be faced with substantial cost.

10 Lord Hodge in *Barnardo's v Buckinghamshire* [2018] UKSC 55 at [14].

11 Some drafters argue that their clients' interests are served by a measure of deliberate ambiguity in the drafting: giving them room to argue, once the contract has been signed, that it should be interpreted in line with their own best interests. The author suspects that this is usually too clever by half, and provokes more disputes than it solves. A cynic might reflect that members of the legal profession have less of an interest in avoiding disputes than do their clients.

A party who has to argue for an implied term is fighting an uphill battle. The normal position is that if a contract is silent in relation to some matter, no term is to be implied to cover it. In Lord Hoffmann's words:

> The question of implication arises when the instrument does not expressly provide for what is to happen when some event occurs. The most usual inference in such a case is that nothing is to happen. If the parties had intended something to happen, the instrument would have said so. Otherwise, the express provisions of the instrument are to continue to operate undisturbed. If the event has caused loss to one or other of the parties, the loss lies where it falls.[12]

So for example, where a charterparty contained no promise on the part of the charterers that they would nominate only a safe berth for loading, no such promise was to be implied: the loss lay where it fell, on the owners.[13]

It is therefore dangerous for a party to rely on an implied term: a drafter whose client needs to argue for an implied term has done a feeble job. To get rid of gaps in the contract, the drafter's main technique is to ask as many of what this work terms 'What if?' questions as possible. In other words, the drafter needs to exercise a degree of imagination and try to make sure that in all foreseeable future events, the contract makes sensible provision for how, if at all, the contractual terms should flex so as to fit the new circumstances. This is an important arrow in the quiver of the effective drafter: it is the subject of Chapter 13 below.

In some cases, being explicit is not merely a question of avoiding a need to rely on inference. It goes to the root of the drafting's effectiveness. Drafting intended to confer rights on a third party is of that type. The Contracts (Rights of Third Parties) Act 1999 requires that the third party who is to benefit must be expressly identified.[14] The right of the third party must also fall within s 1(1), requiring either that the contract expressly provides for the third party to enforce the term or that the term purports to confer a benefit on the third party. And *expressly* providing that the party may benefit is a clearer way of conferring a right on the third party than the alternative of *impliedly* doing so by purporting to confer a benefit on the third party but without making the right to enforcement express (s 1(1)(b)).[15]

[12] *Attorney General of Belize v Belize Telecom Ltd* [2009] UKPC 10: Lord Hoffmann at [17].

[13] *Mediterranean Salvage and Towage Ltd v Seamar Trading & Commerce Inc* [2009] EWCA Civ 531.

[14] The identification must be 'by name, as a member of a class or as answering a particular description' (s 1(3)).

[15] The alternative route depends on examining the contract as a whole to see if the parties, in purporting to confer the benefit, nonetheless intended that the third party should not have the right to enforce it – in which case s 1(2) makes it clear that the third party cannot do so. This is a more nuanced question (see, for example, *Nisshin Shipping Co Ltd v Cleaves & Co Ltd* [2003] EWHC 2602 (Comm)) and obviously less clear-cut than express provision would have been.

Any mistake corrodes credibility

1.5 Strikingly often, a judge in a contract dispute case will refer in passing to an aspect of the drafting that is, both parties acknowledge, obviously wrong and a mistake.[16] Self-evidently, nothing turns on the mistake as far as the parties are concerned: their dispute relates to something else in the contract.

Nonetheless, two separate considerations mean that mistakes of any type should matter for a drafter.

First, it is only with hindsight that a drafting mistake can be seen to be inconsequential. Any mistake could easily turn out to lie at the heart of a dispute. It is only chance and the course of events that make some mistakes crucial and others trivial.

Second, if a document is riddled with mistakes, it is only natural for a judge to treat the whole document as suspect and to be reluctant to allow any particular language to decide the issue in dispute.[17] In other words, in a poorly-drafted contract, a passage where the drafter has (unusually) accurately expressed the parties' wishes is more plausibly open to challenge by whichever party it is that now sees an advantage in contesting that the passage in question means what it says. In such a case, the judge is more likely to depart from the language the drafter has used and treat the parties as bound by contractual obligations that the judge has simply inferred they must have meant instead.[18]

The corollary is that a well-drafted document is more resilient to criticism, and its language correspondingly more likely to be respected.[19]

[16] One recent example among many is *Saxon Woods Investments Ltd v Costa* [2024] EWHC 387 (Ch): 'As a preliminary point, there is a manifest error in the drafting of Clause 6.2' (Simon Gleeson at [12]).

[17] See, for example, Whipple LJ in *Nord Naphtha Ltd v New Stream Trading AG* [2021] EWCA Civ 1829 at [48]: 'These introductory words are, in my judgment, one of several examples of clumsy wording in the Contract' (in a paragraph that concluded that the language in question 'could have been left out or perhaps more clearly or appropriately worded').

[18] '... the poorer the quality of the drafting, the less willing the court should be to be driven by semantic niceties to attribute to the parties an improbable and unbusinesslike intention, if the language used, whatever it may lack in precision, is reasonably capable of an interpretation which attributes to the parties an intention to make provision for contingencies inherent in the work contracted for on a sensible and businesslike basis' (Lord Bridge in *Mitsui Construction Co Ltd v Attorney General of Hong Kong* (1986) 33 BLR 14). More pithily, Lord Neuberger in *Arnold v Britton* [2015] UKSC 36 observed at [18]: 'I accept that the less clear [words] are, or, to put it another way, the worse their drafting, the more ready a court can properly be to depart from their natural meaning.'

[19] See, for example, *Maranello Rosso Ltd v Lohomij BV* [2022] EWCA Civ 1667 (Phillips LJ, in endorsing the High Court judge's interpretation of a settlement agreement, observing: '... the Judge (as he was both entitled and obliged to) had regard to the nature of the drafting, placing particular weight on the text due to the fact that it was formal and high quality' ([58(ii)])).

Anticipate how a judge will think

1.6 Much of this work is directed to help drafters express themselves so clearly and explicitly that there is no realistic prospect of doubt about what the language means. But modern drafters should temper their confidence by remembering how judges resolve disputes about contractual language. English judges self-consciously adopt what they call an iterative approach to interpreting a disputed provision in a contract. By this is meant that a judge must not consider the disputed language in isolation, but must test a tentative conclusion as to its meaning by cross-checking it against the overall purpose of the contract, determined by considering it as a whole in the context of the background that the parties could be expected to have had in mind when they entered into it.[20]

The drafter must be alive to the risk that, however clearly a particular provision has been drafted, its apparent meaning risks being subverted if its commercial effects could appear, to a judge, surprising. This point has important ramifications for the drafter: see **1.24** below.

STANDARD FORMS AND PRECEDENTS

Original drafting is the exception, not the rule

1.7 Only rarely does the modern drafter create a contract from scratch. It is quicker and more efficient (and will therefore spare the pocket of the drafter's client) if the contract is based on a precedent of some type. The digital age allows drafters to access ready-made standard agreements at will. If the drafter works in a law firm, the precedents will often have been developed by the firm itself from its own experience.

The drafter can tap other sources for precedents. Trade associations and similar bodies develop their own forms for use in their particular sector. Commercial publishers also make precedents available to drafters who are willing to pay to get access to them. Promoters of AI are increasingly confident.

There are infinite variations on this theme. The drafter may start with a standard form and adapt its wording for use in a particular transaction. The parties will end up with a contract contained in a single document. Or the drafter may use the standard form without amending it, and construct a document which both invokes that standard form but engrafts onto it some special terms that build on what the standard form says. These 'special terms'

[20] *Wood v Capita Insurance Services Ltd* [2017] UKSC 24: Lord Hodge at [12].

may not be bespoke to the transaction, but themselves represent one party's preferred terms to deal with one particular aspect of the transaction.[21]

As an alternative, the parties may enter into a framework agreement that sets out some expected standard terms for multiple successive contracts of a particular type that the parties contemplate entering into. In that type of arrangement, the framework agreement may expressly acknowledge that any bespoke terms agreed for any particular contract will prevail over anything contained in the framework agreement. This can be seen in *Yieldpoint Stable Value Fund LP v Kimura Commodity Trade Finance Fund Ltd*,[22] a case that illustrates how likely disputes are to arise if the terms of any particular transaction do not fit readily within what is contemplated by the framework agreement itself.

Drafters who rely on a precedent, or a standard form, need however to think about a number of issues if they are to be used safely.

Be careful: adapting a standard form or other precedent is a risk area

1.8 A drafter who uses a standard form or other precedent will feel comforted by using drafting that has a reputable origin and has been used before. To do so feels safer than drafting a provision on a blank piece of paper and relying on the drafter's own wits to come up with something that unambiguously and accurately meets the parties' needs. But, lulled by that apparent safety, drafters often make simple errors. As Chadwick LJ remarked in *Taylor v Rive Droite Music Ltd*:[23]

> The process of adaptation from other documents lends itself more readily to sloppy and careless draftsmanship than the process of drafting as a coherent whole.

What can easily happen is illustrated by *Holding & Barnes Plc v Hill House Hammond Ltd*.[24] Seven leases of property were entered into as part of the sale of an insurance services business. Five of the leases related to parts of a building; two to a whole building. The landlord's repairing covenant was different as between the five part-building leases and one of the whole-building leases. But the *other* whole-building lease inexplicably used the version of the covenant from the part-building leases, not the one from the other whole-building lease. It was very difficult to make sense of the drafting; the Court of Appeal ended up by interpreting the language as if the drafter had picked the right

21 See **1.12** below for the case where the parties compete as to whose standard terms should be chosen.

22 [2023] EWHC 1212 (Comm) (framework agreement containing 'Template Offer' which would, when used, prevail over the framework itself: see from [24] in the judgment of Stephen Houseman KC).

23 [2005] EWCA Civ 1300.

24 [2001] EWCA Civ 1334.

version of the language rather than the wrong one. Peter Gibson LJ resignedly observed:

> The problem which arises is a good illustration of the dangers of the use of the word processor to produce a draft which is then copied to provide other drafts to be adapted for the purpose of other cases.

Before the word processor and the days of creating documents through 'cut and paste', one of the main risks was that a typist copying a precedent from another document accidentally missed out some words appearing in the original between one iteration of a particular words and the next.[25] Technology has largely dissipated this risk: a precedent clause can be transliterated into a new document instantly and without error.

But different risks remain. So the drafter in *Company Developments (Finance) Ltd v Coffee Club Restaurants*[26] provided that the liability of guarantors under personal guarantees in favour of a landlord lasted only during a 'Liability Period'. But the definition of 'Liability Period', seemingly borrowed from another transaction, led nowhere: it stipulated a period applicable in the case of some secondary guarantors but did not, as drafted, apply to the original guarantors at all. The drafter had not bothered to check that the provisions worked properly in the context of the proposed transaction, and they did not.[27]

Nor are standard forms and other precedents infallible

1.9 However carefully they are prepared and however eminent their provenance, standard forms do not always work as predictably as might have been expected.

For example, the LMA[28] standard form used in syndicated loan transactions was generally thought by market participants to give each lender separately enforceable rights against a borrower in respect of what amounted to a separate loan. But a court in Hong Kong held[29] that this was not so as a matter of Hong Kong law. In response, the LMA – though keen to deny that the Hong Kong finding would be followed by an English court – was driven to suggest

25 '...the omission was explained by the phenomenon, technically known as homoeoteleuton, where one sentence contains a word which closed the preceding sentence and the transcriber's eye has wandered from one to the other, leading to the entire omission of the whole passage lying between them' (Lord Bingham *in Homburg Houtimport BV v Agrosin Ltd (The Starsin)* [2003] UKHL 12 at [22]).

26 [2011] EWCA Civ 766.

27 Though the drafter was saved from total embarrassment by the court finding that it was clear enough what the missing 'Liability Period' would have been if the drafter had included it, and so the guarantee was enforceable against the guarantors.

28 The Loan Market Association, based in London.

29 *Charmway Hong Kong Investment Ltd v Fortunesea (Cayman) Ltd* (Hong Kong Special Administrative Region, court of first instance: Miscellaneous proceedings no 3234 of 2013).

revisions to its own forms to 'further emphasise'[30] the generally understood position.

Other illustrations are not hard to find. In *Sutton Housing Partnership Ltd v Rydon Maintenance Ltd*,[31] the parties based their contract on a form issued by the National Housing Federation, but still stumbled into a dispute. And in *Soufflet Negoce SA v Fedcominvest Europe Sarl*,[32] Eder J had to interpret a provision from GAFTA,[33] which although a standard form contained a clear 'uncertain modifier' problem of the type discussed in Chapter 7 below.[34]

The lesson is that the good drafter is a sceptical drafter. The general consensus as to the meaning of standard forms can be wrong. A drafter should not assume that the effect of standard language is what the herd thinks it is. No judge who had to rule on it would shrink from challenging preconceptions about the effect of the language used, however widely they had been shared. Drafters need a similar level of intellectual courage.

Consider how far the standard form fits your transaction

1.10 Standard forms are created precisely so that they can be used for a range of possible contracts. They are not bespoke. And they come, or should come, with a health warning to drafters who base their contracts upon them. The standard form represents a starting point, not a contractual destination.

Another case involving an LMA standard form[35] demonstrates the point. An original lender had lent money to a borrower on terms that if the borrower chose to redeem the loan early, the borrower had to pay a substantial premium. The original lender then used an LMA standard form to sell on to a purchaser, M, part of its participation in the loan. The borrower then *did* choose to redeem the loan early – but only after M had itself on-sold the participation it had bought to a third party. So it was the third party, not M, who received the premium from the borrower. Despite that, the original lender claimed that the LMA standard form required *M* to pay over to it an amount equivalent to the redemption premium: money that M had never received.

The problem was that nobody had seemingly thought of how the premium fell to be dealt with under the LMA standard form. The standard form did not seem to contemplate that the borrower might have to pay any sort of premium, let alone a substantial one. And nobody could criticise the LMA for

30 LMA publication of 28 October 2015: 'LMA Facility Documentation – Supplement to Finance Parties' Rights Clauses'.
31 [2017] EWCA Civ 359.
32 [2014] EWHC 2405 (Comm).
33 The Grain and Feed Trade Association.
34 See **7.2** et seq.
35 *Tael One Partners Limited v Morgan Stanley International PLC* [2015] UKSC 12.

failing to address the question. Indeed, the standard form contained, in bold lettering at the top of page one, the following:

> For the avoidance of doubt, this document is in a non-binding, recommended form. Its intention is to be used as a starting point for negotiation only. Individual parties are free to depart from its terms and should always satisfy themselves of the regulatory implications of its use.

No reasonable outsider could think that the LMA could have done much more to take care with the standard form. Nonetheless, it is easy to see how the drafters of the *Tael* contract may have fallen into the trap of assuming that the LMA's 20 pages of high-quality drafting must have been adequate to cover any eventuality. But they were wrong.

Had the parties not reached for an LMA standard form but documented the sale themselves from scratch, they might perhaps have thought to deal explicitly with the consequences for the transaction terms if a substantial premium did arise. After all, the premium was plainly a significant feature of the underlying loan. If that is right, it suggests that the parties may have been lulled by using an LMA standard form into overlooking the need to think through the fundamentals of their deal so as to make sure the contract worked properly.

Parties who are not adept in the English language may be particularly at risk of assuming, sometimes over-optimistically, that the standard form must by its very nature be framed so as to achieve their particular commercial objectives.[36]

Do not leave a blank in a standard form

1.11 Standard forms sometimes contain blanks to be filled in by the users of the contract to reflect the particular transaction which is being documented. It is particularly embarrassing if the information filled in is wrong, or the relevant space is simply left blank. The law may sometimes afford a sensible remedy here if it is obvious from the surrounding circumstances what has been left out.[37] And the benefit of this type of drafting of a standard contract is that it makes it obvious that *something* should appear in the blank: the omission must, a court would be impelled to find, be accidental rather than deliberate.

But the point for the drafter (here meaning the person adopting the standard form for the transaction, rather than the person responsible for drafting the standard form itself) is straightforward: if there is a blank, what should go in it?

[36] Such as the Korean defendant bank in *W S Tankship II BV v The Kwangju Bank Ltd* [2011] EWHC 3103 (Comm): see the comments of Blair J at [7] and also **11.22** below.

[37] As, for example, in *Clydesdale Bank Plc v Weston Property Company Ltd* [2011] EWHC 1251 (Ch) (failure to fill in box identifying borrower where debts secured by a third party mortgagor).

Whose standard form should be used?

1.12 Sophisticated commercial parties may often be wedded to standard terms that they have either drafted themselves or otherwise satisfied themselves give them adequate protection. If both parties to (say) a sale of goods are in this position, their negotiation can become an attritional exchange – a so-called 'battle of the forms' – in which the parties trade communications in an attempt to ensure that it is their own standard terms, rather than the other side's, that make it into the final contract. This may descend into an unedifying process of each party trying to make the last communication before the contract is performed, so that the performance represents acceptance of an offer on that party's proffered terms.

If a party wants to resist being saddled with the other side's standard terms, the following uncompromising language discussed in one 2022 case[38] may be a useful starting point:

> ...only terms which have been expressly agreed by both parties, at the time of trade or subsequently, shall be binding for the agreement. We hereby reject any proposed amendments unless expressly agreed by us in writing. Neither failure or delay in responding, nor performance of the agreement, shall constitute acceptance to [sic] any terms which have not been agreed between the parties.

BASIC ASPECTS OF STRUCTURE AND STYLE

What 'structure' and 'style' mean for a drafter

1.13 For a drafter, structure merges into style. A drafter's decision as to whether to group all the contractual provisions into a single document, or separate them into discrete documents, is easily characterised as a structural decision. A linguistic choice between two words with subtly different nuances of meaning is more stylistic. But between these two extremes are examples that it is harder to label. How should different clauses be grouped and in which order should they appear? Should the drafter use headings? What other devices can the drafter use to make sure that a reader can navigate through the contract without unnecessary difficulty?

Many of these issues are addressed in later chapters. But some general observations deserve to be mentioned at this stage.

38 *BP Oil International Ltd v Glencore Energy Ltd* [2022] EWHC 499 (Comm), quoted at [69]. The contractual process was not treated as a classic 'battle of the forms' because the parties had agreed to contract principally on the basis of BP's terms ([115]), but the language quoted above was decisive ([130]).

The usual contents of a contract

1.14 A conventional English law contract opens by recording the names of the parties. Their addresses also appear. For a party that is a company, the address is usually its registered office. It is usual, for a company, also to state the territory under whose laws it is incorporated and, for a company incorporated in England and Wales, its registration number.[39]

The list of parties is often followed by a brief statement of the background to, and purpose of, the contract. These are often, to the bewilderment of users of the contract other than lawyers, headed 'Recitals',[40] though 'Background' would be a more modern heading. Chapter 2 below discusses their use.

The reader then usually finds a 'definitions' clause. It provides that where particular words or expressions (usually identified by initial capital letters) are used in the contract, they are to be interpreted so as to carry a predictable defined meaning: ('Excluded Assets shall mean the assets listed in Schedule II'). A discussion of the drafting of the definitions clause, and of definitions generally, appears in Chapter 4.

Next usually come the contract's 'operative' clauses – the meat of the contract, containing the obligations the parties agree to undertake. The operative clauses also include boilerplate clauses that deal with some matters that are common to many or most contracts, but are no less important on that account.

After the operative clauses comes a clause (in traditional lawyers' Latin parlance a 'testimonium' clause) that records how and by whom the parties executed (signed) the contract, and who if anyone witnessed the execution.

A contract may also contain *schedules* which follow the main body of the agreement, and contain matter considered not important enough to be awarded star billing in the body of the contract. A schedule may itself have subsidiary parts which do not form part of the schedule: one of those is usually termed an 'appendix' (plural 'appendices'), an 'annex' or an 'attachment'.

39 It is common for businesspeople to think conceptually that a group of companies (holding company plus its subsidiaries) can be party to a contract. But as any lawyer knows, that is not true: each company is a separate legal entity. One of the drafter's basic tasks is to reflect this and make sure that the right company or companies are parties to the contract. For the types of difficulty that can arise if this is not made clear, see *Estor Ltd v Multifit (UK) Ltd* [2009] EWHC 2565 and *George on High Ltd v Alan Boswell Insurance Brokers Ltd* [2023] EWHC 1963 (Comm).

40 According to David Mellinkoff in *The Language of Law* (Resource Publications, 2004, p 190) the term comes from sixteenth century borrowing from Latin or French. The essence of the term is that a recital was something repeated rather than newly appearing, which is explicable in the sense that the operative provisions of the contract did not exist before the moment of contract, whereas the background did. The rationale for including them was originally, Mellinkoff asserts, no more than to pad out the contract and reward lawyers and clerks whose fees swelled with the length of the documents.

The orthodox nomenclature is, as the above suggests, that the separate units of drafting into which the body of the agreement are termed 'clauses', whereas the equivalent units in a schedule are 'paragraphs'.[41]

One document or more than one?

1.15 With a complex set of contractual arrangements, the drafter may sometimes have to choose whether to record the agreement in one contract or more than one.

The choice can matter. For example, if the arrangements are confined within the four corners of a single document, the document can conceptually have only a single meaning. By contrast, there is nothing to prevent two agreements containing provisions inconsistent with each other, even if the parties to the two agreements are the same. Also, if the drafter chooses two contracts, a defect in one contract that prevents it being enforceable will not affect the enforceability of the other. If the drafter had chosen a single a contract, the same error might have vitiated the whole of it.

A drafter should not, however, assume that separate agreements will be construed independently in all respects. In *Winnetka Trading Corporation v Julius Baer International Ltd*,[42] a relationship between a bank and its customer was recorded in two separate agreements. In interpreting one of the agreements, a banking mandate, the judge was plainly influenced by some of the contents of the other document, an investment mandate, nominally separate though the two mandates were. In particular, two expressions ('negligence' and 'gross negligence') had been used in the investment mandate. The two expressions plainly therefore meant something different ('gross negligence' must mean something going beyond mere 'negligence' on its own). That was relevant to what 'gross negligence' must mean in the banking mandate.

Generally, each of a number of agreements entered into as part of the same transaction will influence the interpretation of the others,[43] representing part of the background of fact that the courts are directed to take into account under the line of authority culminating in the *Investors Compensation Scheme* case.[44]

However, even if separate agreements are entered into as part of a single transaction, that influence may be limited. For example, in *Cherry Tree*

41 Thus broadly reflecting the equivalent language in the context of statutory drafting, at least up to the date of enactment (when a clause of a bill becomes a 'section' of the Act of Parliament it turns into).

42 [2011] EWHC 2030 (Ch).

43 See Sir Kim Lewison, *The Interpretation of Contracts* (8th edn, Sweet & Maxwell, 2023) from para 3.06, the principles of which were cited with approval in *AstraZeneca Ltd v Tesaro Inc* [2023] EWHC 803 (Ch) (Richards J at [67]).

44 *Investors Compensation Scheme Ltd v West Bromwich Building Society (no.1)* [1998] 1 WLR 896.

Investments Ltd v Landmain Ltd[45] the Court of Appeal refused to allow an unregistered facility agreement to influence the interpretation of a charge that had been lodged with the Land Registry and was thus a public document. The decision was made against the background that the Land Registration Act 2002 expressly required any variation or extension of a mortgagee's power of sale to be contained in the charge itself: here, it was not but was contained in a separate facility agreement. So even though the documents were admittedly part of a single transaction, the drafter's decision to separate the arrangements into separate documents had real consequences.

The decision in *Cherry Tree*[46] reflects a wider principle: documents that may affect third parties to whom they are negotiated or assigned, or who otherwise become parties to them, are more likely to be interpreted solely by reference to the words used in them than by reference to the background, even if the background is otherwise admissible. Particular examples of this type of document are the constitutional documents of a company,[47] the terms and conditions of a bond issue,[48] and a bill of lading.[49] So with documents of that type, a drafter has at the same time a more straightforward and a more daunting task: straightforward, because the language of the document itself cannot be blown off course by background material; daunting, because the drafter's choice of language is more than ever likely to fall under the analytical spotlight.

Why might you prefer a single document?

1.16 The possible reasons for preferring one document include:

1. To collect all the arrangements in a single document reduces the risk of overlooking any one aspect of them: with a single document, it is easier to identify any gaps.
2. In particular, a separate document risks being accidentally omitted from a package of separate documents intended to constitute the overall agreement: if that happens, a dispute can arise over whether it is truly part of the agreement or not.[50]
3. If the arrangements in their totality are intended to stand or fall together (the termination of arrangement B should bring arrangement A to an

45 [2012] EWCA Civ 736; the Court of Appeal's approach in that case was followed in *Mostyn Estate Management Co Ltd v Youde* [2022] EWCA Civ 929 (Asplin LJ at [44]–[48]).

46 ibid.

47 *Egyptian Salt and Soda Co Ltd v Port Said Salt Association Ltd* [1931] AC 677.

48 *LBG Capital No 1 Plc v BNY Mellon Corporate Trustee Services Ltd* [2016] UKSC 29.

49 *Homburg Houtimport BV v Agrosin Private Ltd* [2004] 1 AC 715.

50 As happened in *Phoenix Interior Design Ltd v Henley Homes Plc* [2021] EWHC 1573 (QB) (contractor's standard terms described as appearing 'overleaf' but not appearing on the signed copy ([74])).

end as well), it is conceptually easier to achieve this if everything is in a single document.

4. In particular, if *breach* of any one of the arrangements should allow termination of all the arrangements, again it may be simpler for all the arrangements to be collected in a single document.

5. Judges tend to construe a single document as far as possible in a way that avoids internal inconsistencies. So to group all the arrangements together may help them be interpreted as a single coherent whole.

6. If different but overlapping aspects of a single relationship are catered for in separate agreements, those agreements can easily deal in a different way with issues that could arise across the breadth of the relationship (for example, how to resolve disputes). That can lead to uncertainty as which regime applies in any particular case.[51]

7. Separate agreements tend to develop their own vitality, so that it becomes difficult to focus, when developing the drafting of one agreement, on whether making changes to it might not have some unfortunate knock-on consequence in another.[52]

8. If an overall arrangement is provided for in more than one document, it becomes more likely that inconsistencies between them can give an aggrieved party the opportunity to argue that one of the documents has a disproportionate significance.[53]

Why might you conclude that separate documents would be better?

1.17 The factors that might point towards this choice include:

1. The contractual arrangements are not all agreed at one time but piecemeal, so that it makes sense for a series of contracts to be prepared, recording the agreements entered into at the various different stages.

2. If not all parties to agreement A are party to arrangement B (because if so it saves the parties who are not involved in arrangement B spending time

51 Leading for example to the type of dispute seen in *Surrey CC v Suez Recycling and Recovery Surrey Ltd* [2021] EWHC 2015 (TCC) (provision for arbitration in an initial agreement not repeated in a deed of variation: dispute as to whether arbitration required).

52 So in *CDV Software Entertainment AG v Gamecock Media Europe Ltd* [2009] EWHC 2965, the parties' main agreement contained a definition of 'Delivery Dates' that both parties were forced to admit was too inflexible to work in the context of a separate agreement expected to be entered into with a third party to develop certain video games.

53 As was argued, albeit unsuccessfully, in *Lord v Maven Wealth Group Ltd* [2021] EWHC 2544 (Comm) (argument that because the definition of 'Fair Value' for the purposes of pre-emption provisions was contained in an option agreement rather than the articles of association, the procedure for determining Fair Value necessarily followed the option agreement).

considering the documentation of B if the arrangements are separately documented).

3. If the A arrangements are private and the parties do not want them disclosed to the parties to the B arrangements.
4. If the A arrangements are private, but the B arrangements have to be made public or disclosed to competitors.
5. If tax characterisation or sequential logic dictates that the A arrangements be clearly separate from (happen before) the B arrangements.
6. If it is wished to provide for separate time limits on different aspects of a deal.
7. If it is helpful to facilitate substitution of new parties or assignment of the particular rights involved with (say) the B arrangements but not the A arrangements.

Amending agreements tend to go wrong: you are better to amend and restate

1.18 When an existing agreement is amended to reflect a fresh consensus of the parties, one particular risk needs careful attention. Of necessity, the amendment agreement[54] is a separate agreement from the original agreement. Accordingly, the drafter is tempted to accomplish the change by referring to the original agreement and specify some amendments to it. This is very often the technique of the statutory drafter.

But it is easy to blunder when doing this. Faulty cross-referencing can cause the amendment to appear to have an entirely unexpected meaning. This happened in *Dalkia Utilities Services Plc v Celltech International Ltd*.[55] A finance lease was amended to reschedule the amounts payable by the lessee. The amount payable on termination was expressed by simply cross-referring in the amendment agreement to a particular sub-clause in the original lease. That was, however, the wrong sub-clause: it referred only to an interest amount, not (as the parties would surely have expected) the amount of finance as yet unrecovered by the lessor.[56]

54 Which will itself need to be in writing if the original agreement contained the common provision that amendments, to be valid, must themselves be in writing: *Rock Advertising Ltd v MWB Business Exchange Centres Ltd* [2018] UKSC 24.

55 [2006] EWHC 63 (Comm).

56 In the case, the judge found that the result was so bizarre that he refused to give effect to it: an example of a drafting error so egregious in its purported effect that the parties escaped the consequences of the drafter's inattention. But to recommend to a drafter that grotesque errors are safer than apparently trivial ones would be controversial advice.

The practical solution for the drafter here is never to rely on an amendment agreement alone, but to restate the original agreement in its entirety. That way, the parties will have a chance to read through the restated agreement to check that it correctly reflects their new consensus. That reduces the risk that the amendment accidentally subverts some important aspect of the original contract which was meant to be retained.[57]

Decide what belongs in the body of the contract and what in schedules

1.19 At the most general level, the drafter has to decide what material should appear in the body of the contract and what, if anything, should be relegated to schedules.

The virtue of such a relegation process is that the main body of the contract can be kept shorter. It is attractive for a reader who may not have been engaged in drawing the contract up if the body of the contract is short enough for its overall shape to be appreciated at a single initial leaf-through.[58]

Schedules are appropriate for provisions which are in some sense secondary: perhaps the provisions are only relevant in some circumstances which the parties want to cater for but do not expect to apply; or they contain self-contained material;[59] or they contain material which will involve specialists to apply it (the specialists will be grateful if they only have to consider a particular schedule); or the schedules are necessary to explain in detail a particular provision whose essence can be more succinctly contained in an operative provision which directs the reader to the schedule for fuller detail.

Deal with separate matters coherently, grouping clauses into sections if possible

1.20 It makes sense for a drafter to deal with issues discretely rather than haphazardly. If a single clause or group of clauses deals comprehensively with some contractual issue, users of the contract who need to address the issue have a chance of discovering first time what the contract has to say about it, without having to navigate backwards and forwards within the contract to do so.

57 For another case where a difficulty was caused by the parties proceeding by amendment agreements rather than a comprehensive restatement, see *Surrey CC v Suez Recycling and Recovery Surrey Ltd* [2021] EWHC 2015 (TCC) (the parties did prepare a restated version of the original agreement, but merely exhibited it in an amendment agreement and had not in any event carried out the amendment exercise thoroughly ([85]).

58 Or perhaps 'scroll-through' is today a more realistic term.

59 Warranties and representations given by the parties to each other, for example.

The virtues of coherence go beyond just making the reader's life easier. As discussed at **1.23** below, where a drafter places the contract material can also affect what the contract actually *means*.

Coherence matters at every level in a contract. So although drafters will often think of a clause as the basic unit of drafting, the instinct towards coherence should persuade the drafter to try to group together clauses into larger groups of clauses that belong together. For example, an agreement for the supply of services could deal in Section A[60] with preliminary matters that have to be satisfied before the services begin to be provided; Section B with the services themselves and the standards that the supplier must meet; Section C with price, invoicing and payment; and Section D with duration of the contract, including termination for breach.

A considerate drafter will naturally tend to group the sections in the most natural order, reflecting (as in the example in the previous paragraph) the sequence in which the sections are expected to prove relevant. An alternative principle for the grouping of sections is to rank them in order of likely importance, which might point towards consolidating the clauses dealing with the services and the price for them into Section A, relegating preliminary issues to a schedule and perhaps treating invoicing and payment as matters of process to be dealt with later in the body of the contract, if not even in a schedule.

Do not expect a reader to know already what only comes later

1.21 Drafters should imitate skilful writers of English in non-contract writing and avoid, so far as possible, requiring a reader of any clause to anticipate information that is only given later on. So far as possible, in other words, a contract should read like a story: it should be able to be read from front to back without a reader having to run ahead to make sense of it.

This is a counsel of perfection, and will be difficult to achieve. It may not fit perfectly with other principles that guide the drafter as to order the contract (for example if the drafter is trying to deal with issues in order of their likely importance). But it has some consequences for how contracts are put together. For example, it suggests that the definitions clause should appear at the beginning of the contract, not the end. This gives a chance that a reader

[60] Or perhaps Part A (or Section I or Part I). There is no magic in the labels: the important thing is that they are used consistently.

who encounters a defined expression in an operative clause will already know what it means.[61]

Use headings

1.22 Good drafters use headings for the sections into which the clauses of the contract are grouped, and indeed use headings at other organisational levels within the contract, such as individual clauses,[62] schedules and parts of schedules. The intention is not usually that the headings have any contractual force, but rather to help a reader. Particularly with a contract of any length, the headings can be grouped together in a contents list with page numbers at the start of the contract, allowing a reader to find easily the part that is relevant to any particular enquiry. Other general language outside the operative clauses, themselves, for example explanatory or descriptive language included in a title to the agreement, may have a similar status.[63]

Because the headings are intended simply to be helpful rather than to change the meaning of the provisions they introduce, drafters often include among the boilerplate a provision along the following lines:

> Clause headings shall not affect the interpretation of this Contract.

That language has some force,[64] though judges have been known to dismiss it in a case where the clause heading seems to give a clue to a clause's real meaning.[65]

Do not 'bury away' important material

1.23 Judges are from time to time persuaded by arguments that, because of where in the contract it appears, some apparently clear language cannot be taken at face value.

[61] The counterargument is that if an expression has capital letters, a reader knows that it is defined in the definitions clause, and can easily find it if the definitions appear as the final clause or even in a schedule. Proponents of this drafting style have a point if there are so many definitions that their appearance at the front of the contract would defeat any reader's attempt to assimilate them on a read-through. In the contract at issue in *Amey Birmingham Highways Limited v Birmingham City Council* [2018] EWCA Civ 264, for example, the definitions ran to over 200 pages.

[62] Or even perhaps sub-clauses, if it helps more reliable cross-referencing (cf **1.27** below).

[63] *Thurcroft Power Ltd v Volta Energy Group Ltd* [2022] EWHC 338 (Comm) (at [139] and [144]).

[64] It was, for example, expressly respected in the High Court decision in *ABC Electrification Ltd v Network Rail Infrastructure Ltd* [2019] EWHC 1769 ([30.5]); and it was assumed to be effective in *Phoenicks Ltd v Bullock Property & Facilities Management Ltd* [2021] EWHC 2639 (Comm) ([80]). The Court of Appeal noted the presence of similar language, and impliedly at least took it into account, in interpreting a provision in *Kudos Catering (UK) Ltd v Manchester Central Convention Complex Ltd* [2013] EWCA Civ 38: Tomlinson LJ at [23].

[65] See, for example, Eder J in *Aston Hill Financial Inc v African Minerals Finance Ltd* [2012] EWHC 2173 at [32].

In *Charter Reinsurance v Fagan*,[66] the House of Lords refused to interpret the words *actually paid* to demand that money was paid over. In part, this was because in Lord Mustill's words the expression was 'buried in a provision such as clause 2...rather than being given a prominent position on its own'. So the position of the language in the contract influenced how it was to be interpreted. In saying this, the judge was prepared to overlook that clause 1 was expressed to be 'subject to the following terms and conditions' and that he had supplied the numbering of the clauses *himself* (in the original, the words were not in a clause numbered separately from what he decided was clause 1).

Charter Reinsurance may strike the drafter as a worrying decision. But it is arguably less worrying than the more recent case of *Re Sigma Corporation (in administrative receivership)*.[67]

In that case, a special purpose vehicle had become hopelessly insolvent. A security trustee acted for the vehicle's secured creditors. The question for the courts was to determine which categories of creditors the security trustee should distribute the vehicle's remaining assets to. The trust deed at first glance gave a clear answer. It directed the security trustee, during a particular period:

> so far as possible [to] discharge on the due dates therefor any Short Term Liabilities of the Issuer.

The reader might have thought that this was an unequivocal direction to the trustee as to what to do. Lord Mance, however, had other ideas. He thought that this language could not, given the overall 'scheme' of the document, mean what it appeared to mean. To enforce the language according to its terms

> may, therefore, involve a similar risk to that identified by Lord Mustill in *Charter Reinsurance* – that of giving to a sentence, buried in a provision like clause 7.6 concerned essentially with a different situation, the effect of changing fundamentally the apparent financial structure of the relationship.[68]

It did not matter that the clause was headed 'Enforcement' and that the dispute took place against a background where the security was being enforced. For Lord Mance, it was enough that the drafter had probably not foreseen that, as actually happened, the security might prove inadequate to pay all the secured creditors. That meant that the drafting, though expressed with total clarity and on its face clearly applicable, could not sensibly have been intended to apply in that extreme case.

66 [1997] AC 313.
67 [2009] UKSC 2.
68 ibid at para 14.

In a more recent example, the court in *Acerus Pharmaceuticals Corporation v Recpharm*[69] declined to apply the clear language of one particular provision of an agreement (clause 9.3) as if it were freestanding (which would arguably have given one party the ability to walk away from the agreement without liability). The meaning of clause 9.3 could be established only in the context of the other provisions of clause 9, with a much more limited effect. So where the provision appeared was, again, critical.

The 'buried away' concept also featured, though not in so many words, in litigation in which the Supreme Court considered the wording of business interruption insurance policies following the Covid-19 pandemic.[70] An exclusion for epidemic and disease, appearing on page 93 (out of 93) of one of the policies, was too deeply interred for the Supreme Court to accept that it could negate cover that specifically related to business interruption covered by a 'notifiable disease' such as Covid-19.[71]

'Burying away' is also the term that judges use when considering the linked, but conceptually separate, question of whether a particularly onerous or unusual clause will be incorporated in a contract if it has not been fairly and reasonably drawn to the attention of the unsuspecting party affected by it. Terms of this type must not be 'buried away' either: see, for example, *Blu-Sky Solutions Ltd v Be Caring Ltd.*[72]

Drafters ignore this type of case at their peril. The cases show that judges can be tempted to regard where language appears in a contract to be just as important as (in *Sigma*, indeed, more important than) what the language actually says. The risk is greater the higher up the court system the disputed contract is taken. Judges in the highest courts are not short of intellectual self-confidence, and may be more willing to override the natural meaning of language in a quest to impose what they consider an equitable solution to the problem of interpretation with which they have been presented.[73]

To guard against a judge assuming that a particular clause intended to be of general application is to be more narrowly construed, explicit language may be useful. This can be overtly hierarchical:

> Notwithstanding anything else in this contract[74]

or can simply seek to remove the implication that the provision is, by being 'buried away', intended to be of more limited effect than it is:

69 [2021] EWHC 1878.

70 *Financial Conduct Authority v Arch Insurance (UK) Ltd* [2021] UKSC 1.

71 Lord Hamblen and Lord Leggatt in their joint judgment at [75]–[78].

72 [2021] EWHC 2619: Stephen Davies at [59] and [112] (provision for an 'administration charge' on cancellation held 'buried away' and 'concealed' within some standard terms).

73 Judges may also apply the same principle the other way round, and accord more status to a provision to which the drafter gives prominence: see, for example, the importance ascribed by Cooke J to a term contained in the frontispiece to the contract in bold type (*SNCB Holding v UBS AG* [2012] EWHC 2044 at [76]).

74 See also Chapter 12 below at **12.21**.

> This sub-clause [x], despite appearing in the context of a clause generally dealing with the position if [name of regulatory authority] has given permission for the sale of the Assets to proceed, shall also apply if that is not the case.

But to give the contract the greatest measure of apparent coherence, it may be best to arrange the drafting in such a way that provisions intended to be of general application cannot be accused of being 'buried away' at all. If a provision is of general application, bring it to the fore. Most drafters would instinctively, if the parties were happy to agree on a statement of overriding principle by reference to which the whole of the contract should be interpreted, to state it at the beginning. Even if there is no such overarching principle, provisions of more or less general application could usefully be grouped together in a clause introduced by the following:[75]

> The following provisions of this clause [1] shall, except if and to the extent that they are expressly qualified, be generally applicable throughout the life of the contract.

That type of language should deter any judge from finding that such a provision could not have been intended to mean what it said. And the reference to express qualification enables the drafter to identify and cater for those particular cases where it is agreed the language should not apply, or should apply only with modifications: see Chapter 12 below.

Take care with 'surprising' provisions – even if not 'buried away'

1.24 The courts' reluctance to apply 'buried away' provisions unreflectingly is only one manifestation of their eagerness to interpret contractual provisions in their proper context. As Lord Neuberger said in the leading case of *Arnold v Britton,*[76] 'disputed words in a contract need to be interpreted in their *documentary*, factual and commercial context'.[77]

This necessarily involves the court looking at the *whole* of a contract, not just a part of it. The rigour with which the courts do so is graphically illustrated by *Triple Point Technology, Inc v PTT Public Company Ltd,*[78] where Lady Arden commented that she had found it 'helpful' to see the entire 507-page contract rather than the trifling 74-page extract that had been made available to the Court of Appeal.

[75] If the contract, as discussed in **1.22** above, contains a provision directing clause headings to be ignored, this would be better than relying on a clause headed something like 'Generally Applicable Provisions'.

[76] [2015] UKSC 36.

[77] ibid at [15]: emphasis added.

[78] [2021] UKSC 29 at [50].

English courts also respect, as a fundamental principle, the parties' freedom to agree whatever they like. English law generally imposes no overriding criterion of reasonableness: it is left to the parties to guard against onerous outcomes arising from the contracts they enter into.[79]

While the courts will usually, therefore, enforce the bargain that the contract records, drafters need to bear in mind a certain prejudice among judges against untidiness. In particular, judges have an instinct that a contract is likely to reflect consistently a set of principles, with the rights and obligations that the contract contains reflecting those principles pervasively and consistently. But (as judges often, to their credit, explicitly recognise),[80] the parties to the contract may well have arrived at their contractual consensus through a more haphazard process of give and take, in which a concession in one area may have been traded for a victory in another.

So a contract may often contain some drafting on a particular issue which looks illogical against a set of surrounding provisions that seem otherwise to embody a consistent principle. The drafting on that issue seems to stick out like a sore thumb. That 'illogicality' can give a disaffected party the beginnings of an argument that, because the 'sore thumb' drafting is inconsistent with the principle that can be discerned in other provisions, 'something must have gone wrong with the language'.[81] The provision is, in the context of everything else in the contract, *surprising*. The judge who concludes that something has gone wrong with the language is preparing to substitute some other words that work better.

A provision may be surprising not only when compared with other provisions in the contract. It can be surprising because it represents *in itself* an unlikely thing for the parties to have agreed. For example, parties may exclude liability for their own negligence. But for many years, the courts have been reluctant to conclude that they have achieved this unless they use express language or the language they use necessarily implies that they meant to do so.[82] And in an

79 Although statutory protection for consumers has long been in place, reflecting the unequal bargaining power as between consumers and what Lord Denning used to call 'the big concern': see *George Mitchell (Chesterhall Ltd v Finney Lock Seeds Ltd* [1982] EWCA Civ 5 – see now especially the Consumer Rights Act 2015. And, of course, the courts have other non-statutory law tools to protect unwary parties from being unfairly taken advantage of: estoppel, for example, and the ability to set aside contracts entered into under duress or under undue influence.

80 Lord Neuberger in the Court of Appeal in *Sigma* [2008] EWCA Civ 1303 at [100].

81 Lord Hoffmann in *Investors Compensation Scheme Ltd* v *West Bromwich Building Society (no. 1)* [1998] 1 WLR 896, repeated (by Lord Hoffmann himself) in *Chartbrook Ltd v Persimmon Homes Ltd* [2009] UKHL 38 at [14] (and, in only slightly different language, at [25]).

82 *Canada Steamship Lines Ltd v The King* [1952] AC 192. Modern judges tend to see this principle as subsumed within a wider principle that without clear wording to the contrary, parties will be presumed to have intended to contract on a 'normal' basis (see Lord Leggatt in *Triple Point Technology Inc v PTT Public Company Ltd* [2021] UKSC 29 at [109], citing *Modern Engineering (Bristol) Ltd v Gilbert-Ash (Northern) Ltd* [1974] AC 689 as the leading source of the principle).

insurance contract, it may be[83] that the parties can agree that the insurer is to remain on risk even if the insured is guilty of a fraudulent misrepresentation or non-disclosure. But that is such an unlikely bargain for the parties to have made that it would require to be expressed 'in clear and unmistakable terms on the face of the contract'.[84]

Drafters need therefore to take particular care to put beyond challenge provisions that do form part of the parties' consensus but are, in these terms, a surprising thing for them to have agreed.

One way of doing this is through an explicit acknowledgement of the inconsistency, for example:

> Even though, in accordance with sub-clauses (1) to (4) above, the risk of withholding tax applying to payments by the Customer is generally to be borne by the Supplier, in relation to Finnish withholding tax, the Customer shall bear the risk and accordingly [language imposing a grossing-up obligation].

Or drafters could consider a more thoroughgoing provision intended to influence the interpretation of the contract as a whole. Perhaps this could take the form of a recital recording that the contract has been entered into after extensive and detailed negotiation; that the process of negotiation has involved compromise on both sides in relation to specific points; and that the parties acknowledge that the contract does not always reflect application of a set of overriding principles, but that (despite this) the parties wish each provision of the contract to be enforceable in accordance with its terms.

A drafter who leaves any gaps has particularly failed if what is missing (or only sketchily covered) would, if it had been fully and expressly provided for, have been 'surprising' in the sense used in this paragraph. The party who would have benefited from the missing or defective provision can only argue that what is missing item is an *implied* term of the contract. But a court faced with an argument that a term should be implied will not imply a term that is inconsistent with the express terms of the contract. So the party who wants to rely on an implied term is doomed to fail.

Do not repeat yourself

1.25 Most readers of contracts would prefer them to be shorter than they are. So why do drafters so often disappoint by serving up longer ones? The

83 The point having been left open in *HIH Casualty & General Insurance Ltd v Chase Manhattan Bank* [2003] UKHL 6.

84 Lord Bingham in the *HIH* case (ibid) at [16]. See also *Stocznia Gdynia SA v Gearbulk Holdings Ltd* [2009] EWCA Civ 75 (language purporting to limit purchaser's rights under shipbuilding contract held not clear enough to displace right to recover damages for loss of bargain).

hallmark of the second-rate drafter is to load the contract with overlapping provisions which deal with the same issue in slightly different language.

Readers of contracts, who often find contractual language baffling and difficult to follow even when it appears only once, are not gratified to be served up a double dose. Nor is the problem merely that it wastes a reader's time. If two clauses deal with the same issue, they will usually do so in slightly different language, and are therefore likely to be inconsistent with one another. And the characteristic of this sort of careless drafting is that the drafter does not acknowledge the overlap, still less make it clear which, if inconsistencies exist, is the language that prevails.

The practical explanation for this phenomenon is twofold. First, lawyers are by nature and training conservative and cautious. They are more frightened of overlooking something than of confusing readers by repeating themselves, or nearly doing so. Second, contracts that are based on templates or precedents tend to grow by accretion, as those charged with maintaining a current version identify a new provision which looks as if could improve the agreement. It is easier to insert a whole new provision as it stands than it is to perform the delicate surgery necessary to introduce only those parts of the new provision that are needed, cutting out the bits that are otiose and adapting the new material to fit into the existing contract without duplicating it or conflicting with it.

Although judges are used to dealing with drafting that repeats itself, the conscientious drafter avoids what Lord Neuberger calls a 'belt and braces approach'[85] and Lord Hoffmann, more vividly, calls 'torrential' drafting.[86] The paradoxical difficulty with what Lord Hoffmann elsewhere described[87] as the drafter's 'determination to make sure that one has obliterated the potential target' is that it becomes harder rather than easier for the drafter to be confident both that everything that needs saying has been said, and that there is no confusing inconsistency between the overlapping provisions.

One particular version of this problem is the so-called 'argument from redundancy'. Although some judges acknowledge that drafters' caution can lead to superfluous drafting, and that any overlap is no more than an unfortunate accident, others feel more nervous about accepting that some parts of a legal agreement are simply 'surplusage' – an unnecessary waste of ink or pixels.

This leads the judge to preferring an interpretation of the language that would give it *some* meaning rather than one that would leave it bereft of *any*. That the issue can be put in this way shows that the issue arises only where

85 *Macquarie Internationale Investments v Glencore UK Ltd* [2010] EWCA Civ 697.

86 *Norwich Union Life Insurance Society v British Railways Board* [1987] 2 EGLR 137, cited by Lord Neuberger in the *Macquarie* case referred to in n 85: see **12.11** below.

87 In *Arbuthnot v Fagan* [1995] CLC 1396 at [1404].

more than one interpretation of the language is feasible: in other words, only when the drafter has already lapsed into ambiguity.

The 'argument from redundancy' is one that many judges view with scepticism, but one can still see it surfacing and proving influential. For example, Arden LJ, construing a disputed trust deed in *Singapore Airlines Ltd v Buck Consultants Ltd*:[88] 'It is highly unlikely that the drafter would have inserted a wholly redundant Limb 2 between operative Limbs 1 and 3'.

Two Supreme Court cases make the point as well.

In *Kookmin v Rainy Sky*,[89] the court considered how to interpret a performance bond issue by a bank. Lord Clarke remarked that 'the strength of the [b]ank's interpretation is that it is not easy to see the point of paragraph [2] of the Bonds if the Buyers' interpretation of paragraph [3] is correct'.[90]

In *Tael One Partners v Morgan Stanley & Co International PLC*,[91] Lord Reed was considering the drafting of an agreement for the sale of a loan participation. He took pains to explain why he did *not* consider that his conclusion as to the meaning of some particular language rendered it partly redundant. The clear subtext of what he said is that if he *had* thought that his conclusion would have had that effect, he might have reached a different one.

Be careful that being specific does not disguise holes in contractual coverage

1.26 The more specific that drafting is, the more likely it is that the drafter has dealt clearly with its subject matter. But a danger lurks in drafting that is *uneven* in the level of detail with which it deals with different issues.

The danger is most clearly seen if one issue is dealt with in detail, but another issue, superficially similar, is not dealt with at all.

A drafter able and conscientious enough to have provided in detail for one set of circumstances is not likely to have ignored another set of circumstances by accident. The very detail of the drafting for the circumstances that *are* covered implies that it is deliberate that the other set of circumstances are ignored.

McKillen v Misland (Cyprus) Investments Ltd[92] is a good example. A contract contained some pre-emption provisions that imposed strict requirements on

[88] [2011] EWCA Civ 1542 at [39].
[89] [2011] UKSC 50: see also below at **7.12**.
[90] Though in the end his Lordship, together with the other members of the court, found against the bank on other grounds.
[91] [2015] UKSC 12 (at [45]); see also **1.10** above.
[92] [2011] EWHC 3466 (Ch): 'The absence of provisions dealing with a sale of a corporate shareholder is, objectively speaking, consistent with a decision by the parties not to include them' (David Richards J at [102]. The decision was upheld in the Court of Appeal: [2012] EWCA Civ 864.

transfers by any shareholder in a particular company called Coroin. But the drafter had not sought to control at all disposals of shares in a company that *itself* held shares in Coroin. The court inferred that the parties could not have intended the pre-emption restrictions to operate at that level, even though that offered an easy way to circumvent the commercial effect of pre-emption.

This phenomenon has been encountered so often by the courts over so many years that it has been dignified by its own Latin tag: *expressio unius est exclusio alterius.*[93]. Modern English judges would deny it the status of a 'canon of construction', to be followed unthinkingly. It now more represents a common sense way of trying to divine the intention of a contract that is uneven in its coverage.

Examples abound, and the characteristic consequence is that where express language is found in one clause, it cannot be implied in another. Two will suffice.

In *BDW Trading Ltd v J M Rowe (Investments) Ltd,*[94] an agreement for development of a site in Watford gave BDW a right to rescind it. But the right to rescind was excluded 'where [BDW] is in default of its obligations under this clause 6.2'. The question arose: by dealing specifically with clause 6.2, did the agreement impliedly allow BDW to rescind if it had breached not clause 6.2 but some *other* provision? It was held that the answer was yes: by dealing specifically with clause 6.2, the drafter had signalled that other breaches should not affect the right to rescind.[95]

In *Brookfield Construction (UK) Ltd v Foster and Partners Ltd,*[96] some clauses placed time limits on obligations, but others did not. Coulson J held that no time limit should be implied into the clauses which lacked an express limit: 'where the parties wanted to place time limits on ...performance of specific obligations, they did just that'.

As this quote attests, a judge who applies the principle often credits the drafter with having put the contract together with scrupulous care. Cynical observers of the drafting process may harbour a suspicion that this is not always justified. May it not often be that the drafter did not notice that the level of detail was uneven? The provisions that contain the level of detail may just be those which the parties, in negotiation, cared particularly about, without anybody thinking about whether the attention lavished on them should also apply to other areas of the contract.

93 Broadly, coverage of one thing implies another is not covered.

94 [2011] EWCA Civ 548.

95 See also *Cattles plc v Welcome Financial Services Ltd* [2010] EWCA Civ 599 at [49] (references to 'liabilities under this deed' showed that 'where the draftsman intended to refer to liabilities arising under the deed he could and did so': Lloyd LJ); see also *Shell UK Ltd v Total UK Ltd* [2010] EWCA Civ 180 at [83]: 'the argument that the draftsman when he intended to indemnify a party against that party's own negligence expressly so provided is still a compelling argument'.

96 [2009] EWHC 307 (TCC) see [29].

It follows that a drafter must consider whether the level of detail with which one issue has been dealt with may imply that other provisions may be misinterpreted. In particular, if one particular provision has attracted considerable attention and that has resulted in very detailed drafting, is that disproportionate? Are there elements of, or principles underlying, that detailed drafting that also apply more widely, but without them being expressly provided for?[97] If so, the drafter should modify the drafting to cope.

Double check cross-references

1.27 A drafter will often need to cross-refer in one clause another clause in the same contract or another contract.

This seems a straightforward process, but its success depends, obviously enough, on the cross-reference being accurate. If it is not, the drafter may fail to achieve the desired result. If the drafter has made a simple and obvious mistake, the court may sensibly substitute the correct cross-reference as a matter of construing the document as it stands. But it is embarrassing to rely on the court mercifully correcting a drafting mistake, and could be dangerous too. It may be arguable that the cross-reference was not made by mistake was not made by accident but deliberately. This happened in *Bishops Wholesale Newsagency Ltd v Surridge Dawson Ltd*,[98] when a reference in a later clause to 'clause 9.3.2(ii)' was held to mean what it said, and not to be a mistakenly over-precise cross-reference to the whole of clause 9.3.2 (including therefore sub-paragraph (i) as well). On this narrow point turned a difference of £2.5 million in the price payable on exercise of a put option over shares in a private company.

One difficulty with cross-references is that the drafter may have drafted them accurately in an early draft of the contract, but later changes render them out of date. Some programmes support the updating of cross-references, but the cautious drafter will want to make sure before the execution of an agreement to make sure that the cross-references are all accurate. This may best be carried out as a discrete task by a fresh pair of eyes at some point when the document is, the drafter hopes, in final form.

One technique that can help is to frame a cross-reference to another provision not simply in terms of the number of the clause (which may change as provisions are added to or deleted from successive drafts) but also to the name or title of the provision in question. To do so provides some sort of insurance against the numbering changing with unforeseen effect, as it

97 For example, in *McKillen* (n 92), was the true principle underlying the contract that the parties wanted to control the change of ownership of a shareholder's interest in Coroin, whether directly *or* indirectly?

98 [2009] EWHC 2578 (Ch); see also *Dalkia Utilities Services Plc v Celltech International Ltd* [2006] EWHC 63 (Comm).

becomes easier to pick up if a simple mistake in cross-reference has been made, or the contract has changed so as to make an originally accurate cross-reference now a misleading one. But it also helps explain the rationale of the reason for the cross-reference:

> If the Supplier believes that a Force Majeure Event has occurred, the Supplier shall within seven days deliver a notice under clause 14.2 (Procedure in Force Majeure Event) to the Customer.

This of course depends on the contract awarding headings to its provisions, here not merely at the level of the clause but also at the level of sub-clauses. This is a recommended technique.[99]

Do not draft in slabs

1.28 Present-day English lawyers understand better the benefit of clear writing[100] in communicating with their clients. They recognise that if they write in short sentences and avoid legal jargon, they are more likely to make themselves understood. They also recognise that only by putting themselves into the shoes of their readers can they give their clients the service that the clients want.

But many lawyers have made less progress in making their *contracts* easy to understand. Too often, contracts are characterised by slabs of drafting written in dense and intricate style. No attempt is made to control the length of the sentences into which the drafting is divided, and punctuation is either erratic or non-existent.[101]

One can speculate on the reasons why the profession has made less progress in modernising contract drafting than in other forms of writing. One possibility is that lawyers have always regarded contracts as a particular legal preserve: if they are disputed, it is another lawyer (a judge) who will decide what they mean. There is no need to inhale the fresh air of the world outside the law.

Another possibility is that lawyers, members of a profession that is by nature conservative, are at their most conservative when they come to consider drafting. They worry that if a form of words has been used before, it would be dangerous to depart from it. In tinkering with the language, they might be doing so in the face of judicial precedent and cause the drafting to miss the mark. It is safer to stick with something they have seen before, even if it is difficult to explain why.

99 See also **1.22** above.

100 Aided by the efforts of organisations such as Clarity, an international organisation that promotes the use of plain legal language, and the Plain English campaign.

101 A separate flaw, but one that contributes to the impenetrability of slablike drafting: see **1.30** below.

Another argument is that obscurity is inevitable, because drafters need to use technical legal language to record the agreement economically and accurately, and language of that type is not easy for someone who is not a trained lawyer to follow. But even if that is true to some extent, it does not excuse needless complexity of style.

It is no surprise that the drafting that leads to disputes is very often slablike in this fashion. The drafter has, by adopting the style, made it too hard for anyone reading it through in advance to spot that it does not make sense, or hides an unresolved ambiguity.

The point is too obvious to need much elaboration, but two examples may help.

First, in *Investors Compensation Scheme v West Bromwich Building Society (no. 1),*[102] a release document provided in part that

> I.C.S. agrees that the following claims shall not be treated as a 'Third Party Claim' [as defined in section 4 of this form] for the purposes of this agreement and that the benefits of such claims shall enure to you absolutely:
>
> > ...any claim (whether sounding in rescission for undue influence or otherwise) that you have or may have against the West Bromwich Building Society in which you claim an abatement of sums which you would otherwise have to repay to that Society in respect of sums borrowed by you from that Society in connection with the transaction and dealings giving rise to the claim (including interest on any such sums).

This drafting contains 109 words. It is not wholly bereft of punctuation: the drafter was prepared to concede the use of a colon and two sets of brackets. But the relentlessness of the drafting makes it difficult to focus adequately on any particular part of it. So nobody apparently noticed, although this was a commonly-used document that must have been signed up to many times, that the language in the first set of brackets ('whether sounding in rescission for undue influence or otherwise') was in itself difficult to understand (as Lord Hoffmann remarked, 'the words have not been used in a natural and ordinary way').[103] The oddity of language would have been more likely to have been identified if not embedded in a slab of drafting.

Second, consider the drafting of an asset sale agreement:[104]

[102] [1998] 1 WLR 896.

[103] The drafter has the consolation prize of being responsible for giving the House of Lords the opportunity to deliver a decision that is regarded as among the most authoritative and influential in the field of contractual interpretation.

[104] From *Rhodia International Holdings Ltd v Huntsman International LLC* [2007] EWHC 292 (Comm).

> If, and provided that the Purchaser shall have performed its obligations pursuant to Clause 15.1.2, the rights and obligations of [the Second Claimant] under any of the Novated Contracts listed in Schedule 14 cannot be transferred to the Purchaser whether by way of novation or assignment within six months of the date of Completion, then the Purchaser will be entitled by notice to [the Second Claimant] in writing to require [the Second Claimant] to exclude such Novated Contract from the sale of the Business Assets whereupon, unless the other party to such Restricted Contract has indicated to the Vendors in writing or to the Purchaser that it is not willing to consent to the assignment or the novation of the relevant Novated Contract principally because of the identity of the Purchaser or any other members of the Purchaser's Group, the Vendors shall pay to the Purchaser an amount equal to the diminution in the value of the Surfactants Operations caused by the fact that such Novated Contract was not novated or assigned, such diminution in value to be calculated using the discounted cash flow method set out in Schedule 19 and neither [the Second Claimant] nor the Purchaser shall have any further obligation to any other party to this [Sale and Purchase] Agreement in related to such Novated Contract and the provisions of Clause 15.1 shall cease to apply to such Novated Contract.

This drafting contains 233 words in a single sentence. The drafter has at least here used some commas, but the length of the sentence must surely have contributed to the feature that neither side to the contract identified that the drafting embodied an ambiguity in its language (of the 'uncertain modifier' type discussed at **7.2** below).[105]

In both the above examples, the meaning of the drafting could not be agreed without resort to a judge, or more than one judge. It is apparent in each case that the drafter's unsympathetic drafting *style* must be identified as the chief culprit. A drafter should strain to avoid serving up indigestible slabs. Drafting should be broken down into shorter units of meaning, separately numbered or lettered in a coherent hierarchy to make their meaning clear.

If this point needs any further reinforcement, it is worth reflecting that when judges are faced with slab-like drafting, they often divide it up *themselves*, using

[105] The issue is that it is unclear whether: (a) the consequence in the last few lines ('no further obligation…') depend simply on the first few lines of the clause (from 'if' to just before 'whereupon'); or (b) that consequence is also contingent on the 'unless' condition which follows 'whereupon'. This is an ambiguity that can only be seen with difficulty, often not before the third or fourth reading. But that is rather the point.

lettered or numbered sub-paragraphs, in order to analyse the drafting issues or to explain the reasons for them deciding the case in a particular way.[106]

If judges responsible for resolving ambiguities use this technique, drafters themselves should surely emulate it if they are to avoid ambiguities arising in the first place.

Remember that separate units of drafting are self-contained

1.29 Slabs of drafting are difficult to read and, for that reason, tend to conceal any ambiguity. The solution is, as discussed, to divide the drafting into shorter units. But a drafter should bear in mind that separate units of drafting are regarded as self-contained. It is not legitimate to 'read across' from one sub-paragraph, say, into another. Language that appears in sub-paragraph (a) but not in sub-paragraph (b) will not be taken as applying in the circumstances dealt with in (b). Indeed, the very absence of the language from sub-paragraph (b) may be argued to represent a deliberate attempt to signify that the language does *not* apply in the circumstances provided for in (b).

This principle can be seen in operation in *NIHL Ltd v Infinite Ltd (in liquidation).*[107]

In paragraph 1 of a consent order lodged with the court as part of a stay of proceedings, the claimant in an action agreed to use reasonable endeavours to reach, by a particular date, a 'full and final settlement' of its claims against the defendant. In paragraph 2, it was agreed that if 'such settlement' was not reached, the claimant would be at liberty to enter final judgment for a stated sum.

The date passed with no settlement reached. The defendant tried to resist the claimant entering final judgment for the stated sum, arguing that 'such settlement' in paragraph 2 meant a settlement that the claimant had used reasonable efforts to have reached, as was required in paragraph 1. But the court did not agree. The only link between the paragraphs was that in paragraph 2, 'such settlement' meant a full and final settlement. The claimant's argument that there was 'no other link' between the paragraphs was correct, and the requirement on the claimant to use reasonable endeavours to reach a settlement, contained in paragraph 1, could not be read across as imposing a condition of its right to enter judgment contained in paragraph 2.

106 See, for example, *Mid Essex Hospital Services NHS Trust v Compass Group UK and Ireland Ltd (trading as Medirest)* [2013] EWCA Civ 200 (Jackson LJ at [97]–[98]); and *Wood v Capita Insurance Services Ltd* [2017] UKSC 24, where Lord Hodge at [29] adopts the version of the disputed language into which Popplewell J had 'helpfully divided' it. In *Travelport Ltd v Wex Inc* [2020] EWHC 2670 (Comm), Cockerill J set out the disputed definition ('Material Effect') 'with line breaks added to the original for ease of reading'. That breakdown produced 14 separate subparagraphs, which suggests how impenetrable the original layout must have been.

107 [2020] EWHC 3136.

This principle can sometimes be overridden by a judge, and 'reading across' allowed, if applying the principle seems to give the 'wrong' answer. In *Phoenicks Ltd v Bellrock Property and Facilities Management Ltd,*[108] for example, Stephen Davies said that not to read across would 'give undue emphasis to the way in which the paragraph [was] set out'. But in so deciding, the judge acknowledged that the principle exists.

Drafters are recommended to respect the principle rather than relying on a merciful judge to rescue the meaning they intend.

The principle operates only as between units of drafting that are at the same level of hierarchy, for example between numbered sub-paragraphs. It is easy to draft so as to override the principle by taking care with the layout of the drafting. For example, say that a drafter wants to make clear that some language applies equally to both sub-paragraphs (a) and (b) of a single paragraph. The drafter can indent sub-paragraphs (a) and (b)[109] and, rather than stranding the language in either of the sub-paragraphs, include it in a preamble or postscript that precedes or follows the sub-paragraphs and is not indented to the same degree. It is then plain that the language applies to both sub-paragraphs.

Punctuate

1.30 Punctuation is a valuable tool for the drafter. Punctuation marks 'serve to give indications of the grammatical structure and/or meaning of stretches of written text'.[110] Punctuation can therefore, in the hands of a careful drafter, function in a similar way that layout (separating the contractual language into separately numbered or lettered paragraphs or subparagraphs) does to make clear the interrelationship of components of the drafting and in particular, to reduce the chances of uncertain modifiers making the meaning unclear.[111]

Nonetheless, many drafters of legal documents traditionally drafted without punctuating at all, or used punctuation minimally. Many lawyers, even in today's profession, retain a lurking doubt as to whether it is legitimate to rely on punctuation to help convey meaning, dimly recollecting perhaps that English statutes were traditionally unpunctuated.

However, if drafters do think this, they are wrong.[112] Nor are judges interpreting a contract required to ignore punctuation, though they may do so for two

108 [2021] EWHC 2639 (Comm) at [77]).
109 Most normal IT programmes will of course automatically do this.
110 Huddleston and Pullum, *The Cambridge Grammar of the English Language* (Cambridge University Press, 2002) p 1724.
111 See from **7.2** below.
112 Their error was described by David Mellinkoff in *The Language of Law* Chapter X (n 40), as 'a canard of venerable but undetermined vintage'. Since Mellinkoff was writing in 1963, the canard deserves to smell pretty rank by now.

reasons. One is that the drafter's control of punctuation is so slipshod that in any particular case, it would be dangerous to assume that the presence or absence of a punctuation mark is deliberate.[113] The second is that there are other reasons to doubt whether the punctuation was intended to have any significance.[114] But these are exceptions, not the rule.[115]

Practitioners in some areas are more likely to omit punctuation than others. Real estate lawyers have a particular blind spot. For example, in *Morris v Blackpool BC*,[116] one paragraph of a lease read:

> The Lessee shall comply with and observe any reasonable regulations which the Council may consistent with the provisions of this Deed make to govern the use of the Flats and Reserved Property Such regulations may be restrictive of acts done on the Property detrimental to its character or amenities Any costs or expenses incurred by the Council preparing or supplying copies of such regulations or in doing works for the improvement of the Property providing services or employing gardeners porters or other employees shall be deemed to have been properly incurred by the Council in pursuance of its obligations under the Eighth Schedule hereto notwithstanding the absence of any specific covenant by the Council to incur them.

Gloster LJ observed:[117]

> I comment that although upper case letters were used at the start of what appear to be separate sentences in this paragraph, consistently with the rest of the lease, no full stops or commas were used anywhere in this paragraph.

The reader of the lease finds it hard to follow: a reader of the judgment is left in no doubt as to what her Ladyship thought about the drafter's prowess.[118]

113 See *Mapeley Acquisition Co (3) Ltd v City of Edinburgh Council* [2015] CSOH 29, where Lord Doherty described at [20] the punctuation in the lease he was considering as 'throughout… variable'.

114 Such as that it may have been no more than an accident of the process of document production: see the Privy Council in *Sammut v Manzi* [2008] UKPC 58 (Lord Phillips at [8]).

115 For recent examples of judges taking punctuation into account in determining the meaning of a disputed clause, see *CC Construction Ltd v Mincione* [2021] EWHC 2502 at [96] (language of qualification enclosed by commas and construed as referring to what followed); *Rolls-Royce Holdings PLC v Goodrich Corporation* [2023] EWHC 1637 at [98(i)] (comma indicating a natural break); *Al Mana Lifestyle Trading LLC v United Fidelity Insurance Company PSC* [2023] EWCA Civ 61 at [66] (punctuation in jurisdiction clause taken into account despite an obvious error); and *Angeliki Frangou v Ioannis (John) Frangos* [2023] EWCA Civ 1320 at [57] (position of wording relating to time before a comma clearly therefore not controlling the part of the sentence following the comma).

116 [2014] EWCA Civ 1384.

117 ibid at [7].

118 In a similar vein, Sedley LJ introduced his discussion of some disputed inadequately drafted provisions as follows in *Goldmile Properties v Lechouritis* [2003] EWCA Civ 49 by observing 'The lease, in familiar form (including the traditional eschewal of punctuation, however convoluted the clause), contained the following provisions…'.

Similarly, consider the drafting of a sub-underlease in *KPMG LLP v Network Rail Infrastructure Ltd*:[119]

> If the Tenants shall be desirous of determining the said term hereby granted at any time after the expiration of the third thirteenth and twenty third years of the said term and of such desire shall give to the Landlords not less than six calendar months' notice in writing (such notice to expire on any quarter day and to be given within a period of six months following the determination of the reviewed rent to be payable from the expiration of the first eleventh and twenty-first years respectively of the said term and thereafter during the year immediately preceding the eleventh and twenty-first years respectively of the said term) then on the expiration of such notice as aforesaid the said term shall cease and determine but without prejudice to the rights and remedies of either party against the other in respect of any antecedent claim or breach of covenant.

This drafting contains 149 words and is again, apart from some brackets, unpunctuated. The language had been substantially repeated from an earlier version of the document,[120] but some words were omitted, possibly by accident.[121]

In the Court of Appeal, Carnwath LJ said:

> It is indeed surprising, as the judge said, that no-one gave the paragraph sufficient attention to work out precisely what it meant. It is perhaps even more surprising that it was again overlooked by both sides when, in 1984, it was revised, and the dates were altered, following the splitting of the term.

But the style of the drafting is relevant. The lack of punctuation means that the reader's eye tends to slide over the language without finding any purchase. It makes it rather less surprising that both sides failed to notice, before executing it, that it was unclear.[122]

The reader cannot escape the impression that the lack of punctuation caused or contributed to the error being made and escaping detection while there was still time to correct it. The drafter who does not use punctuation is making the drafting harder to follow and is at the same time increasing the chances of error and ambiguity. It is an inexplicable habit.

[119] [2007] EWCA Civ 363.

[120] The drafting of which Carnwath LJ terms 'markedly inelegant' (footnote 1 to his judgment).

[121] The words missing from the passage contained in brackets before the words 'and thereafter' were 'but in the event only that such reviewed rent exceeds the yearly rent payable during the (first) year of the said term': see Carnwath LJ ibid at [6].

[122] For a similar error, see *Homburg Houtimport BV v Agrosin Ltd (The Starsin)* [2004] 1 AC 715.

Chapter 2

Recording the commercial background

Judges take note of the commercial background to contracts. While a contract can itself enshrine general principles, it is in recitals that the drafter often reflects both principles and the agreed commercial background. Recitals can influence the interpretation of the contract, but not override operative provisions; in some types of contracts, they may prove particularly useful.

RECITALS, AND THEIR DISTINCTION FROM OPERATIVE CLAUSES

2.1 A contract's commercial background colours the meaning of its language

2.2 Use recitals to record the agreed commercial background and agreed assumptions

2.3 Use recitals to insulate the drafting against errors within the contract

2.4 Do not locate obligations in recitals: they belong in the operative clauses

2.5 Also put overriding general principles in an operative clause, not the recitals

CIRCUMSTANCES WHERE RECITALS ARE PARTICULARLY USEFUL

2.6 To express the commercial rationale for the whole agreement

2.7 To express the commercial rationale for a specific provision

2.8 To explain adequately some otherwise un- or under-explained matter

2.9 Where the contract is long, complex or enduring

2.10 To acknowledge the parity of bargaining power or the reasonableness of the contract terms

RECITALS, AND THEIR DISTINCTION FROM OPERATIVE CLAUSES

A contract's commercial background colours the meaning of its language

2.1 A contract exists to record the set of promises that each party to the contract acknowledges, by entering into the contract, it is prepared to be held to. So it is tempting to conclude that a contract should confine itself to recording those promises. Those provisions alone are 'justiciable': they alone can be enforced by a court, or trigger an award of damages if they have been breached.

That conclusion is bolstered when one recalls that the interpretation of a contract is under English law an *objective* exercise. That means that the parties' subjective intentions – what each party in its own mind wanted the contract to achieve, or thought it meant – are irrelevant when a court comes to interpret it.[1] Equally irrelevant is evidence of any negotiations leading up to the contract. The courts recognise that the parties' negotiating positions are fluid, and that a party may offer a concession at one point in the negotiations, only to withdraw it later.[2]

But this overstates the case. It is true that in refusing to admit evidence of a party's subjective intentions, the courts recognise that the parties will have different intentions – so to interpret a contract simply so as to meet one party's objectives might be to disappoint another's. But the same cannot be said about the parties' *shared* intentions. Indeed, a common purpose is an important part of the background matrix that the court must take into account as part of the process of interpretation.

Use recitals to record the agreed commercial background and agreed assumptions

2.2 Accordingly, if there is any evidence of a common understanding about the commercial background (what happened before the contract that caused the parties to want to enter into the contract, for example, and what its overall purpose is), this can influence a court faced with the task of deciding what the contractual language means.

The most natural place for such a statement of common understanding is in the contractual document itself, usually in a set of 'recitals' which precede

1 See, for example, Lord Hoffmann's extensive review of the principle in *Chartbrook Ltd v Persimmon Homes Ltd* [2009] UKHL 38.

2 Lord Wilberforce in *Prenn v Simmonds* [1971] WLR 1381, quoted at length by Lord Hoffmann in *Chartbrook* (ibid) at [31].

the operative terms of the contract and are introduced by the old-fashioned introductory word 'Whereas'.[3] Modern drafters may prefer simply to label the recitals 'Background', but the traditional term remains popular among drafters and is for that reason adopted below.

The drafter who records in recitals a statement of common understanding of the agreed contractual purpose is effectively insuring the contract against incompleteness. If the operative provisions do not deal with a particular circumstance, the recitals can fill the gap and point towards how it should be filled. Because the recitals appear in the contract itself, neither party can plausibly deny that they represent the parties' common understanding.[4] So by including the recitals, a drafter reduces the chances of either party later being tempted to argue that the contract's operative terms should lead to an outcome inconsistent with the common understanding expressed in the recitals.

For example, if the parties have, before instructing their lawyers to draw up a formal contract, already drawn up a 'heads of terms' or similar document, designed to set out the bare bones of the agreement they have reached, why not set that heads of terms document out as a recital to the main contract? To do so may boost the parties' confidence that a contract whose detailed provisions may appear dauntingly technical is a reliable expression of the agreement they have reached. Or if the parties to a joint venture agreement share a vision of what they want the joint venture to accomplish, why not record that in the recitals? It may throw light on how one of the operative provisions in the contract should be interpreted.

Contracts may not, however, reflect any underlying principle consistently. They are more haphazard than that. Party A may be prepared to offer an ad hoc concession to party B on a point B cares about, in exchange for a concession on another point that A thinks is more important. The process of negotiation of a contract can thus throw up many inconsistencies, embodying a set of mini-agreements on particular issues, each of which may stand out as 'surprising'[5] in the light of the agreement reached on other related issues, or when considered in the context of the contract as a whole.

With such a contract, it would be misleading for a recital to suggest that the contract reflects a set of underlying principles at all. Instead, as suggested in **1.24** above, the drafter should consider a recital acknowledging that the parties have fully negotiated the contract, and that they want each clause to be interpreted according to its terms.

A drafter should also consider recording in the recitals any common factual assumptions that the parties have made, also including an acknowledgement

3 Often in trademark capital letters, which serve only to reinforce a pointless sense of antiquity.
4 Nor are they vulnerable to being disregarded as irrelevant on the grounds of an 'entire agreement' clause, being contained in the very document that contains that clause.
5 See **1.24** above.

that each of the parties is entering into the contract on the basis that the assumptions are accurate. If the parties choose to contract on the basis that the assumptions are accurate, that represents an agreed basis of contracting that should bind them both even if the assumptions turn out to be inaccurate.[6]

If factual assumptions can be verified before the contract is signed, it reduces risk for this to be done before the contract is signed: see **13.3** below. Or the parties may agree that one party or another should bear the risk of an assumption proving incorrect, which may point to that party making an express warranty or representation in relation to the facts in question. But that may not always be commercially feasible. What then happens if a common assumption proves incorrect? Is the contract void from the start? The answer to this will be yes only if the assumption is of fundamental importance and so meets the tests laid down in *Bell v Lever Brothers*.[7] In circumstances where this question arises, disputes are highly likely: it will often suit one party either to assert that it did not share the assumption, or to deny that it was important enough to meet the stringent *Bell v Lever Brothers* test: that its failure was enough to defeat the contractual purpose.[8] But if the drafter records the shared assumption in the recitals and it is acknowledged to be of fundamental importance, the matter will be put beyond doubt.

Use recitals to insulate the drafting against errors within the contract

2.3 In *Dalkia Utilities Services PLC v Celltech International Ltd*,[9] an agreement amending a finance lease recited the background to it, and in particular that the parties

> have entered into this Amendment Agreement for the purposes of providing for the rescheduling of the Finance Element and the New Works Charge.

In the operative provisions, however, a faulty cross-reference, read literally, would have led to a radical reduction in the amount of the termination sum payable on a termination of the lease by the lessor. This was a consequence not alluded to in the recitals. In finding that a mistake must have been made in the drafting and could be corrected as part of the court's process of

6 'Parties can agree that their dealings shall be conducted on a particular basis of fact (including as to what has or has not occurred) even if the true facts are different and that, if they do, a contractual estoppel will arise' Christopher Clarke J in *Raiffeisen Zentralbank Oesterreich AG v The Royal Bank of Scotland Plc* [2010] EWHC 1392 (Comm) at [250]. See also **13.3** below.

7 [1932] AC 161.

8 See *Great Peace Shipping Ltd v Tsavliris Salvage (International) Ltd (the 'Great Peace')* [2002] EWCA Civ 1407.

9 [2006] EWHC 63 (Comm): see also **1.27** above.

interpretation, the court was influenced by the recitals. Christopher Clarke J observed:

> The manifest purpose of that agreement was to provide for the rescheduling of the Finance Element and the New Works Charge. Recital D says as much.[10]

Similarly, in *BS & N Ltd (BVI) v Micado Shipping Lines (Malta) ('The Seaflower')*[11] the drafting was unclear generally, and did not address a crucial 'What if?' question.[12] In the Court of Appeal, Jonathan Parker LJ pointedly stated:[13]

> the draftsmen of the clause gave insufficient consideration to the precise meaning and effect of the terms in which it is framed. That being so, it seems to me that... the court should focus rather more closely than might otherwise have been appropriate on what may be taken to be the parties' underlying commercial aims and objectives in entering into the charter (with particular reference to the obtaining of the approvals of the major oil companies), and rather less closely on the precise words which the parties have chosen to use to express their contractual intention.

The natural place for recording those 'underlying commercial aims and objectives' would have been the recitals. But no such recital appears to have been included. So when a dispute arose, the commercial background could only be inferred. The drafter had not only drafted unclearly generally, but missed a trick in not setting out the background in a recital, which might have avoided landing the parties in a dispute.

Do not locate obligations in recitals: they belong in the operative clauses

2.4 Carefully used, recitals can therefore be a useful guide. A judge will recognise that they record the parties' objectives.[14]

However, recitals and operative clauses fulfil different functions. Whereas operative clauses impose obligations, recitals normally do not. Indeed, if there is a direct conflict between an operative term and a recital, the operative term

10 ibid at [112].

11 [2001] CLC 421.

12 The contract in question was a charterparty, which provided for particular consequences to flow if the vessel 'lost', following the start of the charter term, certain approvals granted by the oil majors. But the drafter did not ask the question: 'what if one of the approvals is not withdrawn during the charter period, but is not even in place when the charter begins?' – which proved to be the case. See **13.3** below.

13 [2001] CLC 421 at [82].

14 'The starting point when construing the Agreement is the recital' (Arnold J in *Omega Engineering Inc v Omega SA* [2010] EWHC 1211 (Ch).

will prevail: *Gallaher International Ltd v Tlais Enterprises Ltd.*[15] It follows that if a provision is intended to record an obligation, the drafter should locate it in the operative clauses, not in a recital.

The *Gallaher International* case[16] illustrates the pitfalls if a recital gets ideas above its station and purports to do the work of an operative clause. In the contract under review in the case, a recital contained the type of detailed provision for the duration of the contract that would expect to be found in the operative clauses of the contract itself. And indeed, the contract *did* contain such a provision – in terms inconsistent with the recital. It was asking for trouble to try to deal with a question of that level of granularity, a natural fit for the operative clauses, in the recitals. And because operative clauses trump recitals, the recital was ignored.

For another case where the judge refused to allow a recital to be interpreted as if it were an operative provision, see *Fairstate Ltd v General Enterprise and Management Limited*:[17]

> In a formal contract such as this, which has been drafted by a lawyer, the section containing the recitals is not the part of the agreement in which the substantive obligations are usually expressed. It is therefore inherently unlikely that the parties intended any of the matters recited to give rise, by itself, to a substantive obligation.

Although a recital is ill-equipped to contain a promise to perform an obligation, it may sometimes contain a promise of a different type. An example is the promise that a party will behave under the contract as if a particular state of affairs exists. As noted in **2.2** above,[18] this can ground a contractual estoppel, and can readily appear in a recital as well as an operative clause: see *Rolls-Royce Holdings PLC v Goodrich Corporation.*[19]

The corollary to all this is that if something is *not* intended to be legally binding, the drafter would do better to put it in a recital rather than in the operative clauses. An illustration is *Honeywell Control Systems Ltd v Multiplex Constructions (UK) Ltd,* [20] a case arising out of the construction of the new Wembley Stadium. Multiplex had been employed as the main contractor for the work, and Honeywell was one of its subcontractors. A dispute arose about whether Honeywell had an ongoing right to inspect the main contract under which Multiplex agreed to carry out the work for its employer. Contending

15 [2008] EWHC 804 (Comm), Christopher Clarke J citing on this point (at para 997 of his judgment), among other cases, *Re Moon ex p Dawes (1886)* 17 QBD 275 (if the recitals are clear but the operative clauses are ambiguous, the recitals will control the interpretation: Lord Esher M.R. at [286] and Lopes LJ at [289]) and *Young v Smith* (1865) LR 1 Eq 180 (recital cannot operate to introduce a wholly new operative provision).

16 ibid.

17 [2010] EWHC 3072 (QB); (2010) 133 Con LR 112 at [74] (Richard Salter QC).

18 See n 6 above.

19 [2023] EWHC 1637 at [49].

20 [2007] EWHC 390 (TCC).

that Honeywell had no such right, Multiplex argued that the right relied on by Honeywell, although contained in an operative appendix to the Multiplex/ Honeywell sub-contract, was 'in the nature of a recital'. It was, Multiplex said, limited to signifying by way of background that Honeywell had seen a copy of the main agreement before the subcontract was entered into, rather than giving an ongoing right to inspect it. The judge gave this argument short shrift:

> the fallacy in [Multiplex's] argument, if I may respectfully say so, seems to me to be this. Part 1 of the Appendix is not a recital and it is not in the nature of a recital.[21]

It followed that the provision was operative and that Honeywell, as it had for its own part argued, did indeed have an ongoing right to inspect the main agreement.

So the *Honeywell v Multiplex* case shows that it would be a drafting error to include within an operative provision something that is intended not to be legally binding. Sometimes this type of error is more benign. The drafter of the contract that was before the court in *CIS General Insurance Ltd v IBM United Kingdom Ltd*[22] had set out in an operative clause a list of benefits expected to accrue to one party from entering the contract. This was in some ways a harmless error: it could scarcely be contended that a list of expected benefits was binding in any meaningful sense. But even if harmless, it was untidy: it was material that belonged, if anywhere, in the recitals.

Also put overriding general principles in an operative clause, not the recitals

2.5 The parties may want a generally expressed set of principles to control the contract: to prevail over any specific operative clause that might be seen as conflicting with those principles. If so, the drafter should include the principles in the operative provisions themselves. The recitals would not be the right place to put a set of overriding principles, because of the rule discussed in **2.2** above that operative provisions prevail over recitals. A statement[23] that a clause setting out general principles is intended to control any other provision in a contract will displace the normal rule[24] that specific provisions are taken to prevail over general ones.

[21] ibid at [55].
[22] [2021] EWHC 347 (TCC): see [64].
[23] See generally Chapter 12 below for language to answer the question 'What prevails?'.
[24] Often expressed by judges in terms of the Latin maxim 'generalia non specialibus derogant': loosely translatable as 'general provisions do not undermine specific ones'.

An example of how a general principle can control the contract is the drafting in *Masri v Consolidated Contractors International Co SAL.*[25] The drafting of an agreement relating to the participation by Mr Masri in the exploitation of a Yemeni oil field stated, at the beginning of the agreement:

> Basic principle is for Masri to receive 10% of CCC's 10% or a 1% overall interest in the Block for Masri subject to the following conditions, payments and adjustments.

The contract went on to list various types of receipts by CCC (as Mr Masri's counterparty was referred to) that triggered Mr Masri's rights to receive his 10% entitlement. That list conspicuously omitted any reference to recoveries of operating costs. CCC argued that this omission was deliberate. But the general principle was held to prevail, so that Mr Masri was entitled to share in receipts in the form of recovered operating costs, even though they were not on the specific list.

Masri shows that drafters need to consider carefully whether to state an overriding principle. If they do, the inference is that it will apply unless it is expressly provided to the contrary. If the drafter had wanted to achieve the position that CCC was arguing for in the case, the drafting would have had to provide a specific carve-out, along the lines of:

> Notwithstanding the basic principle referred to above, [Mr Masri] shall not be entitled to share in any operating cost recoveries received by CCC

to show that the basic principle was overridden in that particular respect.

CIRCUMSTANCES WHERE RECITALS ARE PARTICULARLY USEFUL

To express the commercial rationale for the whole agreement

2.6 A court will readily conclude that recitals can explain the overall purpose of an agreement. For example, in *Schofield v Smith and Boardman,*[26] commenting on a settlement agreement, Newey LJ commented:

> There is no relevant doubt as to the 'aim', 'object' or 'purpose' of the Settlement Agreement. As the recitals to it confirm, the Settlement Agreement was evidently intended to settle the dispute between [specified parties].

[25] [2007] EWCA Civ 688.

[26] [2022] EWCA Civ 824 at [38(iv)]; see also *PA (GI) Ltd v Cigna Insurance Services (Europe) Ltd* [2023] EWHC 1360 (Comm) (Dame Clare Moulder at [61]).

In the nature of things, cases of 'missing recitals' do not advertise themselves. One can, however, be seen in *Al Sanea v Saad Investments Co Ltd*.[27] Mr Al Sanea's vehicle held a sizeable stake in B, a quoted company. To underpin the value of the B stake in the vehicle's balance sheet during the 2008 financial crisis, Mr Al Sanea himself granted the vehicle a put option over the stake. The put option envisaged the possibility of cash settlement as an alternative to physical settlement, though that was not a feature that was necessary to achieve the balance sheet objective and may have been no more than an afterthought to make the option look as convincing as possible. The recitals to the put option referred to the stake in B. But they did not refer to the balance sheet objective. Nor did they explain that the cash settlement was simply a possible method of satisfying what was essentially an obligation to deliver B shares, not a separate obligation of independent vitality that could survive the vehicle's disposal of the stake in B.

If a recital had made clear either of these points, the vehicle (now controlled by liquidators) could not plausibly have argued that the cash settlement was intended to have an independent existence at a later date, after the B stake had been sold off. If only the recitals had been clearer, the liquidators' arguments would have been strangled at birth, and much difficulty for Mr Al Sanea avoided.[28]

To express the commercial rationale for a specific provision

2.7 An example of how recitals might have helped in this respect is *BMA Special Opportunity Hub Fund Ltd v African Minerals Finance Ltd*,[29] which related to a complex financing facility for a project in Sierra Leone. The drafting of the facility ran to nearly 150 pages. It included provision requiring the borrower to pay the lenders a fee of 6% if the loan was prepaid in certain circumstances. Despite the best efforts of an army of drafters,[30] it was not clear whether, when the facility was indeed prepaid less than 12 months later, those circumstances applied or not. Both sides argued that 'commercial common sense' favoured their own view: that the fee was payable (as the lenders unsurprisingly argued) or (as the borrowers equally unsurprisingly contended) that it was not.

It would surely have been helpful if the underlying purpose of the prepayment fee had been set out in the recital: what was the principle that the drafters

[27] [2012] EWCA Civ 313.

[28] This was a particularly unfortunate omission, since at the time of drawing up the put option, Mr Al Sanea appears to have been, in a sense, negotiating with himself (he controlled the investment vehicle) – so it would have been freely open to him to have included a fuller and more helpful set of recitals.

[29] [2013] EWCA Civ 416.

[30] Six sets of lawyers, charging aggregate fees of approaching $2 million (ibid at [8]).

were trying to reflect?[31] And, even more important, it would have reduced the chances of a dispute arising in the first place. Faced by a recital recording the *principles* behind whether the fee was payable, the parties would have a chance to check, before signing the agreement, that whether they agreed with it. If they did not, they could say so when there was still time to change the agreement. This would surely have been better than the question being buried away somewhere in the midst of 150 pages of technical legal drafting (and even then, not clearly addressed).

To explain adequately some otherwise un- or under-explained matter

2.8 Some cases show that a less than fully-thought through set of operative clauses could benefit from the help of some recitals to guide the reader as to what they mean. *Square Mile Partnership Ltd v Fitzmaurice McCall Ltd*[32] is a stark example. The circumstances were as follows:

- the dispute related to the financial terms of an agreement for the sale of the entire share capital of a company;
- just before – indeed the very day before – the sale, a series of transactions were carried out to strip value out of the company being sold;
- the individual responsible was conscious that the pre-sale transactions were rough and ready, so that some sort of further adjustment might be needed after the sale had taken place;
- the sale agreement referred in its operative clauses to the presale transactions, but only in the most general terms ('[the seller] has prior to this Agreement removed certain assets from [the target]');
- the sale agreement also referred to the possibility of an adjustment, but only again in the most general terms;
- the individual carrying out the pre-sale transactions did not keep a record of what had been done or why.

It is not only with the benefit of hindsight that it seems to have been tempting fate not to have set out in a set of recitals what the pre-sale transactions were, what they were meant to have achieved, and what the intention of the parties was when they allowed in the operative provisions for the possibility of a subsequent adjustment. Evidence of the pre-sale negotiations, which might have thrown light on those questions, was of course inadmissible.[33]

[31] A sophisticated 'What if?' question maybe? (see generally Chapter 13 below).
[32] [2006] EWCA Civ 1690.
[33] See **2.1** above.

As it was, the individual responsible for the pre-sale transactions had to give evidence in court nearly three years after the event[34] in an attempt to reconstruct what he had done and how and why the various transactions had been carried out. Quite apart from the stress this must have given rise to, the court was faced with the unappetising task of deciding what had happened (or perhaps one should say what it considered most likely to have happened) before it could resolve the dispute.

Where the contract is long, complex or enduring

2.9 Contracts that display any one or more of these characteristics[35] may cry out for explanatory recitals. Consider the contract which fell, perhaps predictably, into dispute in *Amey Birmingham Highways Ltd v Birmingham City Council*.[36] It was a PFI contract under which Amey agreed, for a 25-year period, to maintain and operate the road network in Birmingham. The contract was described as a 'formidable document',[37] which is something of an understatement as it ran to over 5,000 pages (over 200 of which were taken up with definitions). It was 'a massive and convoluted contract, containing many oddities and infelicities'.[38]

Against that background it is not surprising that the contract gave an opportunity for Amey to argue that they were not required to perform their services in exactly the way that the council expected. The main issue turned out to be whether or not a particular set of data fell to be updated as survey results came in. But the answer to whether that set of data fell to be updated was not made clear anywhere in the 5,000 pages of the contract.[39] And nowhere does it appear that the contract recorded that the overall purpose of the contract was to require Amey to maintain the road network based on data that was constantly updated so as to present an up to date picture of the network from time to time. Had it done so (and a recital seems the obvious place for such a statement of purpose to appear), it seems likely that the argument that Amey advanced – that no updating was contemplated – would not realistically have been tenable.

34 The agreement was entered into at the end of May 2002; the court hearing at which the evidence was given was in early May 2005.

35 A contract intended to create a long-lasting relationship is sometimes referred to as a 'relational contract' by academics and others.

36 [2018] EWCA Civ 264.

37 ibid at [10].

38 ibid at [38].

39 The metaphor that a reader of the contract could not see the wood for the trees seems more than usually apt, given how many of them must have been felled to provide the paper to print it.

To acknowledge the parity of bargaining power or the reasonableness of the contract terms

2.10 If parties are of comparable bargaining power and have negotiated a contract freely, they are more likely to be able to agree the basis on which they are contracting than if they are of unequal power.

This could affect for example their freedom to agree

> that no representations (or none other than honest belief) are being made or are intended to be relied on. Such parties are capable of distinguishing between statements which are to be treated as representations on which the recipient is entitled to rely, and statements which do not have that character, and should be allowed to agree among themselves into which category any given statement may fall.[40]

Furthermore, the Unfair Contract Terms Act 1977, s 2, allows provisions in non-consumer contracts restricting liability for negligence (other than liability for death or personal injury) to be enforceable in accordance with their terms only insofar as they satisfy a test of reasonableness. The same test applies to provisions designed to restrict liability for liability for pre-contract misrepresentations.[41]

The reasonableness test is objective, but if parties are of comparable bargaining power and consider the terms of the contract on which they have agreed as being fair and reasonable, the courts are less likely to regard those terms as unreasonable. They will instead be disposed to enforce them, recognising that it is desirable for contracting parties to be able to contract with certainty.[42] It follows that if the parties want that certainty, it can do no harm to include a recital to the effect that the parties are of comparable bargaining power and believe the provisions to represent a reasonable allocation of risk.43

40 *Raiffeisen Zentralbank Oesterreich AG v The Royal Bank of Scotland PLC* [2010] EWHC 1392 (Comm): Christopher Clarke J at [317].

41 Under the Misrepresentation Act 1967, s 3 (as amended).

42 See, for example, Chadwick LJ in *E A Grimstead & Son Ltd v McGarrigan* [1999] EWCA Civ 3029.

43 And in principle, the drafter can go beyond reciting the parties' joint belief that the terms were reasonable, and also record in the recital specific factors believed to be relevant to reasonableness, including the matters identified in the Unfair Contract Terms Act 1977, Sch 2.

Chapter 3

Enforceability: binding or non-binding?

Because a contract exists only if the parties intend to become legally bound, disputes arise if the parties do not make it clear whether they do so. Making a document 'subject to contract' is normally a clear sign that no contract yet exists, but is not failsafe. The 'subject to contract' formula usually suggest that a contract is contemplated in the future, so is not suitable if the parties never intend to become legally bound. The drafter can use other techniques to signify in a document that the parties do, or do not, intend it to bind them, but need to bear in mind that courts prefer to uphold contracts than to strike them down. Uncertainty risks a contract or part of it being unenforceable; a drafter can reduce the risk by suitable drafting. 'Endeavours' clauses can help to achieve enforceability in uncertain future circumstances.

DRAFTING TO MAKE CLEAR WHETHER PARTIES INTEND TO CREATE LEGAL RELATIONS

UNCERTAINTIES MAY PREVENT AN ARRANGEMENT BECOMING BINDING

DRAFTING TO MAKE CLEAR WHETHER PARTIES INTEND TO CREATE LEGAL RELATIONS

Make clear whether the parties intend to be legally bound

3.1 Law students learn early on that an 'intention to create legal relations' is a necessary ingredient to the formation of a legally-binding contract.

The question whether the parties to an 'arrangement', to use a neutral term, want it to be legally binding is not decided by what they subjectively intend. In line with English law's general approach,[1] what matters is whether the language the parties use signifies that, looked at objectively, they should be taken to have intended to be legally bound.

Use 'Subject to contract' to avoid creating a binding contract, but beware its limitations

3.2 If a document is silent on whether the parties intend it to be legally binding, the risk of dispute naturally arises if one party thinks that it was intended to be binding but the other does not. Faced with a dispute about that, a court has to consider the language of the document to evaluate whether, looked at objectively, the language is more consistent with the parties having intended to become legally bound, or with them having stopped short of that Rubicon.

The dispute is particularly messy, and correspondingly expensive to sort out, if the existence or otherwise of a contract has to be determined not by looking at a single document, but a whole series of correspondence, to which is often added evidence from the parties of what passed between them at meetings.

1 See, for example, **2.1** above.

The rule that evidence of negotiations is inadmissible in interpreting a contract does not apply to prevent a court looking at the logically anterior question of whether a contract exists in the first place.[2] The court has at the same time to analyse whether, and if so at what point, one party made an offer to the other that was subsequently accepted.

People in the commercial world often try to save money by negotiating a proposed deal to a relatively advanced stage before involving a lawyer. They may get as far as exchanging 'heads of terms'. If they were asked whether they were legally bound, they might often say that the heads of terms contained everything meaningful about their deal. But in the next breath they might add (paradoxically) that they believed that they would not be legally bound until a lawyer had cast it in a 'proper' legal form.

Drafters should be alive to the risks this ambivalence creates. Several cases reach the courts every year in which the central point of dispute is whether the whole of a document, or some part of it, is legally binding.

It is routine for drafters to include the words 'Subject to contract' in correspondence that is not intended to give rise to a legal relationship.[3] And this is generally a simple and effective way of insulating negotiations from accidentally giving rise to a binding contract.[4]

Similar language may achieve the same result in other contexts. So in a real property transaction the words 'subject to lease' may be used, and in a ship chartering transaction 'subject to details'.[5]

But a drafter should not regard the formula 'subject to contract' as conclusive. If a document includes the formula but also contains language suggesting that, despite it, the parties *do* owe one another enforceable obligations, the 'subject to contract' formula may be outweighed. A court will interpret a document that might be a contract in the same way as it does an undoubted contract: by trying to make sense of it as a whole. If, in Lord Hoffmann's words in the *Investors' Compensation Scheme* case,[6] 'something must have gone wrong with the drafting', the offending words may be ignored.

2 'Whether there is a binding contract between the parties and, if so, upon what terms depends upon what they have agreed. It depends not upon their subjective state of mind, but upon a consideration of what was communicated between them by words or conduct, and whether that leads objectively to a conclusion that they intended to create legal relations' (Lord Clarke in *RTS Flexible Systems Ltd v Molkerei Alois Müller GmbH & Co* [2010] UKSC 14 at [45]).

3 For examples, see *Generator Developments Ltd v Lidl UK GmbH* [2018] EWCA Civ 396 ('The meaning of the expression is well-known' (Lewison LJ at [79]); and *Joanne Properties Ltd v Moneything Capital Ltd* [2020] EWCA Civ 1541.

4 As also would seem to be the equally straightforward labelling of, say, some 'heads of terms' as '*non-binding* heads of terms'. The label 'heads of terms' is not of itself inconsistent with their being binding: the extra adjective is needed to convey that meaning.

5 *Star Steamship Society v Beogradska Plovidba (The Junior K)* [1988] 2 Lloyd's Rep 583 (Steyn J at [588]), cited in *Nautica Marine Ltd v Trafigura Trading Inc* [2020] EWHC 1986 (Comm) (Foxton J at [44]).

6 *Investors' Compensation Scheme Ltd v West Bromwich Building Society (no. 1)* [1998] 1 WLR 896.

A drafter should be careful if the parties to a 'subject to contract' document want to bind themselves immediately in some aspects of their relationship.

Commonly, for example, a transaction involves one or both parties providing the other with some confidential information, with the other party acknowledging that it is legally bound not to pass it on. The duty to keep the information confidential is intended to be immediately enforceable. So there is a two-headed problem if the drafter includes the non-disclosure obligations in a 'subject to contract' document. If the words 'subject to contract' mean what they say, the non-disclosure obligations are unenforceable, which is at odds with what the parties want. But if a judge considers the obligations are enforceable despite the 'subject to contract' formula, the formula is subverted to some extent at least. The door is open for one party to argue that the document was intended to be fully binding, and that the words 'subject to contract' might have been included simply by mistake.[7] The formula is so short and simple[8] that it is easier to conclude that it might have been accidentally included than would be the case with more elaborate language.

The solution may be, as is indeed often done, to isolate the immediately enforceable obligations in a separate contract. An alternative would be to draft something that acknowledges and resolves the inconsistency, perhaps along the lines of the following:

> [X] These [heads of terms], with the exception of paragraph [Y] (confidential information), are not intended to be binding on the parties but are subject to contract. This paragraph [X] is intended by the parties to override any implication to the contrary contained anywhere else in this document.

The unusual case where the parties never intend to become legally bound

3.3 In most cases, a document is 'subject to contract' in the sense that the parties view the document as an interim staging post on a journey that will lead eventually to a formal written contract that binds them. At that point, the interim document becomes irrelevant, particularly if the formal contract contains an 'entire agreement' clause that expressly consigns the interim document, together with any other earlier material, to the waste-paper basket.

But occasionally, the parties *never* intend to become legally bound. The heads of terms represent the destination, not a stop on the way. In a case

7 As apparently happened in *Richards (Michael) Properties Ltd v Corporation of Wardens of St. Saviour's Parish Southwark* [1975] 3 All ER 416.

8 Though that does not mean that everyone in the commercial world understands what it means: the evidence in *Confetti Records v Warner UK Music Ltd (trading as East West Records)* [2003] EWHC 1274, for example, suggests that some do not.

like that, the words 'subject to contract' are not appropriate: no *contract* is ever contemplated to which the heads of terms are in any sense *subject.* To include 'subject to contract' would be to imply that the parties intend to take a future step which they do not in fact contemplate taking. Furthermore, in a case where the words 'subject to contract' appear, they are apt to lose their potency if the parties later behave in such a way that it suggests they *do* regard themselves as contractually bound.[9]

To reflect that kind of arrangement, a drafter would do better to use language which expressly denies the intention ever to create legal relations, such as the following:[10]

> This document records the current intentions of the parties as to the matters contained in it, but
>
> (a) it is not intended to be legally binding or, in particular, to give either party the right to enforce its terms; and
>
> (b) the parties intend that (a) will remain the case, even if both parties observe the terms of the arrangement as fully as they would have been obliged to do if the document had instead been legally binding.

Other techniques to avoid creating a binding contract

3.4 A drafter who wants to avoid a document crossing the line so as to become legally binding should bear in mind, as well as the 'subject to contract' formula, the following points:

- The more comprehensive the document (the less it contains gaps that a formal contract would normally address), the more pressure is put on 'subject to contract' language. A drafter might in such a case consider an explicit acknowledgement that the document contains most of what a legally-binding agreement would contain, but state that nonetheless, the parties did not intend to be legally bound. That would draw the sting from any potential argument that 'subject to contract' did not mean what it said.
- A drafter should avoid phrasing the document as an 'offer'. Under English law, there is of course a sense in which an offer *is* subject to contract: the offer requires to be accepted before a contract comes into existence. If 'subject to contract' is interpreted in that sense, a document that calls itself an 'offer' is, even if expressly stated to be 'subject to contract', susceptible of being turned into a contract simply by being accepted.

9 As happened in the *RTS Flexible Systems* case (n 2).

10 Loosely based on language to this effect in *Rose & Frank Co v JR Crompton & Bros Ltd* [1925] AC 445.

Language which refers to the document being 'accepted', perhaps by the counterparty signing a copy, is also better avoided.

- A document that embodies only some basic terms is better described as 'heads of terms' than as an 'agreement'.[11] Still less should the document refer to itself as a 'contract'.
- Express reference to contractual concepts like 'consideration' or which otherwise smack of legally binding obligations (such as 'guarantee'[12] or 'indemnity') is unhelpful: it is better to use the language that business people would naturally use ('be responsible for', 'cover the cost of') rather than lawyers' terms of art.
- The 'look and feel' of the document should be sharply distinct from a contract. It is better, for example, for the document not to formally identify the parties with their company numbers and the registered offices; nor to use systematic definitions; nor to contain a formal attestation clause.
- It would help to tone down language that suggests that it is inevitable that agreement will be reached in a formal document. For example, it would be better to precede a list of boilerplate points with 'Any contract would include terms dealing with the following matters' than with 'The formal written contract will contain terms dealing with the following matters'. For the same reason, it is better to use modal verbs[13] sensitively to accord with the lack of an existing agreement: 'the price for the works *would* be determined as follows', for example, rather than 'the price for the works *will* be determined as follows'.
- The drafter will need to consider the commercial context in framing any document, because that context may affect how likely it is to create legal relations. For example, insurance contracts are often created through a two-stage process (initialling of a 'slip' followed by a more formal document), but the slip is regarded as contractually binding in itself. By contrast, a 'letter of comfort' designed to reassure a potential creditor about the debtor's creditworthiness may not be intended to create legal liability.[14]

11 For example, in *Branca v Cabarro* [1947] KB 854 a document calling itself a 'provisional agreement' was held immediately binding: Lord Greene MR noted, in reaching this conclusion, the absence of 'the familiar words "subject to contract"' (at [857]). To label a document a 'letter of comfort' is to imply that it is not binding (*Associated British Ports v Ferryways NV* [2009] EWCA Civ 189 (Maurice Kay LJ at [27]). But that label is not determinative: the document must always be interpreted as a whole.

12 In *Attrill v Dresdner Kleinwort Benson Ltd* [2013] EWCA Civ 394, a bank was held to have intended to create a legally binding obligation when it referred to the 'guaranteed' level of a bonus pool.

13 See Chapter 6 below.

14 Though ultimately it is a question of construing the document as a whole (*Associated British Ports v Ferryways NV* [2009] EWCA Civ 189): which reinforces the view that careful attention to the language is essential.

- It may also help to make it clear that a formal step, such as both parties signing the final agreement, must be taken before it is to be regarded as binding. In *Jamp Pharma Corporation v Unichem Laboratories Ltd*,[15] a provision to this effect helped to save a chain of emails from crossing the line prematurely and amounting to a contract on their own.[16]
- Sometimes the parties may not be ready to enter a full contract, but wish part of what they have so far discussed to be legally binding (for example, an obligation to keep information confidential, or a 'lockout' agreement to forestall negotiations with someone else). To achieve this, it is neater to isolate the binding provisions in a separate document[17] (otherwise, the risk is that the whole document is binding).
- When a document is in the course of negotiation, the 'track changes' facility is often used to show readers how successive drafts of a proposed agreement differ from earlier versions. It would be unusual for a 'track changes' version to be legally binding: the arrangements are clearly 'in a state of flux'.[18]

How to do the reverse: how to make a document binding

3.5 The drafter who wants to emphasise that a document is binding should, unsurprisingly, use the mirror image of the above techniques. In particular, it helps for a document that is intended to be legally binding to describe itself as a 'contract'. In practice, many drafters do not quite go that far, but observe the convention that a contract describes itself as an 'agreement' (opening accordingly 'This Agreement is made on [date] between…').

This is perhaps a bit lazy, or at least misses an open goal. Linguistically the term 'agreement' can embrace a case where the parties are fully in accord, but do not want the agreement they have reached to be legally binding, either at any stage or at least for the time being. That this is so can be seen from the point that an 'agreement subject to contract' is a feasible concept. But the notion of a 'contract' that is not legally binding is less easy to recognise. So it

15 [2021] EWHC 1712 (Comm).

16 By contrast, in *Mahmood v Big Bus Co* [2021] EWHC 3395 (QB), a reference in a 'Heads of Terms' to preparation of 'contracts' as a future step was not enough to prevent some of the provisions of the Heads of Terms being binding themselves.

17 This recommendation was not followed in *Pretoria Energy Company (Chittering) Ltd v Blankney Estates Ltd* [2022] EWHC 1467 (Ch) ('Heads of Terms' containing a plainly binding lockout agreement; argued that other terms in same document were inferentially also binding, though on the facts this argument was rejected in the High Court, a decision supported in the Court of Appeal at [2023] EWCA Civ 482).

18 The phrase used by Picken J in *Avonwick Holdings Ltd v Azitio Holdings Ltd* [2020] EWHC 1844 (Comm) at [669]. But if all the essential terms have been agreed, exchanges of drafts while only minor issues are being finalised may be consistent with an agreement having already been concluded: *Black Sea Commodities Ltd v Lemarc Agromond PTE Ltd* [2021] EWHC 287 (Comm) (from [14]).

can only help to emphasise that a document is intended to be legally binding if it styles itself a 'contract'.

All the characteristics that the drafter should shun if trying to prevent a document[19] being legally binding should be embraced if the intention is to create a legally-binding relationship:

- The formalities common to a contract (recitals, definitions, formal identification of the parties and a careful attestation clause) are entirely appropriate.
- An explicit acknowledgement that the document is intended to be legally binding, either immediately or upon satisfaction of some specified conditions, is useful, particularly if for whatever reason the document bears a more equivocal title like 'heads of terms'.
- A governing law clause will point in favour of a binding contract, since the clause would be all but meaningless otherwise.[20]
- A document that contains warranties and representations that the parties have capacity to enter into it suggests a binding agreement.[21]
- There is no reason to steer clear of formal vocabulary ('consideration' for example), though a drafter will want to avoid going overboard on this.[22]
- Language that implies a non-binding relationship is correspondingly unhelpful. For example, to state that a payment is 'ex gratia' suggests that it is voluntary; an 'indulgence' is not something contractually required;[23] and a statement of 'current intention' implies that the intention may change, and that if it does, what the parties may be required to do may itself change.
- The involvement of lawyers in drawing a document up suggests in itself that a document is intended to be legally binding.[24]

19 The absence of a document *of any type* may itself suggest that no binding agreement has been reached: see, for example, *Asher v Jaywing PLC* [2022] EWHC 893 (Ch) at [140].

20 See the observations of Christopher Clarke J in the High Court in *RTS Flexible Systems* (n 2) at [34].

21 *Avonwick* (n 18) at [664].

22 Formal vocabulary is not necessary for a contract to be binding, and legalistic vocabulary will alienate the commercial businesspeople who need to understand the contract. This issue is relevant not just to be able to apply it later without seeking further legal advice on what it means, but more importantly to verify, before the document is signed, that it fully reflects their commercial objectives. See Chapter 11 below.

23 *Broadwick Financial Services v Spencer* [2002] EWCA Civ 35.

24 *Barbudev v Eurocom Cable Management Bulgaria EOOD* [2012] EWCA Civ 548: 'It is very clear from the terms of the Side Letter itself that the parties intended to create legal relations. For a start, it was drafted by Freshfields' (Aikens LJ at [37]).

Remember that courts prefer to uphold agreements than to strike them down

3.6 Judges are reluctant to find an agreement void for uncertainty if it was plainly intended to be binding.

Partly, this reflects a feeling that to do so subverts the parties' subjective intentions. It is rare for subjective intention to matter under English law: the court interprets a document based not on subjective intention but an intention objectively determined. Nonetheless, if it is evident that both parties went into an arrangement thinking they were contractually bound, a judge may feel that the law is in a sense letting down the party that adheres to its original intention if the court refuses to enforce the bargain. It is an unattractive conclusion to find in favour of a party that alleges, as a pretext to avoid being held to its word, that the agreement it signed up to was not legally binding.

Judges are particularly reluctant to strike down for uncertainty agreements that have already been partly performed.[25]

Do not jump the contractual gun

3.7 Because drafting a contract takes time, business people may grow impatient with the process and want the arrangements to start before a contract is concluded. This carries its own dangers.

The parties may use a draft contract which they are still negotiating as the basis for what is foreseen as a temporary arrangement pending the conclusion of a formal contract. In such a case the parties may refer to the draft contract and agree that it is to apply during what is hoped to be a temporary period. But that may take the urgency out of the negotiations of the contract proper, and lead to questions of whether all the provisions of the draft contract apply during the temporary period, or only some of them (and if so, which).[26] Or the parties, expecting to conclude a contract, may embark on a contractual relationship under the terms of a letter of intent, but never get around to concluding an actual contract because negotiations falter. In such a case it may suit one party to argue that the relationship never had contractual status, but only ever amounted to an inchoate series of offers and counter-offers. In *RTS Flexible Systems,*[27] a case in which arguments of this type surfaced, Lord Clarke observed:

> The different decisions in the courts below and the arguments in this court demonstrate the perils of beginning work without agreeing the

[25] *Mamidoil-Jetoil Greek Petroleum Co SA v Okta Crude Oil Refinery AD* [2001] 2 Lloyd's Rep. 76.
[26] See, for example, *Skanska Rashleigh Weatherfoil Ltd v Somerfield Stores Ltd* [2006] EWCA Civ 1732.
[27] [n 2]: the quote from Lord Clarke is from the opening paragraph of his judgment.

precise basis on which it is to be done. The moral of the story is to agree first and to start work later.

Given that the case went as far as the Supreme Court, with all the cost implications of that process, the moral Lord Clarke draws is a forceful one.[28]

UNCERTAINTIES MAY PREVENT AN ARRANGEMENT BECOMING BINDING

If the aim is to be binding, provide enough certainty

3.8 None of the above strategies discussed in **3.5** above, aimed at making a document binding, will work if gaps or uncertainties make it too uncertain to be enforced. A court will not enforce an agreement if it cannot feel confident about what obligations the parties intended to bind themselves to.

Only a rash drafter would assume that, just because the two parties clearly agree to bind themselves when they enter into the contract, they will always maintain that stance. A contract of any material duration often turns out, because of circumstances unforeseen and perhaps unforeseeable at the time of execution, to favour one party over another. The disadvantaged party will then have an incentive to argue that the contract, or at least obligations that remain to be discharged, is or are too uncertain to be enforced.

In the nature of things, it is harder for the drafter to specify obligations that will arise only in future uncertain circumstances. The drafter is in especially hazardous territory if the parties are contemplating a legal relationship that will last several years into the future, at which point their initial assumptions may well not hold good.

If there is uncertainty, what is void: the whole agreement, or only part?

3.9 A court weighing up how to treat uncertainty in a contract has an alternative to finding that it is a complete nullity. The alternative is less drastic: a court may decide that the uncertain provisions can be 'severed' – cut out of the contract – but as a life-saving amputation, leaving the rest of the contract alive and well. This may seem to the court an attractive alternative to unscrambling entirely an already partly-performed agreement.

[28] For an example of a relationship where a party supplying services repeatedly failed to secure a contract that would fully protect its interests, see *CLS Civil Engineering Ltd v WJG Evans & Sons* [2024] EWHC 194 (TCC) (cap on payments by its counterparty increased four times, but no full contract ever agreed, despite repeated requests).

A drafter should also recognise that uncertainty can arise both in relation to what the contract says and what it does *not* say. The drafter may attempt to deal with an issue in the agreement, but do so too vaguely or incoherently for a court to be satisfied as to what it means. Or the drafter may simply leave too much unsaid for the court to feel confident that, in filling in the gaps, it is upholding what, considered objectively, the parties can be regarded as having agreed.

Use a severability clause to limit the impact of any uncertainty

3.10 The idea of a severability clause is to reinforce the power a court has anyway if any uncertainty does not go to the root of the contract.

A severability clause tries to flag to the court that the parties would prefer the court to save the contract rather than killing it. Such a clause provides explicitly that if any part of the agreement is unenforceable (for example as being contrary to public policy, or simply illegal), the unenforceability is not to be regarded as vitiating the whole contract. Instead, the contract should be regarded as having been executed with the offending part excised.

Most cases relating to severability arise in the context of restrictive covenants which try to prevent ex-employees harming their former employers' businesses. Severability allows an employer to enforce constraints on an ex-employee that the law regards as reasonable – not in other words open to being struck down as an unreasonable 'restraint of trade' – while consigning to the waste bin any constraints that go too far. But questions of severability can arise in many other contexts too.[29]

The principle of severance allows particular words in a set of (say) restrictions to be struck out under a 'blue pencil' test, so long as the striking out does not cause any major change in the overall effect of the restrictions.[30] But the test does not allow words to be interpolated or added: only struck out.[31] As a legal doctrine, the test must accordingly be regarded as something of a blunt instrument. Whether the test can operate to save the unaffected part of a provision will turn on the way the drafter has constructed the provision and the language it contains: whether the drafter has been careful enough to ensure that the blue pencil can be wielded so as to leave intact something

29 *Tillman v Egon Zehnder Ltd* [2019] UKSC 32: Lord Wilson at [54].

30 ibid at [87].

31 Confirmed ibid at [85]: a notable contrast to how freely a court can 'rewrite' contracts as part of the process of interpretation if 'something has gone wrong with' the language of the contract ('there is not, so to speak, a limit to the amount of red ink or verbal rearrangement which the court is allowed' – Lord Hoffmann in *Chartbrook Ltd v Persimmon Homes Ltd* [2009] UKHL 38 at [25]). Perhaps it is all to do with the colour of the ink or the pencil.

meaningful after removal of the offensive words. The careful drafter will have this principle in mind.

Drafters of severance clauses sometimes try to sidestep the blue pencil test by explicit language to the effect that if a provision overreaches itself and strays into unenforceable territory, it remains enforceable 'to the extent' that it remains the right side if the line. The idea is, it seems, to preserve maximum enforceability. In other words, even if the blue pencil test could not preserve any of the effect of the provision, because no simple striking out of language could leave behind an enforceable residue, the provision's inoffensive aspects should be treated as ring-fenced and left to operate unchallenged. How far the courts would accept this stratagem remains unclear, although it has been cautiously endorsed by the Competition Appeals Tribunal.[32]

Characteristics of arrangements that the courts refuse to enforce

3.11 Arrangements that the courts refuse to enforce on the grounds of uncertainty are a particular version of 'agreements to agree', which the courts consistently refuse to enforce. The concept of a binding agreement to reach agreement is a legal nonsense, and unenforceable. How can the courts sensibly enforce an obligation to reach an agreement?

One common feature of agreements that the court strikes down on this basis is that the drafter has used an inherently broad or flexible concept without specifying enough details of what is meant. The drafter has, as it were, referred to a genus when what was needed is a reference to a species or sub-species.

Two examples of this type of defect can be given.[33]

In *G Scammell and Nephew Ltd v HC and JG Ouston*[34] an order for a lorry was given

> on the understanding that the balance of the purchase price can be had on hire purchase terms over a period of two years.

But no detail of what those hire purchase terms might be was given, nor any parameters of what would distinguish acceptable terms from unacceptable ones. The House of Lords declined to enforce the bargain.

[32] *Alex Neill Class Representative Ltd v Sony Interactive Entertainment Europe Ltd* [2023] CAT 73 from [146] (status of litigation funding arrangements as an unenforceable 'damages-based agreement' under the Courts and Legal Services Act 1990, s 58AA).

[33] Reassuringly for members of the legal profession, in neither case does a lawyer seem to have been involved. Note that both involved agreements that had not in any meaningful sense already been performed (see **3.6** above).

[34] [1941] AC 251.

In *Dhannai v Crasnianski*,[35] two businessmen were proposing to establish a private equity fund. But although some structural features of the proposed fund had been agreed, there were many more aspects that were uncertain: again, the court declined to find that there was a binding contract.

Other cases do not involve reliance on an over-broad *concept*, but instead fail because the drafting relies on some defective *machinery*.

For example, in *The Pensions Regulator v A Admin Ltd*,[36] a trust deed relied on a method of computing pension benefits 'prescribed by Part 4 F[inance] A[ct] 2004'. But Part 4 of that Act did no such thing. The trust deed was consequently void for uncertainty.

Similarly, in a Privy Council case, a provision in a loan agreement that said that the bank could charge its customer interest 'at the Bank's usual rate of interest on overdrafts' was held void when it emerged that the bank had in fact no such rate.[37]

One critical point for a drafter is that an obligation to *do* something is enforceable (provided it is certain enough what that something is). A drafter who wants to make an obligation enforceable and who is naturally drawn to drafting in terms of an obligation to *agree to* something rather than to *do* it is treading on dangerous ground.

Long-range provisions are particularly vulnerable

3.12 It is naturally harder for the drafter to specify obligations that, because they will fall to be performed a long time in the future, will be set in a context that is at the outset inherently unknowable. The drafter has to try to describe obligations with enough specificity to make them enforceable. And as time passes, it becomes increasingly likely that by the time the obligations fall to be performed, one of the parties will simply want to walk away from the contract.

Before a contract is signed, a drafter may find it harder to persuade the parties, who will be mainly concerned with the immediate future, to focus on what might happen in several years' time.

That makes *extensions* to contracts a particularly sensitive area. For example, in *Grow With Us Ltd v Green Thumb (UK) Ltd*,[38] the uncertainty related to what was to happen at the end of a franchise contract period. And in *BJ Aviation Ltd*

35 [2011] EWHC 926 (Comm).
36 [2014] EWHC 1378 (Ch).
37 *Financial Institution Services Ltd v Negril Negril Holdings Ltd* [2004] UKPC 40. While the bank was in the end allowed to levy a *reasonable* rate of interest, the lesson for the drafter remains a stark one: do not rely on non-existent machinery in drafting a contractual term.
38 [2006] EWCA Civ 1201.

v Pool Aviation Ltd,[39] the uncertainty related to the extension of a lease of an airport after an initial agreed period.

The effect of an uncertainty problem at the end of any initial period is likely to be limited to making the extension void rather than making the whole relationship void. This is both because the extension is easily severable from the initial period, and because courts are less willing to strike the whole contract down when it is already partly performed (still less when it is substantially performed).

Be explicit to achieve certainty

3.13 A drafter who wants to draft an enforceable contract can adopt some strategies to reduce the risk of the agreement being void for uncertainty.

First, the drafter should be as explicit as possible about those features of the deal that *are* agreed. To do so reinforces the sense that the parties intend to be bound.

Second, the drafter could consider an explicit acknowledgement that the parties regard themselves as bound, notwithstanding that there remain some details to be agreed.

Third, in respect of the items not yet agreed, the drafter should not simply ignore the issue. It is better to give some indication of the general thrust of the provision yet to be agreed. An example may be helpful. In *British Electrical Industries Ltd v Patley Pressings Ltd*,[40] the drafter provided that an agreement was to be subject to 'force majeure conditions'. But this vague formula was fatal to the enforceability of the arrangement. The drafter might have done better to have mentioned the principles that the parties agreed should be reflected in the clause whose detail they had yet to agree. For example, the drafter could have provided that neither party should be responsible for circumstances beyond its reasonable control, perhaps with examples of the type of circumstances that would qualify. Or again, the drafting could have stated that if circumstances beyond the parties' control made performance of either party's obligations impossible for a specified period, the contract should be suspended, or come to an end.

Another strategy is to invoke the type of provision that is customary in transactions of that particular type,[41] or to provide that the missing provision

[39] [2002] EWCA Civ 163.

[40] [1953] 1 WLR 280.

[41] Generally, agreements entered into in the course of a trade, the customs and practices of which are well-known to those involved in the trade, are more likely to have any gaps filled in by a court so as to uphold the contract: *Hillas Ltd v Arcos Ltd* [1932] 147 LT 503. The depressing corollary for the drafter of a bespoke contract that falls outside any established trade context is that it will stand or fall on its own merits, without any help from the customs or practices that a trade contract can fall back on.

should match up to a standard of being fair and reasonable to both sides. A court could then hear expert evidence on these criteria and determine how the gap was to be filled with more confidence than if the nature of the missing provision was simply left at large by the drafting. Even if the contract is one affected by a statutory implied term[42] of reasonableness, such as the Sale of Goods Act 1979, s 8(2) (implied term of a 'reasonable price' where the price is not fixed otherwise), it can do no harm to acknowledge *explicitly* that the price should be a reasonable one.

Alternatively, if a mechanism is in place which would fill the gap in the contract if the parties cannot agree themselves on a particular issue, the uncertainty risk is mitigated. So if the parties cannot come to terms, the question could be referred to a person who could determine what was reasonable. And a dispute resolution mechanism in the form of arbitration or expert determination points in the same direction, towards enforceability.[43]

Cable & Wireless Plc v IBM United Kingdom Limited[44] shows how a provision that risks straying into 'agreement to agree' territory can nonetheless be upheld held if enough care is taken with the drafting. A party that would have preferred simply to litigate was forced to participate in an alternative dispute resolution procedure using a particular mediation mechanism. A bare agreement to try and negotiate a settlement of the parties' dispute might well have been void as an agreement to agree;[45] but the parties had specified enough details for the procedure to be binding on them. The result can be contrasted with *Children's Ark Partnerships Ltd v Kajima Construction Europe (UK) Ltd*,[46] in which a contractual dispute resolution procedure was not clearly enough drafted to be enforceable. So the level of detail can be crucial.

Use 'endeavours' clauses to help achieve enforceability

3.14 Drafters often have to cater for the circumstance that the parties are agreed that a particular objective is desirable or necessary for their contract to work as intended, but it is not clear, because of the inherent uncertainty of future events, exactly what each should be obliged to do to achieve that objective.

42 The drafter should always consider the statutory context. If something repugnant to the law purports to be agreed, the contract itself falls into doubt, and there is fertile ground for a dispute.

43 As, for example, in *Tramtrack Croydon Ltd v London Bus Services Ltd* [2007] EWHC 107 (Comm) (obligation 'in good faith [to] agree, acting reasonably, the financial arrangements to be put in place to compensate' one party for certain specified events, with a backup of expert determination if they could not agree).

44 [2002] EWHC 2059 (Comm)

45 *Walford v Miles* [1992] 2 AC 128.

46 [2022] EWHC 1595 (TCC): see [61].

In the nature of things, this is likely to happen most often when the objective is outside the control of the contracting parties because it depends on securing agreement from a third party. But that is not essential. It could be, for example, that the objective relates to some other criterion, for example a threshold level of sales being achieved in the early stages of the contract.

The drafter's usual technique in this type of case is to state the objective as clearly as possible (this is usually not contentious) and then to provide that one or both parties, depending on the context, is obliged to use 'reasonable endeavours' or 'best endeavours' to achieve the objective. Other formulations include an obligation to use 'all reasonable endeavours' or to do 'all things reasonably necessary' to achieve the stated objective.

This type of language implies that at the date of contract, it is not possible to describe with any confidence exactly what steps might turn out to be needed. But that uncertainty should not, the drafter hopes, cause the agreement to fail as being too vague to be enforced. What amounts to 'reasonable endeavours' (or 'best endeavours' for that matter) is an objective test, and therefore one that the court therefore regards itself as equipped to decide.

Drafters may refer to 'reasonable endeavours' in other contractual contexts. For example, the applicability of a force majeure clause may depend on whether the party affected can overcome the force majeure event by 'reasonable endeavours', as *MUR Shipping BV v RTI Ltd.*[47]

'Endeavours' clauses often seem to end up in disputes. The battleground is usually that when it comes to discharging the relevant obligation, the parties cannot agree what the test, however it has been formulated, requires.

The drafter might hope that, in the light of a plethora of decided cases on the various versions of 'endeavours' clauses, the meaning of the various formulations used by drafters is reliably established. But that is not quite true. The difficulty is that the context in which the tests have to be applied depends so heavily on the specific facts of the case that clear principles do not readily emerge. But some principles do emerge from the mist, and can help the drafter.

The meaning of 'endeavours'

3.15 None of the formulations allows the relevant party to offer a merely cursory effort, or to give up if it does not instantly work. An 'endeavour' connotes more diligence and persistence than that.

47 [2024] UKSC 18: the Supreme Court held that a party cannot, by reason of an obligation to use reasonable endeavours to overcome the force majeure event, be required to accept non-contractual performance.

Perhaps nervous of the meaning of the term 'endeavours', however it is qualified, drafters sometimes prefer to use the term 'steps' and oblige a party to 'take all reasonable steps' to achieve the desired result. There is a suggestion that to use that formula may impose a lower degree of determined effort than does an obligation to use (say) 'best endeavours': *CIS General Insurance Ltd v IBM United Kingdom Ltd.*[48]

An obligation to use 'all reasonable endeavours' or 'best endeavours' imposes a more onerous standard on the obliged party than does an obligation merely to use 'reasonable endeavours'.[49] A party that has agreed to the more exacting 'best endeavours' or 'all reasonable endeavours' formulation should be prepared not to leave unturned any stone which it is reasonable to turn over in the quest to achieve the objective.

Many of the decided cases turn on how far the party under the obligation in question is required to spend its own money, or otherwise act contrary to its own financial interests, in pursuing the objective. The issue here is that the word 'reasonably' is at best a blunt instrument when evaluating that question.

Be as explicit as possible when using 'endeavours' clauses

3.16 The more that *specific* steps can be predicted and provided for, the better. For example, if an agreement for the sale of land depends on a developer obtaining residential planning permission, the temptation may be to start with drafting to the effect that the developer should use its 'best endeavours' to obtain it. But it would be better to provide explicitly for the developer to submit an application to the planning authority by a particular date, relating to a specific number of dwellings, and consistent with an architect's outline plans referred to in the contract. This benefits both parties: the landowner can be confident that as a minimum, the developer will take those steps, but the developer also knows that if it does so, it has discharged that part of its obligation.

A drafter should also try to peer into the future and cater for a plan B if the initial efforts prove unavailing. A particular Plan B will reduce the risk of the party under the obligation trying to avoid doing anything further on the grounds it is being sucked into a never-ending series of obligations.[50] For example, if in the above example the planning authority refuses to give consent, should the developer appeal, and if so how far? Or is there a different agreed fallback, such as the submission of a less ambitious or less controversial application?

48 [2021] EWHC 347 (TCC) at [418].

49 *Rhodia International Holdings Ltd v Huntsman International LLC* [2007] EWHC 292 (Comm).

50 In *Phillips Petroleum Company United Kingdom Limited v Enron Europe Ltd* [1997] CLC 329, a fallback date for a trigger event under a contract weakened the demands imposed by the parties' obligations to use 'reasonable endeavours' to agree an earlier date.

One aspect of drafting for a Plan B is that the party under the obligation will want a time limit on its obligation: in other words, if by a particular date the party's efforts have proved unavailing, it will want to be able to move on without being in breach of the contract. That will require care on the part of the drafter to make clear whether the contract is then wholly brought to an end, or whether it survives in an adapted form.

Although the input of an expert is not required to make an 'endeavours'-type obligation enforceable, it may nonetheless be useful to require the reasonableness of a particular step to be subject to verification on the part of an acknowledged expert. For example, if the parties are not agreed on the likely prospects of an appeal, should an opinion be sought from a senior lawyer with suitable experience, or perhaps another expert?

Even if it is not certain enough that the parties will want to compel a particular course of action, it would help set the standards of reasonableness if the contract specified *examples* of the type of step that is in their contemplation at the date of contract.

Finally, given that so often the dispute centres on the financial effects for an obligor, drafting will minimise the risks of dispute if it makes clear what the parties consider reasonable in this context. For example, how much money should the party be required to spend? Can a value be ascribed to the management time the party spends in pursuing solutions and if so, what amount of time of that value should the party be committed to? If pursuing the agreed objective has some measurable impact on the party's business (for example, it is forced to keep open a facility that otherwise it would close down as not central to its business), what is the threshold at which the party can say that it is not reasonable to go any further? The more this type of issue is thought through and agreed in advance, the less likely a dispute becomes.[51]

An agreement to use reasonable endeavours to achieve a particular objective is binding. But a 'reasonable endeavours' clause will not save an agreement from being void for uncertainty if it amounts to no more than an agreement to agree. So when parties agreed to

> use reasonable endeavours to agree the terms of a joint venture regarding Cardiff and Belfast Airports having regard to the principles set out in the note in the agreed form

the reference to the agreed principles could not save what was in substance merely an agreement to negotiate, and so the arrangement was unenforceable.[52]

51 If a party is not expressly required to incur any expense, the inference will arise that the scope of its obligations are correspondingly limited, almost to vanishing point: see (albeit in a case not in terms purporting to require a party to use 'endeavours', but purporting to impose an obligation) *De Havilland Aircraft of Canada Ltd v Spicejet Ltd* [2021] EWHC 362 (Comm) (at [21]).

52 *London & Regional Investments Ltd v TBI Plc* [2002] EWCA Civ 355.

By contrast, in another (Scottish) case[53] a contract was entered into between a seller and a purchaser, but before the seller had itself acquired the land. The seller undertook an obligation to use 'all reasonable endeavours' to agree a purchase price with the existing owner. This was held enforceable (and in particular not tainted by any 'agreement to agree' defect that might have arisen if the agreement to be reached would subsist between the very same parties required to 'endeavour' to reach it). But even in cases involving using reasonable endeavours to reach agreement with a third party, the overriding question remains: is the objective clearly enough defined, and are there criteria that allow the court to measure satisfactorily whether the person concerned has met the requirement to use 'reasonable endeavours' to achieve it? Only if the answer to both questions is yes will the obligation be enforceable.[54] Again this points towards a drafter being as specific as possible in relation to both these requirements.

53 *R & D Construction Group Ltd v Hallam Land Management Ltd* [2010] CSIH 96.
54 *Dany Lions Ltd v Bristol Cars Ltd* [2014] EWHC 817 (QB).

Chapter 4

Definitions

Drafters should use definitions, with the definitions clauses cross-referring to any terms defined within the operative clauses. Even straightforward expressions may need to be defined. Drafters should avoid confusing readers by making sure that all defined expressions are used, and all capitalised terms defined. Definitions should not contain obligations. Drafters should consider defining parties by name rather than role, and take care if parties play more than one role. Borrowing statutory definitions carries its own risks. Definitions must be adequately specific, with a coherent word order. Judges respect definitions, so drafters should use them consistently and so as to denote a single concept. The wise drafter checks that the definition works wherever it is used, including in successive redrafts. Overusing definitions risks confusion.

DEFINITIONS GENERALLY

4.1 Use definitions

4.2 Consider defining some expressions 'locally' within the clause they are used in…

4.3 …but do not rely only on local definitions

4.4 Do not assume that the meaning of terms is too obvious to be defined

THE CONTENT OF THE DEFINITIONS CLAUSE

4.5 Do not include in the definitions clause a defined term that is not used elsewhere in the contract

4.6 Do not use capitalised expressions if they are not defined…

4.7 …or otherwise suggest that a term is defined when it is not

THE DRAFTING OF DEFINITIONS

4.8 Be consistent with how definitions are phrased

4.9 Choose a defined term to reflect the underlying concept

4.10 Do not put obligations in definitions

DEFINITIONS GENERALLY

Use definitions

4.1 A definition provides that where particular words or expressions (usually identified by initial capital letters) are used in the contract, they are to be interpreted so as to carry a predictable defined meaning:

> 'Excluded Assets' shall mean the assets listed in Schedule II.

Having defined a term, the drafter can be confident that it will be understood to bear the meaning ascribed to it. Nobody interpreting the contract has to wonder whether the context of a particular clause might suggest some other meaning.[1] The defined term bears a stable meaning throughout the contract, which helps the drafter achieve the predictability the parties demand.

1 Unless the drafter is ill-advised enough to stipulate in the definitions clause that the defined terms bear their specified meaning 'except where the context otherwise requires' – language which erodes the predictability that is one of the chief attraction of definitions.

Since the defined term is usually shorter than its definition, a drafter using a defined term can express a concept more succinctly. Readers of contracts will welcome the economy of language that results.

Consider defining some expressions 'locally' within the clause they are used in...

4.2 Conventionally, definitions are collected together in a single clause and appear alphabetically, which saves time for readers. The definitions clause usually appears at the beginning of the contract, not the end. This increases the chance that a reader encountering a defined expression in an operative clause will already know what it means.[2]

Drafters sometimes feel that to collect all the definitions together in the definitions clause is heavy-handed. This is particularly the case if a defined term is used only in one particular clause rather than cropping up throughout the contract. The drafter may reasonably conclude that it is more convenient for such a definition to appear 'locally' within that clause itself, rather than being led away to languish in captivity in the definitions clause alongside all the other definitions. Using a local definition allows a user to take in the definition as part of reading the relevant clause, with no need to hunt back through the contract to locate the definition in the definitions clause.

This technique, like anything the drafter does that is calculated to make the reader's life easier, is to be applauded. If a drafter uses it, however, a further element of good practice is to cross-refer to the locally-defined expression in the definitions clause. Customarily drafters use this type of wording:

> 'Withdrawal Notice' shall be interpreted in accordance with clause 6.2

or

> 'Withdrawal Notice' shall bear the meaning set out in clause 6.2.

If the drafter takes the trouble to use this technique, readers who encounter the defined expression, but whose eyes have not been caught by the local definition, are spared the puzzlement that may otherwise follow when they turn to the definitions clause but find that the expression is not referred to there.

[2] The counterargument is that if an expression has capital letters, a reader knows that it is defined in the definitions section, and can easily find it if the definitions appear as the final clause or even in a schedule. Proponents of this drafting style have a point if there are so many definitions that their appearance at the front of the contract would defeat any reader's attempt to assimilate them on a read-through, as for example in *Amey Birmingham Highways Limited v Birmingham City Council* [2018] EWCA Civ 264 (where the definitions ran to over 200 pages).

...but do not rely only on local definitions

4.3 With a contract of any length, it is better to bring the definitions together in a definitions clause. The alternative is to rely on local definitions alone, which implies defining an expression the first time it appears in the contract. But this will make the definition impossible to track down, unless perhaps the technique of providing

> 'X' shall bear the meaning set out in clause 6.2

is applied to all definitions. But this would simply condemn the reader to two sets of page turning rather than just one.

It is recommended to use local definitions only for defined terms used within a very narrow compass, ideally only on a single page in the contract[3] so that whenever it is used, the reader's eye is readily drawn to it.

Do not assume that the meaning of terms is too obvious to be defined

4.4 If a term is defined, the courts will usually take the definition to signify that the parties have concluded that they want the term to bear the specified meaning. But if a term is *not* defined, a creative judge may feel tempted to conclude that it does not bear the meaning it would naturally be expected to have.

For example, in *Sinochem International Oil (London) Co Ltd v Mobil Sales and Supply Corporation,*[4] a majority of the members of the Court of Appeal persuaded themselves that 'party' as used in a particular contract did not mean (as most drafters would routinely expect) only a party to that agreement, but could be read as extending to the 'affiliates' of such a party. The moral is that a drafter should always assume that drafting can never be too explicit: even if to define 'Party' as 'a party to this Agreement' would normally seem too obvious to need saying, to do so would head off the surprising conclusion that it might mean something else.

Because definitions usually define expressions that are nouns or noun phrases, drafters are sometimes reluctant to award other types of phrase the status of a definition. But if they are squeamish about this, unpredictability results.

3 It is dangerous to couch this recommendation in the form that local definitions are appropriate provided the defined term is used in a single *clause,* since one clause can stretch over many pages. For example, in the Lloyd's Bank capital notes case *BNY Mellon Corporate Trustee Services Limited v LBG Capital No 1 Plc* [2016] UKSC 29, the condition (clause) in the bond terms that related to conversion of the notes ran to more than 20 pages.

4 [2000] 1 All ER (Comm) 474.

For example, in *Investor Trading Ltd v City Index Ltd*,[5] a contract used the phrase

> during the term of the agreement

on more than one occasion, without itself defining what the expression meant. Although the meaning was superficially clear, it was unclear whether or not it included a period which was defined in the contract as the 'Wind Down Period'. It was therefore open to one party to argue that, in the various contractual contexts in which it appeared, the expression 'during the term of the agreement' sometimes included the 'Wind Down Period' and sometimes did not. Although the argument was unsuccessful, it would surely never have been advanced if the expression had been defined[6] to make it clear what it meant.

THE CONTENT OF THE DEFINITIONS CLAUSE

Do not include in the definitions clause a defined term that is not used elsewhere in the contract

4.5 It is clumsy, and robs the drafting of credibility, if a term is defined in the definitions clause, only for it not to be used anywhere in the operative clauses of the contract. This can easily happen if the drafter adapts a template agreement by removing an unnecessary operative provision in which the defined term is alone used, but does not follow through by removing the definition from the definitions clause.

A drafter might assume that if this happens, the failing is harmless, since all that happens will be that the otiose definition will itself be struck out of the contract. But this is not necessarily so. An illustration of the inconvenience (and expense) that can arise from this error is *Ellis and Montague (as administrative receivers of Rayford Homes Limited) v Bank of Scotland PLC*.[7] A bank whose own standard form intercreditor agreement contained a defined term[8] found itself in the embarrassing position of having to argue that the term, which was not used in the contract, was meaningless and should be ignored. The embarrassment was that the bank had put forward the contract containing the term itself and had more than once referred to the defined term in correspondence with the customer as if it must have meant *something*.

5 [2011] EWCA Civ 837.

6 The drafter's failure to define it may perhaps have owed something to the difficulty of deciding, if the expression 'during the term of the agreement' was itself to be defined, which if any of the words used should be capitalised. But even though their use is customary and to omit them may be risky (see n 51 below), there is no magic in the capital letters, and it would have been better to define the term without any capitals than not to have defined it at all.

7 [2011] EWHC 1948 (Ch).

8 'BOS Priority', which was apparently defined so as to mean a particular amount (in the case itself, to compound the error, the amount was left blank – itself a blunder: see **1.11** above).

The lesson for the drafter is a simple one. Before an agreement is signed, the drafter should check that every defined term is used at least once in the agreement. If a defined term is not used anywhere, it should be removed from the definitions clause.

Do not use capitalised expressions if they are not defined...

4.6 A corollary is that it is similarly poor technique for a drafter to use a capitalised term that is not defined anywhere. Readers of a contract are used to the convention that if an expression appears with initial capitals in the body of the agreement, that signifies that the expression is defined somewhere. If it turns out not to be defined anywhere, the drafter has condemned users of the contract to a fruitless trawl through the contract in search of a chimera, which is a waste of everybody's time and a further blow to the credibility of the drafting.

In *Vinci Construction UK Ltd v Beumer Group UK Ltd*[9] the parties used capitalised expressions ('Baggage' and 'Remaining Works') to distinguish between categories of construction work at an airport. Different completion dates applied to the two categories, which drove the computation of damages payable if the works were delayed. But the capitalised expressions were nowhere defined, allowing one party to argue[10] that the damages provision was unenforceable.

The lesson for the drafter is, again, clear: if a capitalised expression is used, make sure it is defined.

...or otherwise suggest that a term is defined when it is not

4.7 Anybody reading the drafting in *Whitecap Leisure Ltd v John H Rundle Ltd*:[11]

> After expiry of the defects liability period specified in this agreement the Seller shall be under no further obligation or liability either under the contract or in tort...

would have expected the term 'defects liability period' to be defined somewhere in the agreement, even though it lacks initial capitals. It did not do so, however (giving the lie to the use of the word 'specified'). Drafters should avoid insinuating that an undefined term is defined somewhere when it is not: as this case shows, the cost to the parties may be a distracting and expensive court case.

9 [2017] EWHC 2196 (TCC).
10 Unsuccessfully, but only after a two-day High Court hearing.
11 [2008] EWCA Civ 429; [2008] 2 Lloyd's Rep 216.

Similarly, in *Dwyer (UK Franchising) Ltd v Fredbar Ltd*,[12] a franchising agreement used a capitalised expression[13] without defining it, causing the court to have to infer its meaning in the context of a clause designed to restrict competition with that very business.[14] The drafter had done an incomplete job.

THE DRAFTING OF DEFINITIONS

Be consistent with how definitions are phrased

4.8 Definitions are usually introduced by language such as

> [Defined Term] means [definition]

or

> [Defined Term] shall mean [definition]

or occasionally a simple colon:

> [Defined Term]: [definition].

Untidy drafters are inconsistent and sometimes use one form of introductory language, sometimes another. Though no serious risk of confusion or ambiguity exists, the impression is of carelessness.

A different issue arises if the introductory verb 'means' or 'shall mean' appears instead as 'includes' or 'shall include'. They are different in meaning. The difference is neatly explained by Arden LJ in *Singapore Airlines Ltd v Buck Consultants Ltd*:[15]

> Definitions in statutes and deeds can be exhaustive or non-exhaustive. Non-exhaustive definitions are usually prefaced by the word 'include'. More often, however, a definition is intended to be exhaustive and it will then generally begin with the word 'mean' or 'means'. It is difficult to read a definition which begins with the word 'means' as other than exhaustive.

In other words, use of the word 'includes' before a list naturally tends to suggest that items beyond those enumerated may be included in the general concept that introduces the list: *East of England Ambulance Services NHS Trust v Flowers*.[16] By contrast 'means' (or 'comprises'[17]) is narrower, and seeks to confine the concept to those items appearing on the list.[18]

12 [2021] EWHC 1218 (Ch); [2022] EWCA Civ 889.
13 The 'Drain Doctor Business'.
14 [2021] EWHC 1218 (Ch) at [300].
15 [2011] EWCA Civ 1542 at [15].
16 [2019] EWCA Civ 947 at [19].
17 ibid at [17].
18 See, for example, *Rockliffe Hall Ltd v Travelers Insurance Company Ltd* [2021] EWHC 412 (Comm) (Cockerill J at [60]).

Drafters should therefore consider carefully whether to use 'means' or 'includes' to introduce their definitions. Normally 'means' will be the correct formula. 'Includes' is likely to be relevant only if it introduces a list. The drafter must then consider a further question: whether it is clear enough if anything that is not expressly included on the list is intended to be covered.[19]

A colon is naturally read as equivalent to 'means' rather than 'includes'.

Choose a defined term to reflect the underlying concept

4.9 The meaning of a defined term is predictable. There is no room for nuance if a defined term is used: the meaning of an expression that is defined does not take any colour from the context in which it is used.[20] Taken to an extreme, this might suggest that the actual capitalised expression that is defined is irrelevant, because its only contractual role is to represent the definition of it that appears in the definition clause – so it could as well be a mathematical symbol as a group of words. So the drafter could, for example, replace the defined term

> the Agreed Purchase Price shall mean £1,500,000 plus 20 per cent of the Company's profits for the period ending on 31 October 2023

with

> X shall mean £1,500,000 plus 20 per cent of the Company's profits for the period ending on 31 October 2023,

and instead of

> The Buyer shall pay the Seller the Agreed Purchase Price on the Closing Date

the relevant operative clause could read

> The Buyer shall pay the Seller X on the Closing Date,

with no loss of clarity.

This is right so far as it goes; but it is preferable for a drafter to select, for the term that is defined, an expression that represents as fairly as is feasible the concept that is being defined. Not only does this place less strain on the reader (who does not have to keep in mind what the colourless symbol 'X' represents), but it also runs with the grain of judicial thinking.[21]

19 See from **5.9** below.

20 Unless the drafter is tempted by 'Except where the context otherwise requires': see n 1 above.

21 Lord Hoffmann in *Chartbrook Ltd v Persimmon Homes Ltd* [2009] UKHL 38 addresses this point (at [17]): although it would be possible to use mathematical symbols, 'the contract does not… The words used as labels are seldom arbitrary. They are usually chosen as a distillation of the meaning or purpose of a concept intended to be more precisely stated in the definition.' The same point is made by Lewison LJ in *SAS Institute Inc v World Programming Ltd* [2013] EWCA Civ 1482 (at [106]).

An inappropriately chosen defined term risks confusing the reader. So for example in *Fitzhugh v Fitzhugh*,[22] 'the Licensor' (singular) of a family farm was defined as three named individuals, one of whom was also one of two individuals defined as 'the Licensee'. Predictable difficulties ensued when the two other individuals within the 'Licensor' definition wanted to give a notice to the 'Licensee', which the individual who was within both definitions did not wish to receive. Choosing an essentially singular expression to define a group of more than one individual seems to have blinded the drafter to complications which, with hindsight, were all too likely to arise.[23] A similar issue blighted the drafting in *Mogens Alex Bastholm v Peveril Securities (Dalton Park Retail) Ltd*.[24]

Do not put obligations in definitions

4.10 Drafters risk confusing their readers if they do not confine definitions to performing the function of defining the expression they relate to. In particular, they should not contain *obligations*, as in

> 'Closing Date' shall mean 31 July 2024, when the Buyer shall pay the Purchase Price to the Seller.

The obligation to pay the Purchase Price (a significant obligation – but the principle applies to minor obligations as well) should appear in an operative clause in the body of the contract, not a definition.

In *AIB Group (UK) Plc v Martin*,[25] Lord Millett said of a definitions clause that:

> it is not the purpose of such a clause to enlarge the parties' rights and obligations beyond those provided by the operative provisions.[26]

Admittedly, Lord Millett's qualms were not shared by the other members of the House of Lords, who did not see the clause in question as extending liability so much as identifying the obligors and what they had agreed to pay.[27] But the feature that the drafting caused a disagreement at that judicial level, it is submitted, simply provides support for the drafting recommendation discussed in this paragraph.

22 [2012] EWCA Civ 694.
23 For the choice between singular and plural, see below from **7.19**. The practical difficulties could also be seen as a failure to ask a 'What if?' question (see Chapter 13 below): what if the Licensor wants to give an unwelcome notice to the Licensee?
24 [2023] EWHC 438 (Ch) (five individuals described as 'Seller': uncertainty over whether a notice submitted by only four of them, the other having become bankrupt, was valid).
25 [2001] UKHL 63.
26 ibid. at [8].
27 ibid at [39]–[41] (Lord Scott).

Consider defining parties by their names rather than their roles

4.11 Template agreements tend to use labels for parties to denote their roles within the contractual framework: 'Buyer', 'Seller', 'Customer', 'Supplier.' This is, of course, the very feature that allows the template agreements to function as templates.

Drafters adapting templates of this type are often tempted to define the particular parties acting in those roles as 'Buyer', 'Seller' and so on, partly because it reduces the need to make wholesale changes to the template agreement.

But referring to the contracting parties by their *names* rather than their *roles* is arguably preferable. The parties themselves, in reviewing the draft agreement and in consulting it afterwards, will find it easier to grasp the contractual rights and obligations if the parties' names (whether of individuals or companies) are used rather than labels which force the reader to identify who is playing the role in question.[28]

Make it clear, when defining a party by a label, whether a reference to the party is limited to it in that capacity

4.12 A drafter should take particular care if a party is playing more than one role in a transaction.

Landesbank Hessen-Thuringen v Bayerische Landesbank[29] illustrates the dangers. In a financing transaction, a financial payment waterfall first awarded certain costs (including hedging costs) to the 'Facility Agent'. Bayerische Landesbank (BLB) was acting as Facility Agent, and argued that it was therefore entitled at that stage in the waterfall to all its hedging costs, including amounts incurred in other capacities. But the drafter had anticipated that argument, and had referred to the Facility Agent as follows:

> [BLB] in its capacity as facility agent for the Lenders under the Finance Documents (the 'Facility Agent').

This careful reference was enough to prevent BLB getting what might be described as a windfall from the waterfall.[30] Only its losses in the capacity of

[28] An instance of the drafter using labels rather than names, and then misapplying them, is *Salvage Wharf Ltd v G & S Brough Ltd* [2009] EWCA Civ 21, where the labels 'Owner' and 'Developer' were unfortunately reversed so that a provision made no sense. The chances of someone picking up this error would surely have been increased if the parties' names had been used instead. A similar blunder was made in the drafting in *Littmann v Aspen Oil (Broking) Ltd* [2005] EWCA Civ 1579, where the drafter unfortunately used 'Landlord' instead of 'Tenant' in a termination clause.

[29] [2014] EWHC 1404.

[30] See ibid [26] (Flaux J).

Facility Agent were recoverable at that stage. But if the definition had more carelessly provided that the 'Facility Agent' simply meant BLB (impliedly, arguably acting in any capacity), the arguments would have been more finely balanced.

A similar issue arose in *Cattles Plc v Welcome Financial Services Ltd*,[31] but was resolved the other way. A restriction applying to a 'Guarantor' in one particular clause was held to apply, in the context of the particular drafting, to a Guarantor acting in other capacities as well.

The lesson for a drafter is that as so often, explicit drafting is vital.

Proceed carefully when borrowing a definition from statute

4.13 If a term has been defined in a statute, a drafter may think that it is both economical and convenient to import the statutory definition into a contract. If Parliament has spent time carefully considering how to define terms like 'parent company' and 'subsidiary' in the Companies Acts, and 'connected persons' and 'associates' in tax legislation, why should a drafter spend time and energy re-inventing the wheel?

However, drafters need to tread carefully, for a number of reasons.

First, what the defined term means in the contract can depend on exactly how the drafter adopts the statutory definition.

One choice the drafter can make is to repeat the language of the statute itself. So the drafter could for example write:[32]

> Control, in relation to a body corporate (company A), shall mean[33] the power of a person (P) to secure—
>
> (a) by means of the holding of shares or the possession of voting power in relation to that or any other body corporate, or
>
> (b) as a result of any powers conferred by the articles of association or other document regulating that or any other body corporate,
>
> that the affairs of company A are conducted in accordance with P's wishes.

Where statutory language is, like this, set out in full in the contract, it becomes contractual language like any other. That has implications for what, in that context, the language means. If a dispute arises as to what the language means for the purposes of the contract, it is possible for the contractual meaning to diverge from the statutory meaning. The purposes of the contract and

31 [2010] EWCA Civ 599.
32 The example is taken from the Corporation Tax Act 2010, s 1124 (2).
33 The Corporation Tax Act itself has 'means' rather than 'shall mean' but 'shall mean' is adopted here – see **4.8** above and also Chapter 6 ('*Basic Verbs*') below.

the purposes of the statute are not necessarily the same. If, for example, the language borrowed from the statute conflicts with some other provision in the contract, the court would have to weigh up which should prevail.[34]

The same approach applies if the language is not set out verbatim in the contract, but is incorporated into the contract as if it were. So if the contract invokes language 'set out in' a statute,[35] the contract is treated as if it contained the statutory language set out in full.

An alternative approach is to state that the statutory meaning applies, for example by providing:

> 'Control', in relation to a body corporate, means control of that body corporate for the purposes of section 1124(2) of the Corporation Tax Act 2010.

An incautious drafter might think that there is no difference between these two possibilities. But that is not correct.

If the contract requires an expression to bear its statutory meaning, there is no room for an argument that the language should take its colour from the contractual context, and perhaps have a meaning different from the statutory meaning: 'The same meaning applies in both contexts'.[36]

In most cases, a drafter is recommended to use the former method, and set out the statutory language in full. There are a number of reasons for this recommendation.

First, the reader of the contract does not have to look up the legislation in question to see what it says: all the language that the reader needs is set out in the contract.[37]

Second, the drafter and the contracting parties have insured themselves to some extent against future judicial decisions on what the defined expression means for statutory purposes. The parties have 'domesticated' the statutory language, and preserved for themselves the argument that its meaning should solely reflect their contractual purposes.

Third, the language is fixed if it is set out in full.

If instead the drafter contract proceeds by stating that the statutory meaning applies, various questions arise.

34 *Adamastos Shipping v Anglo-Saxon Petroleum Ltd* [1959] AC 133.

35 As in *Brett v The Brett Essex Golf Club* (1986) 278 EG 1476.

36 *Enviroco Ltd v Farstad Supply A/S* [2009] EWCA Civ 1399 at [21] (Patten LJ); the Court of Appeal's decision was upheld in the Supreme Court.

37 A factor that points the other way is that if the statutory provision is very lengthy, the cross-referencing method is more economical. But a drafter who is nervous about causing the contracting parties to adopt statutory language which may be unfamiliar to them should be made more so if the language is long and detailed.

First: what happens if the statutory definition itself changes? The answer is very often that the contractual meaning will change if the statute changes. That might be because the contract contains some common boilerplate along the lines of:

> References to any statute or other legislation shall include any reference to any amendment, extension, consolidation or replacement of that statute.[38]

But even *without* that language, a statutory change could be argued impliedly to trigger a change to the contractual meaning of the defined term. That could apply because of the application of the Interpretation Act 1978,[39] which provides that where an enactment is repealed and re-enacted, whether with or without modification, a reference to the original Act in any document (sc. including a contract) is to be interpreted as a reference to the re-enacted version. But this in itself leads to some uncertainty: what if the enactment referred to is not repealed and re-enacted, but is simply amended by the addition of some extra provisions? That would seem to be outside the case covered by the Interpretation Act and leave the question of whether the contract should be interpreted in accordance with the old version of the Act or the new one as a matter of interpretation of the contract.[40]

Moreover, even if the statutory language does not itself change, the courts might change their minds about what the statutory definition means. If that happens, the effect is that the expression is regarded as having always borne that meaning.[41]

The drafter can at least make it clear whether a change to the enactment will itself affect what language the contract is to be read as containing. It is open to the drafter to try to freeze the meaning by reference to the statute as it exists at the date of contract:

> 'Control', in relation to a body corporate, means control of that body corporate in the sense provided for in section 1124(2) of the Corporation Tax Act 2010 as that subsection appears on the date of this contract.

This language will have the effect of preserving the original version of the statutory language.[42] This gets close to the position if the actual language appears in the contract, but is not exactly the same. For example, assume that the language of the statute does not change, but a court decision that follows

38 Often this language appears without anybody taking much notice of it, a symptom of how easy it is to underestimate the significance of boilerplate language. It appeared, for example, in the disputed charterparty in the *Farstad* case (sub nom *Farstad A/S v Enviroco Ltd* [2010] UKSC 18): see [3] (Lord Collins).

39 Through a combination of ss 17(2) and 23(3).

40 Slade LJ in *Brett v Brett Essex Golf Club* (1986) 278 EG 1476.

41 *Samsoondar v Capital Insurance Company Ltd* [2020] UKPC 33 (at [13] (Lord Burrows).

42 The effect of the Interpretation Act described applies only 'unless the contrary intention appears': s 17(2).

the contract decides what the relevant language means for statutory purposes. If the statutory language is set out in the contract, that court decision may not determine what it means in the contractual context. But if the contract requires the statutory meaning to be applied, rather than just containing the statutory language, such a decision would inescapably apply for the purposes of the contract as well.

Make definitions specific enough

4.14 A definition helps to make the meaning clear only if it is clear itself. To leave pivotal expressions undefined within a definition causes the definition to lose its power to fix the rights and obligations which the contract gives rise. A drafter cannot in other words assume that merely defining an expression is enough: the definition itself has to be clear and unambiguous. In *Singapore Airlines Ltd v Buck Consultants Ltd*,[43] the drafter of the trust deed governing a pension scheme provided a definition for an important term, 'Earnings':

> 'Earnings' means for each Member the annual rate of his basic remuneration from the Employers.

However, the purported clarity conferred by this definition was illusory: 'basic remuneration' was not itself defined. So a dispute arose about whether certain amounts, including a London weighting allowance, were within the definition or not. The drafter's failure was to fail to subject the language of the definition to the degree of analysis needed to determine whether it was clear.

DEFINITIONS IN THE CONTEXT OF THE CONTRACT AS A WHOLE

Handle definitions with particular care: the respect afforded to them suggests that 'some provisions are more equal than others'

4.15 A court takes particular notice of defined terms, recognising that they have been the subject of unusually close attention by the parties, and deserve on that account to be respected. In *Teesside Power Holdings v Electrabel International Holdings BV*,[44] the judge observed that the technique of defining a term 'is indicative of special thought having been given to the wording of the provision'.

[43] [2011] EWCA Civ 1542.
[44] [2012] EWHC 33 (Comm).

A similar view animated Briggs J in the first instance judgment in *Chartbrook Ltd v Persimmon Homes Ltd*,[45] though the House of Lords had less sympathy with the point.

In the property sale contract under dispute in *CLP Holding Company Ltd v Singh*, [46] the expression 'Purchase Price' was defined as £130,000 – which prevented the purchaser becoming liable for an additional amount in respect of the VAT that was payable in respect of the purchase.

Similarly, when a settlement agreement between a group of companies and their bank contained a wide definition of 'Affiliate' and 'Employee', the result was that the companies to their surprise lost the right to take subsequent action not merely against the bank against which they had taken proceedings, but also the companies' own former administrator whom they separately had considered guilty of malfeasance.[47]

Do not allow a definition to embrace two different meanings in the same contract

4.16 The whole reason for defining a term is to fix its meaning. Arguments that a single defined term can bear one meaning in one clause, but a different meaning in another, are far-fetched. In *Fitzhugh v Fitzhugh*,[48] Rimer LJ described it as 'improbable' that the term 'the Licensor' could in one clause refer to two named people, but in another to only one of them, even though the latter interpretation would allow the license to operate more rationally. A judge may occasionally apply a defined term in more than one sense to avoid an 'absurd' result.[49] But a drafter who has been inattentive enough in defining terms to risk the drafting producing an absurd result has fallen at the first hurdle in any event. And drafters should not rely on a merciful judge to do their job for them.

It is feasible for a drafter to provide explicitly that the same expression should mean two[50] different things in different parts of the contract. However, for a drafter to do this is to court disaster, as seen in *JIS (1974) Ltd v MCP Investment Nominees Ltd*.[51]

45 [2007] EWHC 409 (Ch) at [45].
46 [2014] EWCA Civ 1103.
47 *Schofield v Smith* [2021] EWHC 2533 (Ch).
48 [2012] EWCA 694.
49 *City Inn (Jersey) Ltd v 10 Trinity Square Ltd* [2008] EWCA Civ 156 (Lord Jacob); *Starlight Shipping Company v Allianz Marine & Aviation Versicherungs AG* [2014] EWHC 3068 (Comm) (Flaux J).
50 Or in theory even more than two.
51 [2003] EWCA Civ 721.

Clause 1 of a lease defined 'the defined premises'[52] for the purposes of the agreement generally. In Schedule 2, however, which dealt with rent reviews, a different and narrower definition was given to that phrase 'for the purposes of this Schedule only'.

Meanwhile, clause 5 of the lease purported to confer a right to the tenant to break the lease early. For the purposes of clause 5 break right, the Clause 1 definition of 'the demised premises' applied, but it was almost certainly the wrong one. The Clause 1 definition made the break option practically unworkable, whereas it would have been feasible with the Schedule 2 definition.

The problem would have been less likely to arise if different definitions had been used for the two terms – perhaps 'the demised premises' and 'unlet premises'.[53] And the use of different defined terms would have helped the parties identify, before entering into the lease, the potential for the problem that later arose through the overenthusiastic use of the wider Clause 1 definition.[54]

Use defined terms consistently

4.17 Once a term has been defined, a drafter should use it consistently, in accordance with what Lord Diplock observed in *Prestcold (Central) Ltd v Minister of Labour*:[55]

> The habit of the legal draftsman is to eschew synonyms. He uses the same words throughout the document to express the same thing or concept.[56]

Lord Diplock was not referring here only to terms of the type commonly defined with initial capital letters. His comment was directed to an able drafter's correct instinct that any words, even if not defined, may prove a source of confusion if not used consistently. For a recent case where the courts inferred that a term that was not defined should nonetheless be interpreted as having a consistent meaning, see *Adaptive Spectrum and Signal Alignment*

52 Without the usual initial capitals, which may have contributed to nobody asking the right questions about the significance of the definition.

53 'Unlet premises' would have measured up better to Lord Hoffmann's idea that a definition should function as 'a distillation of the meaning or purpose of a concept intended to be more precisely stated in the definition' (*Chartbrook Ltd v Persimmon Homes Ltd* [2009] UKHL 38 at [17]).

54 See also *Swissindependent Trustees SA v Sofer* [2023] EWHC 12 (Ch) (term defined in one trust instrument inexplicably used to mean something different in another instrument intended to form part of the same arrangement; resolved by preferring the meaning given in the definition).

55 [1969] 1 WLR 89.

56 The habit of the *competent* legal draftsman, perhaps. In *Sutton Housing Partnership Ltd v Rydon Maintenance Ltd* [2017] EWCA Civ 359, the contract used two different expressions ('Levels of Minimum Acceptable Performance' and 'Performance Profit Thresholds') to signify the same thing, leading to predictable confusion: see [16].

Inc v British Telecommunications PLC.[57] But the point is most clearly seen with defined terms.

It is inept, but by no means unknown, for a drafter to define an expression with the customary capital letters, only then to ignore the definition and use the expression without capitals. The technical issue is whether, in using lower case letters, the drafter is trying to signify that the words are being used with a different meaning from the meaning given by the definition.[58] And, if a different meaning is intended, what is it? Is it coloured by the meaning ascribed to those words in the definition, or is the contrary inference to be drawn? More usually the conclusion is that the drafter intended to use the capitalised expression, but has carelessly failed to do so, with a consequent lack of credibility.[59]

There is no conceptual difficulty in making one defined term depend on another. Indeed, with any moderately complex agreement, that is likely to be necessary. In the nature of things, it is likely that if this technique is used, a defined term may be used in a definition before the reader has yet arrived at it, because of the convention that defined terms appear in alphabetical order. For, example, in *Chartbrook Limited v Persimmon Homes Limited*,[60] the contract's definition of 'Price' was

> 'Price' means the aggregate of the Total Land Value and the Balancing Payment.

A reader of the definitions reaching this point would already have come across the definition of 'Balancing Payment', but not the definition of 'Total Land Value' which is yet to come. This offends against the principle that a contract should so far as possible be capable of being read sequentially (so that a reader should not be expected to have advance knowledge of what comes later in the contract).[61] But the confusion that would arise if alphabetical order of defined terms were to be abandoned seems a greater sin.

57 [2023] EWCA Civ 451 at [32] (Birss LJ) (meaning of 'services' in an agreement licensing use of patented processes to enable telephone wires to be used to facilitate internet access).

58 Lord Diplock in the *Prestcold* case (n 55) goes on to say, immediately after the quotation cited, 'and consequently if he uses different words the presumption is that he means a different thing or concept'. In *Pink Floyd Music Ltd v EMI Records Limited* [2010] EWCA Civ 1429, the drafter of a record contract sometimes used 'Records' with an initial capital and sometimes used 'records' in all lower case, which contributed to the difficulty of deciding what the contract meant (and indeed the Court of Appeal was divided as to what it *did* mean).

59 As for example in *Aberdeen City Council v Stewart Milne Group Ltd* [2011] UKSC 56, where among many other drafting howlers the drafter created careful definitions of the capitalised expressions 'Gross Sale Proceeds' and Lease Value', only then to refer in the crucial definition of 'the Profit Share' to uncapitalised terms ('80% of the estimated profit or gross sale proceeds'). Lord Hope comments with admirable restraint that the drafter's many mistakes 'make it easier to attribute the problem that we have to deal with to oversight than to a deliberate choice when the agreement was being drafted'.

60 The High Court decision appears at [2007] EWHC 409.

61 See **1.21** above.

A more serious risk is that two interlinked definitions turn out not to mesh as the draftsman intended them to. The risk of this happening is made more acute by the feature that the drafter is having to shuttle backwards and forwards between the two definitions in a way that would not be necessary if the two definitions were collapsed into a single piece of drafting.

One can see this risk becoming reality in the *Aberdeen City Council* case,[62] where the drafter did not notice that two separate definitions of 'Estimated Profit' and 'Profit Share' both required deduction of a third amount defined as the 'Allowable Costs', which led to an obviously unintended double counting.

Check that the definition works in all the operative clauses in which it is used

4.18 It is axiomatic that a drafter must ensure that when a defined term is used in an operative provision, it works to give the intended result. Because a definition contained in a definitions clause is remote from the operative clause, this needs careful attention.

Decided cases occasionally show that a defined term is painfully at odds with the commercial intention. For example in *Chipasaway International Ltd v Kerr*,[63] a franchisee agreed in a franchise agreement not to compete, after the franchise term, with 'the Business' as defined. The definition of 'the Business', however, referred to the provision by the franchisee of services to customers. So the operative provision, construed literally, would have effectively prohibited only the franchisee competing with himself. The Court of Appeal managed to persuade itself that a more sensible construction could be placed on the drafting, but the drafter had failed to think hard enough about whether the language used in the definition flowed through properly into the operative provision.

Check, as the contractual relationship develops, that the definitions remain relevant

4.19 Definitions risk becoming outdated in a dynamic contractual relationship, so a definition that originally works well to clarify what the contract means can soon become irrelevant and confusing. In *CDV Software Entertainment AG v Gamecock Media Europe Ltd*,[64] the parties used a defined term 'Delivery Dates' to specify dates for delivery of final master versions of certain video games:

[62] n 59.
[63] [2009] EWCA Civ 320.
[64] [2009] EWHC 2965.

> 'Delivery Dates' means the dates for delivery...of the Products set out in Schedule 1.

The specified dates came and went, and the defined term became useless for assessing the parties' rights and obligations after that time. It did not help that the relevant operative clause envisaged 'revised Delivery Dates', without the defined term suggesting any such flexibility. The drafter should have recognised that the original definition was over-specific, and needed to build in some flexibility:

> 'Delivery Dates' means the dates for delivery...of the Products set out in Schedule 1 or such other dates as the parties shall agree from time to time.

Beware over-reliance on definitions: a cascade of interlocking definitions can conceal errors

4.20 Definitions are useful tools, enabling drafters to express and marshal highly sophisticated legal concepts in what should in theory be a predictable way. They are not unlike elaborate pieces of computer coding that are intended to lead to a predictable and desired result, eliminating uncertainties down to the vagaries of language. But if all the work of the drafting is shouldered by the definitions, each of which depends for its meaning on other definitions that themselves derive from others, the very complexity may carry with it the seeds of its own downfall. This is illustrated by *State Street Bank and Trust Co v Sompo Japan Insurance Inc*,[65] in which complicated financing arrangements were provided for in a contract which ran to over 500 definitions, many of them parasitic on others.

When a guarantor Sompo paid out under its guarantee, it expected to be fully reimbursed under its rights in a reimbursement agreement. That this was the parties' intention was evident from a narrative description of the proposed arrangements in the offering circular under which investors were invited to subscribe for notes in the financing. But the definition of a crucial term in the agreement meant that the amount to which Sompo was apparently entitled caused it to suffer a shortfall of $150 million, because the drafting omitted one of the list of defined terms that made up the amount to which the guarantor was entitled.

The court held that it could uphold the parties' intentions, despite the botched drafting of the agreements, on the grounds that to hold otherwise made no commercial sense. It is, however, telling that the drafter's 'obvious mistake' arose in the drafting of the contract, not the offering circular. In other words, when the drafter wanted to give a narrative description of the proposed

[65] [2010] EWHC 1461 (Ch).

arrangements to investors, the description was accurate. The error only crept in when the contractual drafting, which relied on a quasi-mathematical system of interlocking definitions, came to be prepared. The drafter should infer that an extreme level of care is needed if an intricately constructed system of interdependent definitions is to drive a commercial outcome. There is no obvious common sense cross-check that can be applied to drafting of that type to illustrate whether the drafter has (as happened in the *Sompo* case) fallen into error.

Chapter 5

Formulae and lists

Drafters need to be able to handle formulae and lists. Formulae are best expressed mathematically, though alternative methods can be used. Worked examples illustrating the application of the formula can be helpful, as can recording what the formula is designed to achieve. Lists tend to grow longer, and can cause as many problems as they solve. Adding general language to the end of a list in an attempt to make it comprehensive breeds uncertainty, and is best avoided.

FORMULAE

5.1 Draft using formulae to express calculations

5.2 Express a mathematical formula mathematically

5.3 Make it clear in what order a set of steps is to be performed

5.4 Use worked examples

5.5 Use enough worked examples

5.6 Make sure the examples match any mathematical or narrative description

5.7 Consider expressing the principle(s) behind the formula and the worked examples

5.8 Worked examples can throw light on unintended consequences

LISTS

5.9 Do not allow lists to expand so as to create more problems than they solve

5.10 Do not resort to sweep-up language without considering the risk of 'eiusdem generis' interpretation

5.11 Avoid an 'eiusdem generis' problem using these techniques

FORMULAE

Draft using formulae to express calculations

5.1 The most common contractual formulae are used to lay down the way in which an amount payable by one party to the other should be calculated. They are often designed to apply at a stage when the parties' contractual relationship is otherwise largely at an end. For example, in an agreement relating to the sale and purchase of the shares in a private company, a seller of the target company may be entitled to an earn-out payment dependent on the company's post-completion profitability, at a stage where the only other ongoing contractual obligations owed by either party may take the form of exposure to warranty claims, or a lasting obligation to respect the confidentiality of information.

This means that formulae are often contractually relevant in circumstances where the risks of a dispute are greatest. Where the application of a formula determines the amount payable by one party to another, their interests are directly opposed: the payer wants the sum to be as small as possible (ideally nil), and the payee wants the reverse. And if the parties' contractual relationship is otherwise at an end, they have no reason to compromise as they would do if they needed to continue to co-operate.[1]

Additionally, some drafters feel uneasy about drafting formulae, feeling perhaps that their essentially mathematical nature is at odds with a professional expertise that is rooted in, or that ought to be rooted in, command of words rather than numbers. The formula reflects a pure commercial bargain, negotiated between business people who evaluate their success or failure in financial terms and who are comfortable with numbers. The lawyer's particular expertise in applying legal principles to a set of facts is not engaged. All this contributes to the drafting of formulae being a significant generator of disputes.

Decided cases that have involved formulae afford valuable lessons for the drafter.

Express a mathematical formula mathematically

5.2 Faced with trying to draft a formula that is an essentially mathematical calculation, some drafters shun the option of drafting in mathematical terms and prefer to express the formula verbally. For example, in *Chartbrook Ltd v*

1 See, for example, *Pixdene Ltd v Paddington and Company Ltd* [2022] EWHC 2765 (IPEC) (entitlement of Pixdene to 10% of the worldwide merchandising income generated by Paddington Bear: 'the parties do not trust each other' and (quoting Counsel for one of them) 'the milk of human kindness has long since evaporated between them': Melissa Clarke at [12].

Persimmon Homes Ltd,[2] the drafter of a development agreement tried to capture linguistically how 'overage' (a sort of profit share payable by the developer to the landowner) should be calculated. The drafter framed it as a definition of a term described as the 'Additional Residential Payment' or 'ARP'. The ARP was to be

> 23.4% of the price achieved for each Residential Unit in excess of the Minimum Guaranteed Residential Unit Value less the Costs and Expenses.

If one ignores *the 'Costs and Expenses'*, which were not central to the dispute, and uses X and Y respectively for 'the price achieved for each Residential Unit' and the 'Minimum Guaranteed Residential Unit Value', the formula boils down to

> 23.4% of X in excess of Y.

But this is ambiguous. The ambiguity lies in the feature that the formula requires two steps to be performed, but it does not tell the reader in which *order* they are to be performed. It could equally require Y to be subtracted from X first, with the ARP being 23.4% of the result; or require Y to be subtracted from an amount that is 23.4% of X. In other words, it might mean

$$\text{ARP} = 23.4\%\ (X - Y)$$

or

$$\text{ARP} = (23.4\% \text{ of } X) - Y.$$

The difficulty here is on analysis a particular version of the grammatical problem with 'uncertain modifiers', discussed in Chapter 7 below.[3]

The ambiguity is straightforwardly illuminated when the formula is expressed mathematically, and using mathematical notation. As Lord Hoffmann remarked,[4] the defined terms 'might just as well have been algebraic symbols…I strongly suspect that if they had been, they would have made it clear [how the formula was intended to work.]' As the alternative formulations above make clear, if the drafter had drafted algebraically, the use of brackets would have made it clear in which order the steps in the calculation fell to be performed.

In one respect, however, a mathematical formula presents a particular risk. It is in the nature of mathematical or algebraic formulae that concepts – often important concepts – are reduced to a mathematical symbol. This means that it is less easy for anyone to notice if the symbol is omitted, accidentally or otherwise, as the contract moves towards signature.

2 [2009] UKHL 38.
3 See from **7.2**.
4 [2009] UKHL 38 at [17].

In *George Wimpey UK Ltd v VI Construction Ltd*,[5] for example, a formula was designed to reward a landowner if profits from a development exceeded a base figure, rather as in *Chartbrook*. Also as in *Chartbrook*, an adjustment was to be made for 'enhancements' which increased the base figure in the excess over which the landowner was to share. This addition of an important element (£2 million) was represented in successive drafts of the formula by the expression '+E'. In later iterations of the formula, however, the expression '+E' was omitted without the developer noticing. It seems less likely that the omission would have passed unnoticed if it had been labelled as the figure for enhancement rather than as a simple symbol '+E'.

The reduction of the formula to algebraic terms accordingly demands close attention in successive drafts if it is to capture the underlying concepts it was designed to reflect.

Make it clear in what order a set of steps is to be performed

5.3 Although most drafters should be numerate enough to cope with using brackets to make clear in what order the steps in a calculation should be undertaken, there are alternatives. One obvious technique was one of which the *Chartbrook* drafter was aware: to make copious use of definitions. In the *Chartbrook* formula, for example, the expression 'Minimum Guaranteed Residential Unit Value' made use of several other defined terms,[6] some of which themselves referred to amounts which had to be calculated in accordance with their own definitions. So it was obvious that the process of establishing those amounts had to precede the operation of calculating the ARP itself. In other words, the use of definitions can enable a relatively complex calculation to be separated into smaller components, and the order in which they are to be conducted made clear.

A further alternative is to describe the calculation as a series of sequential steps, rather in the same way as a recipe might be written. So the drafter in *Chartbrook* could have provided:

> Step One: find the amount which is 23.4% of the average price for each Residential Unit
>
> Step Two: From the amount found in Step One, subtract the Minimum Guaranteed Residential Unit Value[7]

and so on.

5 [2005] EWCA Civ 77.

6 Specifically 'Residential Unit', 'Total Residential Land Value' and 'Planning Permission'.

7 This was the order which the House of Lords found to be the one signified by the ambiguous formula, which was the one which the developer Persimmon had argued for. The High Court and the Court of Appeal had found the other way. Persimmon saved some £3.7 million as a result.

Use worked examples

5.4 If a formula is so inexpertly drafted as to be ambiguous, trouble awaits. That trouble can, however, be avoided if the drafter takes the trouble, before the contract is signed, to illustrate how the formula is intended to work, based on some assumptions as to the outcome of the events which drive the formula. If the two parties disagree about the outcome, based on the examples, the problem is identified before the contract is signed. The parties then have a chance to reach a consensus as to how the formula should operate, and the drafting can be amended so as properly to reflect that consensus.

Even if the formula as drafted remains technically ambiguous, the parties will, by having agreed that the example reflects their common understanding as to which of various theoretically competing constructions should be used, effectively have closed off the likelihood of any dispute.[8]

The drafter may need to work hard to encourage the parties to devote as much time to the worked examples as they should, given how preoccupied they are with other pre-contract concerns. As Blair J observed in *Starbev GP Ltd v Interbrew Central European Holdings Ltd*,[9] having identified the issues on the formula that the parties disagreed about:

> It is perhaps not surprising that each of these issues raises difficult questions of construction. The parties had clinched their deal, and the question as to how the deferred consideration would work in practice was pushed off into the indefinite future.

But if a worked example *is* included, it will tend to reinforce the credibility of the drafting more generally.[10]

Use enough worked examples

5.5 It is in the nature of a formula of any complexity that the outcome – the result of applying the formula – will depend on the way in which the variable inputs interact in the circumstances that actually unfold. Any one

8 It is noteworthy from the first instance judgment in *Chartbrook* ([2007] EWHC (Ch) 409 at [117]) that the parties *never* discussed a worked example of the formula. Had they done so, it would have been apparent that they each supported a different interpretation of how the formula should work. For another case where the inclusion of a formula would have illuminated that the parties had radically different views of how a formula should work, see *Bishops Wholesale Newsagency Ltd v Surridge Dawson Ltd* [2009] EWHC 2578 (no worked example included to demonstrate how the formula should work in practice; the parties later did not agree that a reference to a particular subparagraph truly reflected their bargain).

9 [2014] EWHC 1311 (Comm).

10 See, for example, *James Kemball Ltd v K Line (Europe) Ltd* [2022] EWHC 2239 (worked example of how a contractual surcharge for a shortfall in orders included 'by way of illustration'; held that the carefully drafted surcharge provisions precluded a party from terminating if the surcharge provisions could operate).

example may not illustrate the specific combination of events that actually transpires and causes the controversy to arise between the parties.

It follows that the drafter should consider including a range of examples, with a view to each illustrating the way in which the formula is agreed to work in different combinations of circumstances. There is then a greater chance of the parties having agreed how the formula will work in the circumstances that actually come to pass. And even if the exact circumstances do not match any of the examples, the preparation of a number of examples may help illuminate the principles that the parties accept should guide the calculation, for example by showing the order in which various steps should be applied to make the formula work in practice.[11]

If the drafter includes only a single example, the impression is given that the drafter has included it as something of a half-hearted afterthought, not truly included to make clear how the formula should work across a range of differing circumstances. The chances of it defusing a potential dispute are much reduced.[12]

Make sure the examples match any mathematical or narrative description

5.6 If there is an inconsistency as between the algebraic representation of the formula (or its narrative description) and the way the examples proceed, the drafter is back to square one: the examples, far from eliminating the chances of confusion and disagreement, have compounded them. It is then unclear whether the examples are to be preferred over the narrative, or the narrative over the examples: a classic 'What prevails?' question of the type discussed in Chapter 12 below.

This fault bedevilled the drafting in *Altera Voyager Production Ltd v Premier Oil E&P UK Ltd*,[13] where the contract included worked examples that included two steps in the calculation that were not mentioned in the narrative. The result, almost inevitably, was a dispute that ended in court: the very result that the examples were intended to guard against.[14]

The moral for the drafter is to make sure that the examples are consistent with the narrative. And whilst it should, if this is done, prove unnecessary, it would also make sense to provide explicitly that if the examples do not reflect

[11] Such as the two steps in the *Chartbrook* formula: see **5.2** above.

[12] Only a single example was given in each of *ING Bank NV v Ros Roca SA* [2011] EWCA Civ 353 and *Starbev GP Ltd v Interbrew Central European Holdings Ltd* [2014] EWHC 1311 (Comm), with neither succeeding in forestalling litigation about the effect of formula to which it related.

[13] [2020] EWHC 1891 (Comm).

[14] The judge decided to follow the numerical examples, accepting the commonsense view expressed by the court in *Starbev* (n 12) that in a contract full of boilerplate, it was reasonable to expect the parties to have given the worked examples special attention (see Blair J at [74]).

the narrative, the examples should prevail. This presupposes of course that the parties have checked the examples to ensure that they properly reflect their understanding of the formula. But it is inherently more likely that the parties will make sure that examples reflecting realistic assumptions do indeed reflects their true bargain than that they will verify in some other manner that an abstract formula does so.

Consider expressing the principle(s) behind the formula and the worked examples

5.7 When trying to draft a formula, drafters seem reluctant to start by answering the basic question: what is the formula trying to achieve? What are the principles underlying it? This is curious, because if the parties themselves were asked to explain to a third party what their formula was intended to achieve, they would express themselves in more general language. Before they explained in detail how the formula worked, they would give an overview of the underlying objective.

If the drafter adopted the same technique, that might on its own help to flush out misunderstandings between the parties as to what the formula was trying to achieve. And it would allow those misunderstandings to be ironed out before the contract was signed.

For example, if the drafter in *Chartbrook*[15] had introduced the formula with language like

> This formula is intended to allow [Chartbrook] to share in any sales revenue from the development that exceeds the amount currently expected by [Persimmon]

it would have been obvious that the drafting was not intended by the drafter to confer on Chartbrook a sizeable reward even if the expected sales income figures were not achieved, as Chartbrook asserted[16] they understood it was intended to mean. It would have been clear, even without any worked examples, that the formula fell to be interpreted in the sense that, in the absence of such a simple statement of intention, it took three court cases and nine judges to establish.

Similarly, in the *Bishops Wholesale Newsagency* case, [17] the dispute was whether an adjustment to an option price should apply to both methods of calculating the price provided for in the contract, or only (as the cross-reference literally

15 [2009] UKHL 38: see **7.2** above.

16 Briggs J found in the High Court that Chartbrook had genuinely believed throughout that the formula was intended to bear this (more generous to them) meaning.

17 [2009] EWHC 2578 (Ch): see n 8 above and also **1.27** above.

provided) to one of them. That dispute would surely have been avoided if the contract had set out what the adjustment was intended to achieve and why.

One reason why drafters may shy away from language of that straightforward type is because they see the general language as dangerously imprecise, and fear that the subtleties of the formula will be lost or overridden by the general statement. But this is surely an exaggerated concern, particularly if worked examples are included. All that the general language does is provide an indication of the general objective. The potential for confusion or inconsistency is dispelled if the drafter acknowledges that the general statement is intended as an expression of the general purpose, and is without prejudice to the operation of the formula in the manner illustrated by the worked examples. This illustrates the point encountered elsewhere in this work:[18] the more the drafter is careful about stipulating how provisions interact, the fewer the chances of misunderstanding or dispute.

If the drafter includes worked examples of the application of a formula, each designed to illustrate a different possible combination of circumstances, the effect is to allow the drafter to identify and answer a number of the 'What if?' questions that are the focus of Chapter 13. For example, if in *Scottish Widows Fund and Life Assurance Society v BGC International*[19] the drafter had thought to include some worked examples, the issue that arose in the case (that the formula was ambiguous as to what happened if rents fell back in one rental period, having risen in the previous one) might have been addressed. And an expression of principle might have headed off the arguments in *Westminster City Council v Sports and Leisure Management Ltd*[20] as to whether payments could flow in one direction only, or two.

Worked examples, in other words, reinforce a skilful drafter's ability to make the drafting comprehensive enough to cover, and provide clearly for, the possible range of future events.

Worked examples can throw light on unintended consequences

5.8 Worked examples can also allow the parties to recognise the effect in practice of the principles which they have agreed on, but without properly thinking through them.

In *Arnold v Britton*,[21] as discussed in **13.2** below, leases of holiday chalets provided for lessees to pay an initially affordable service charge. But the annual charge ratcheted up by 10% every year. By the remorseless logic of

18 See particularly Chapter 12.
19 [2012] EWCA Civ 607: see **13.23** below.
20 [2021] EWHC 98 (TCC): also see **13.23** below.
21 [2015] UKSC 36.

compounding,[22] the lessees were paying £3,000 a year each by 2012. And by 2072, as the leases were coming to an end, the annual charge payable by every lessee would exceed £1 million. If a simple worked example showing the level of the service charge at (say) ten-year intervals had been included in the lease, the lessees' problem would have been identified, and surely sorted out, before the leases were granted.

LISTS

Do not allow lists to expand so as to create more problems than they solve

5.9 Drafters are fond of lists. Part of the drafter's urge towards specificity – the commendable urge to be as explicit as possible when describing any category – is to prefer a list of specific items to a generic description of the category. So a drafter who wants to refer to all of Sandwich, Rye, Hythe, New Romney and Hastings would naturally lean in favour of listing them rather than using the term 'The Cinque Ports'. Perhaps, the drafter worries, there is some interpretation of the term 'The Cinque Ports' that (despite its name) includes only four of them, or includes another so there are six? By naming them individually, the drafter prevents the drafting missing its intended meaning.

In this example, each of the Cinque Ports is mutually exclusive: Sandwich is Sandwich, not Hastings. But the impetus towards lists is not felt only with a list of mutually exclusive items of this type. It is also present with items which conceptually *overlap*. This type of drafting often sees the drafter trying to capture a general concept, and offering examples of that concept as a way of capturing it.

Say that the drafter is trying to trigger a right of pre-emption over an asset if the owner seeks to derive value from it. The most natural way of the owner doing that might be to sell the asset. But a sale is just one possibility. The owner might not sell the asset to another, but transfer it to a creditor in satisfaction of a debt. So the drafter extends 'sell' to 'sell or transfer'. But that is still not enough. The owner might grant an option over the asset, or take some other action that creates a beneficial interest in favour of another, like declaring a trust over it. Or the owner might raise money from the asset by using it as security. So the creation of security interests has to be covered. And the creation of security in itself might take many guises. The owner might mortgage the asset, or pledge or hypothecate it. And what about a case where the owner does not set out to initiate the creation of a security interest, but

[22] A feature which also undermined the formula in *Monsolar IQ Ltd v Woden Park Ltd* [2021] EWCA Civ 961.

carries out some transaction which causes a lien to arise over the asset in favour of another person?

Before the drafter knows it, the list has grown to a length familiar to the drafter, but not welcomed by anyone else. Lord Hoffmann described this type of drafting as 'torrential' and attributed the tendency to multiply overlapping concepts to 'a determination to obliterate the conceptual target'.[23]

Whether the items on a drafter's list are clearly distinct items or overlap, the drafter's objective is, therefore, to avoid leaving anything out. If a list refers only to 'Sandwich, Rye, Hythe and New Romney', but Hastings is left out, a reader infers that the omission is deliberate. The impression is only strengthened by the feature that the five ports often appear all together. This inference, when applied to the interpretation of contracts, is known by the Latin expression 'expressio unius est exclusio alterius'. It is not, any more than any other principle of construction, to be blindly followed. It may be disregarded if it would run counter to the wider context of the drafting, or lead to an absurd result.[24] Most drafters deal with it by ignoring Lord Hoffmann's preference, and instead making their drafting such that to label it as 'torrential' would be an understatement. The drafter appears to have scanned a thesaurus in the search for synonyms and near-synonyms, and the result is very hard to follow.

For example, the term 'Tax' is often defined by language similar to the following:

> 'Tax' means any tax, levy, impost, duty, contribution, withholding, levy or charge of any nature whatsoever, and any fine, penalty, surcharge or interest relating to any of the foregoing and regardless of whether the person concerned is primarily liable or not and includes (without limitation) corporation tax, advance corporation tax, income tax, capital gains tax, VAT, national insurance contributions, capital duty, stamp duty, SDRT, and all other taxes on gross or net income, profits or gains, distributions, receipts, sales, use, occupation, franchise, value added, and personal property, and any other payment which any person is or may be or become bound to make and which is or purports to be in the nature of taxation.

This type of drafting tends only to expand. It is never pruned, even though (for example) 'capital duty' was abolished in the UK in 1988. Its very length suggests that nothing that could conceivably be thought of as tax could escape the definition. But that is not so. For example, language of the type used

23 *Norwich Union Life Insurance Society v British Railways Board* [1987] 2 EGLR 137 at [138D]. Elsewhere Lord Hoffmann bemoaned this type of drafting, optimistically thinking things were getting better: 'The modern English tradition, while still erring on the side of caution, is to avoid the grosser excesses of verbiage and trust to the judges to use common sense to get the message. I think that this tendency should be encouraged' (*Bank of Credit and Commerce International SA (in liquidation) v Ali (no. 1)* [2001] UKHL 8 at [38]). The author is doubtful whether his optimism was well-founded.

24 *East of England Ambulance NHS Trust v Flowers* [2019] EWCA Civ 947 at [19] (Bean LJ).

above was considered in *Teesside Power Holdings Ltd v Electrabel International Holdings BV*.[25] In the case, the question arose whether repayment supplement (the quasi-interest return paid by the UK tax authorities when overpaid tax is returned to the taxpayer) counted. It was held that it did not, the definition suggesting that it covered amounts paid to the tax authorities by the taxpayer, but not the other way round.

Drafters who enumerate as many items as they can of the items on the list – who, in the above example, name as many types of tax as they can bring to mind – are in part trying to counter the 'expressio unius' principle referred to above. As soon as the drafter includes some examples of the phenomenon that the drafting is intended to cover, the principle comes into play. And the more comprehensive the list, the stronger the impression that any omission is deliberate. Only by including every conceivable item on the list can the drafter feel happy that the list is comprehensive.

Do not resort to sweep-up language without considering the risk of 'eiusdem generis' interpretation

5.10 It is natural that drafters, faced with this daunting standard, try to insure their drafting against the possibility that they have missed out one example that they should have covered. The drafter therefore adds some more general language to the end of the list to try to sweep up any overlooked examples. So a drafter, seeking to list the types of cargo that a charterer should not be allowed to carry,[26] identifies a list; 'acids, explosives, arms [and] ammunition'. But, sensing that this is not an exhaustive list, the drafter adds at the end 'or any other dangerous cargo'.

The trouble with this arises when a reader (including a judge) is faced with interpreting a general phrase of this type and has to evaluate whether or not any specific cargo which is not on the list should be regarded as within the 'other dangerous cargo' language. That enquiry naturally develops into asking whether the items on the list display some common characteristic that suggests that the intention of the general language was to embrace only items that also share that same characteristic. For example, did the list of specific items – 'acids, explosives, arms [and] ammunition' – mean that the concept of 'other dangerous cargo' extended to turpentine? Turpentine, a wood-based product, is harmful to humans when ingested, and also inflammable. But it is at least arguable that the list of 'acids, explosives, arms [and] ammunition' suggests that the 'danger' common to each is more a danger to the vessel itself than to humans handling it, and if so the conclusion might follow that

25 [2012] EWHC 33 (Comm).

26 The language is that considered in *Chandris v Isbrandtsen-Moller Co Inc* [1950] 1 All ER 768.

turpentine was not within the 'other dangerous cargo' concept referred to in the charterparty.

This principle – that language following a list can be constrained by the items that appear on the list so as to embrace only items that share that common characteristic – is known to lawyers as the 'eiusdem generis' rule.[27] But to call it a rule is misleading. In *Chandris v Isbrandtsen-Moller Co Inc*,[28] Devlin J referred to it more than 70 years ago as no more than a 'guide', and it is certainly not applied blindly by judges. But nor is it entirely redundant today. In *BOC Group plc v Centeon LLC*[29] Evans LJ referred to it as a factor which, when it is relevant, cannot be ignored:

> the conditions which underlie it are ones which a reasonable man would take into account as a matter of course.[30]

The drafting of general language following a list is naturally framed so as to afford some support to a construction 'eiusdem generis'. Thus, the drafter in *Isbrandtsen-Moller* naturally framed the category as 'acids, explosives, arms, ammunition, or other dangerous cargo'. The word 'other'[31] implies that the items on the list are examples of the category referred to in the more general language that follows. To see the general language itself as limited by an 'eiusdem generis' construction might be said to be looking through the opposite end of the telescope, but is in some ways a natural consequence of the type of 'iterative' construction' favoured by modern judges.[32] In other words, the fact that the drafter sees the items on the list as examples of the general language naturally emphasises the affinity between the general language and the list, and reinforces a sense that the list provides a clue as to how the general language should be interpreted.

Avoid an 'eiusdem generis' problem using these techniques

5.11 A drafter who does not want general language to be construed 'eiusdem generis' can strain to avoid it by using words like 'whatsoever'[33] to emphasise the intended breadth of the general language. But even that is no magic wand, Evans LJ remarking in the *Centeon* case[34] that

27 In Latin, 'eiusdem generis' means 'of the same type'.
28 [1950] 1 All ER 768.
29 [1999] 1 All ER (Comm) 970.
30 ibid at [979].
31 *Fujitsu Services Ltd v IBM United Kingdom Ltd* [2014] EWHC 752 also confirms that 'other' is a word that can be material to the interpretation of a list: Mrs Justice Carr at [75].
32 *Re Sigma Corporation* [2009] UK SC 2 at [12] (Lord Mance).
33 Suggested by Devlin J in *Isbrandtsen-Moller*: he also suggests 'whether or not similar to the foregoing' and 'without prejudice to the foregoing', either of which may strike the modern reader as old-fashioned.
34 *BOC Group Plc v Centeon LLC* [1999] 1 All ER (Comm) 970. 'Whatsoever' was regarded as no more than emphatic in *Reeve v McDonagh* [2024] EWHC 439 (Ch) at [32].

> the meaning of general words, even 'whatsoever', may be limited by the context in which they appear.

An alternative that is sometimes encountered is to provide explicitly in the contract that the contract is intended to be interpreted without the 'eiusdem generis' principle applying. The principle of contractual freedom of contract might suggest that it is open to parties to stipulate how they want it to be interpreted. Judges can and do take notice of some broadly similar stipulations, such as the commonly seen provision to the effect that headings in the contract should be ignored.[35] But it is not an approach calculated to appeal to a judge, who may feel that it is illegitimate for the parties to tell the court to disregard a principle which has been developed over many years by judges keen to resolve ambiguities carelessly left behind by the contracting parties.

The better course for the drafter is to attack the list the other way round. In other words, it is preferable to begin with the general words, and then express any specific items on the list as examples (but as no more than examples; not an exhaustive list) of the category in question. The language in the *Isbrandtsen-Moller* case[36] would then be something like:

> any dangerous cargo of any kind whatsoever, including (without limitation) acids, explosives, arms and ammunition.

Because the word 'includes' normally implies that the examples following it are no more than examples,[37] and because placing the general words up front naturally places more emphasis on them, this type of drafting should avoid the limitations imposed by the 'eiusdem generis' principle.[38]

The drafter can add some boilerplate language that is perhaps more promising than a direction to ignore the 'eiusdem generis' principle. This can take the form of stating that examples in a list following the word 'include' or 'includes' are not intended to limit the meaning of the general expression which of which they are examples, but are merely illustrative. Language of this type is indeed commonly found in commercial contracts, and is respected by judges as effective: see, for example, *Clarence Court Eggs Ltd v Chapman.*[39]

35 See **1.22** above.

36 [1950] 1 All ER 768.

37 *Singapore Airlines Ltd v Buck Consultants Ltd* [2011] EWCA Civ 1542 at [15] (Arden LJ): see **4.8** above.

38 See also *Transocean Drilling UK Ltd v Providence Resources Plc* [2016] EWCA Civ 372 ('without limitation' tends to 'explain and expand' the meaning of the exemplified term).

39 [2022] EWCA Civ 1681 at [57]–[58] (Coulson LJ). The admirably thorough language that the drafter in that case used was '…the word 'including' shall mean including without limitation or prejudice to the generality of any description, definition, term or phrase preceding that word, and the word 'include' and its derivatives shall be construed accordingly'.

Chapter 6

Basic verbs

Contracts exist to regulate future behaviour. But English lacks a future tense, so a drafter must choose carefully which verbs to use in the contract to achieve different results. To draft obligations, a drafter should use 'shall'. But the drafter may need to draft other types of contractual language, without confusing the reader: to convey negative obligations; to frame permissions; to make it clear that a party is free not to do something; to lay down what a party has to do to achieve a particular result; or to express the parties' aspirations. Each requires to be dealt with in a particular way.

VERBS TO IMPOSE CONTRACTUAL OBLIGATIONS

The grammatical tense of contracts: essentially a future tense

6.1 When a contract is entered into, its purpose is to regulate *future* behaviour. It cannot oblige the parties to do something retrospectively, at an earlier date.

Contracts are sometimes entered into with an 'effective date' falling before the date they are entered into. But the effect of this is limited to aligning the position as between the parties to what it would have been if the contract had in fact been entered into at the earlier date from which it purports to take effect. In the construction industry, for example, work may begin on the basis of a letter of intent before the full contract is signed. In such a case the full contract may be said, to that limited extent, to have 'retrospective effect': see, for example, *FM Conway Ltd v The Rugby Football Union.*[1] Such an agreement would not affect third parties. For example, if A enters into an agreement on 31 March to sell a business to B 'as of' *or* 'with effect from' 1 January, the intended effect is that A should account to B for any profits that the business has generated between January and March. But those profits will be taxable in the hands of A, not B. HMRC, a third party, is not bound by the agreement. And if anyone else thinks fit to ask, on 28 February, whose business it is, the answer is A, not B.

A party can at the contract date *represent* that a state of affairs exists, and that state of affairs can include the party *having acted* in a particular way. To that limited extent, a contract can be said to look backwards rather than forwards. But if it turns out that the party did not act in the way it said it had, the innocent party's remedy is in misrepresentation. No action in specific performance could require the offending party to perform the missing action: the party did not promise to *do* the missing act in the contract, but promised that it *had done so already*. In *Lowe v Lombank*,[2] discussing a particular clause in a hire purchase agreement, Lord Diplock explained in the Court of Appeal:

> To call it an agreement as well as an acknowledgment by the plaintiff cannot convert a statement as to past facts, known by both parties to be untrue, into a contractual obligation, which is essentially a promise by the promisor to the promisee that acts will be done in the future or that facts exist at the time of the promise or will exist in the future. To say that the hirer 'agreed' that he has not done something in the past means no more than that the hirer, at the request of the owner, represents that he has not done that thing in the past.

1 [2023] EWCA Civ 418 at [81] (Coulson LJ).

2 [1960] 1 WLR 196; see also *Raiffeisen Zentralbank Oesterreich AG v Royal Bank of Scotland plc* [2010] EWHC 1392 (Comm).

A written contract entered into on a given date D is limited therefore to setting out obligations to be performed either on D itself (after the contract is entered into) or on any future date. But on any later date when the contract is relevant, it nonetheless functions as a set of promises that were made at D, not at the later date when the contract is examined. That is why, for example, if the parties agree that certain warranties are to be deemed to be repeated continuously throughout the period covered by the contract, the drafting has to provide so explicitly. Without the deeming provision, the warranties would speak once only, as at D. This is also why the courts, considering a contract in its commercial context, will look only at facts and circumstances known or reasonably available to the parties 'at the time that the document was executed'.[3]

So a contract is naturally forward-looking. In a grammatical sense it means that the natural tense of contractual drafting used to capture the parties' obligations is the *future* tense.[4]

But English lacks a future tense

6.2 Stepping back for a moment from the special context of contracts, the English language lacks an inflected form of a verb that conveys a future tense meaning. Taking as an example the verb 'make', we have a form that marks the present tense ('I make', or in the third person singular 'he makes' or 'she makes') and a version that denotes the past tense ('made'). But there is no inflection of 'make' itself that conveys the future tense. We need to use an auxiliary verb 'shall' or 'will' to describe the future tense, giving, for example, 'she shall make' or 'she will make'. An alternative is the construction 'is going to', giving the equally unequivocal future connotation of 'she is going to make'.

Since contractual language relates to the future, it is not surprising that this type of language is a candidate for drafters to use to describe the acts which each party binds itself to carry out. But language is not suitable for this contractual purpose if it does no more than signify the future. A contractual statement that a party A 'is going to do X' seems underpowered as a way of signifying that A is entering into a legally enforceable *promise* to A's counterparty B, binding A to do X with the implicit acknowledgement that if it does not, it may have to compensate B or even be forced by a court to fulfil its promise.

3 *Arnold v Britton* [2015] UKSC 36 at [15] (Lord Neuberger).
4 Though recitals which set out the background to the contract will more naturally be couched in the present tense or the past tense (simple past or perfect).

Prefer 'shall' to rival verbs to impose obligations

6.3 So contract drafters turn to modal verbs[5] to impose contractual obligations.

The first two to be considered in this context are 'shall' and 'will'.

Both 'shall' and 'will' can simply indicate the future tense, with no sense of obligation: if I say 'it will rain tomorrow', there is of course no obligation on 'it' to do anything. Similarly with 'shall', particularly when used in the first person: if I say 'I shall go to the cinema tomorrow', I may often just mean that I have decided to go, with no sense that I owe it to anybody else to follow through on my declaration.

But both 'shall' and 'will' can be used in senses going further than simply denoting futurity.

Two particular different aspects[6] of 'shall' make it particularly suitable for contracts. One is that 'shall' has a formal air suitable for the solemnity of a contractual commitment. For example, the Articles of Union between England and Scotland in 1707 provided:

> That the two Kingdoms of Scotland and England, *shall*, upon the first Day of May next ensuing the Date hereof, and for ever after, be united into one Kingdom by the Name of Great-Britain.[7]

And the second is that 'shall' signifies the commitment of the speaker to the outcome described. When the Fairy Godmother says to Cinderella 'You shall go to the ball', we understand that she is doing more than merely making a prediction: she is going to use her magical powers to secure that it happens. Similarly, though a contract is typically expressed in the third person, the parties commit themselves by entering into it to performing their respective obligations. The emphatic quality of 'shall' also confers not merely a sense of obligation, but also the power to discharge it.[8]

'Will' can also carry a connotation going beyond simply signifying that the action described is to occur in the future. An utterance such as 'Oh yes, I will' in response to an instruction not to do something carries a similar sense of emphatic commitment, bordering in this case on defiance. And 'will' can carry a flavour of posing a question in the form of an offer and responding to it, as in 'Will you marry me?' followed by 'Yes, I will' or, less happily, 'No,

5 The definition of modal verb in *The Chambers Dictionary*, 12th edn (2011) is: 'In English, any of the verbs can, could, may, might, will, would, shall, should, must and ought, and sometimes need, dare and used to, which modify the sense of a main verb and express concepts such as politeness, certainty and obligation'.

6 See Huddleston and Pullum, *The Cambridge Grammar of the English Language* (Cambridge University Press, 2016), p 194.

7 Emphasis added.

8 *International Power Plc v Healy* [2001] UKHL 20 at [35] (Lord Hoffmann).

I won't.' But outside those specialised contexts, the normal function of 'will' is the normal neutral sign of futurity as in 'They will be arriving at about six o' clock.' There is a contrast here with 'shall', which does not fit happily into a neutral context like that: 'They shall be arriving at about six o'clock' is unnatural.

Viewed in this light, it is unsurprising that 'shall' has tended to win out over 'will' as the method most commonly used in English law contracts to express obligations.

'Shall' has been criticised, most vocally by writers outside Britain. They argue that it is archaic, overformal, or both. They prefer alternatives. 'Must' and 'will' are the front runners among modal verbs. The reasons for preferring 'shall' to 'will' have already been discussed above. And 'must', though clear enough, carries more of a flavour of a duty imposed from outside rather than a freely-chosen obligation.

Other, more long-winded candidates include 'is obliged to' or 'shall be obliged to',[9] 'promises to', 'is required to' and 'shall be required to'. But they tend to disqualify themselves on the grounds that they are too long, drawing attention to themselves when repeated as often as they would appear if used consistently through all but the briefest contracts. Each laboriously underlines that the contract imposes binding obligations, but that is arguably unnecessary. Most contracts have a general preamble which says something like

> It is agreed as follows:

which is surely enough, in a document otherwise obviously intended to amount to a contract, to leave nobody in any doubt as to its significance. Even less attractive, in the light of such a preamble, is 'agrees to' as language used throughout a contract to signify obligations: 'it is agreed that…'(preamble) followed by 'A agrees to do X' in an operative clause is repetitive and clumsy.

So even if one were to start with a clean slate, 'shall' might emerge as the best word to convey contractual obligation. And of course the slate is not clean. 'Shall' has a long history of being used to impose contractual obligation, and is familiar in that role to lawyers (including judges who would have the task of resolving a dispute about a contract's meaning) and non-lawyers alike. This work accordingly recommends 'shall' to express contractual obligation, despite the reservations sometimes expressed.

Whichever word is used to denote contractual obligation, it is best used consistently. The drafter of the contract in *Schuler (LG) v Wickman Machine Tool Sales Ltd*[10] used indiscriminately the formulations 'will', 'shall', 'agrees to' and 'undertakes to', earning no marks for consistency. And in *Rhodia International*

9 Or, sometimes, in American English, 'obligated to': British speakers usually prefer 'obliged to'.
10 [1972] 1 WLR 840.

Holdings Ltd v Huntsman International LLC[11] the drafter was also inconsistent, providing:

> With effect from Completion...the Purchaser shall...carry out and complete each of the Contracts...and the Purchaser will...duly and punctually performs and discharge each of...the obligations and liabilities under the Contracts.[12]

The inconsistency between 'shall' and 'will' is more than just clumsy. It invites the question why the drafter chose two different terms. Could the difference be signalling some subtle difference in meaning? None was presumably intended, but the drafter has unnecessarily provoked doubt in the reader's mind.

OTHER TYPES OF CONTRACTUAL LANGUAGE

Contracts do not only impose obligations

6.4 Contracts exists principally to regulate the parties' conduct, and that principally takes the form of them promising to do certain things: to undertake positive obligations. But a contract can have other functions as well.

First, a contract may impose a 'negative obligation': in other words a party does not promise to perform the action that is described, but it promises *not* to do it, to *refrain* from doing it. The contract prohibits the action in question.

A drafter may also want to make it clear that a party is free to do something: that it has liberty or discretion to do it. That function is in some ways the opposite of the negative obligation: if a party is allowed to do something, it is the reverse of its being obliged not to do it.

Given that a party is generally at liberty to do anything it is not forbidden from doing, one might ask why it is necessary to consider language – call it 'permissive' language – that confers a liberty or discretion as a separate category. Why not simply draft any language of prohibition or what is termed above 'negative obligation' in a limited way: would not anything lying outside the limits of the constraint *automatically* be allowed, without any need for explicit permissive language? But that is too purist an approach. The drafter may want to suggest that although a particular action is *normally* forbidden, there are circumstances in which it is allowed. The easiest way to convey that may be by making it clear that when the stated circumstances apply, the party is free to take an action that is normally proscribed. Or the drafter may want to make it clear that a particular act is specifically allowed, or that a party has freedom of manoeuvre in what it does, because if the contract was not explicit about that point, an *implication* might arise that the party did not have the

[11] [2007] EWHC 292 (Comm).
[12] Clause 14.1 of the contract, quoted ibid at [7].

right to perform the act, or had to act in a particular way. Or the drafter may want, as with an option, to provide that a party has freedom whether or not to take some step, but that contractual consequences flow for the other party if that voluntary step is taken.

So a drafter may want to craft some 'permissive' language to make it clear that a party is free to do something.

A drafter may also want to make it clear that a party is free *not* to do something. Again, this seems odd at first glance: if a contract is principally concerned to record a party's promise to perform particular acts A, B and C, why bother to specify that a party is free *not* to do act D? Surely the absence of an obligation on the party to do D is enough to make it clear that it is allowed *not* to do D? But again, the drafter often has legitimate reasons for wanting to make it clear that 'not to do D' is allowed. Perhaps the party is normally required to do D, but is allowed not to do D in particular excluded circumstances. It may be helpful, because explicit, for the contract to go beyond merely *implying* that not to do D is permitted in those excluded circumstances and to say straightforwardly that in the excluded circumstanccs, not to do D is allowed. This language might be called language of 'sanctioned omission'.

Again, a drafter may want to provide for what might be called an 'obligation within a discretion': to make it clear that if the party wants to exercise a right or discretion within the contractual framework, the party has to do so in a particular way. An example would be the type of drafting that provides for the steps the holder of an option must take in order validly to exercise it. In other words the contract prescribes a required mode of behaviour if a contracting party to achieve a particular end.

Drafters sometimes ambitiously try to impose the parties' view of events in a way that does not directly impose an obligation on, or confer a discretion on, the parties, but instead acts more of a record of the parties' *intentions* or *aspirations* in an area which it cannot control. For example, a joint venture agreement may very often contain a clause that asserts that the agreement is not to be taken as creating a partnership between the parties. But whether the arrangement is a partnership does not depend on the parties' intentions, but is a matter of law.[13] Similar examples are cases where what might be viewed as a secured financing arrangement purports to take the form of a true sale, or a relationship that looks like one of employment is asserted to be a consultancy instead. This type of provision does not in any meaningful sense affect the contractual obligations of the parties, apart perhaps from impliedly requiring them to refrain from arguing that a different quality attaches to their relationship from the one they have jointly asserted. Language that seeks to record the parties' agreement on this type of issue might be called 'aspirational' language.

[13] Under English law, the question is whether the parties are 'carrying on a business in common with a view of profit' (Partnership Act 1890, s 1(1)): see further **12.28** and **12.29** below.

Do not mix up the different types of contractual language

6.5 Various types of contractual language need therefore to be distinguished. Much of the rest of this chapter is accordingly devoted to discussing how best the drafter can deploy the modal verbs that the English language uses to achieve the different contractual effects that the drafter is aiming at.

It is inherent in this that it is dangerous for the drafter to use language that does not make it clear which contractual effect is intended. An example of this in a statutory context is *Cooke v New River Company*,[14] where an Act of Parliament provided that a water company

> shall, at the request of any consumer of water…, or at their own instance, afford a supply of water by means of a meter.

The problem was that 'shall' suggested an obligation, but 'shall…at their own instance' suggested a choice or discretion. So when faced with that and some other obscurities in the language, the courts were left puzzled as to whether the metered supply was obligatory or discretionary.[15] The moral for a drafter is clear: decide what type of contractual effect you want, and draft clearly for it, avoiding language that might suggest that you are aiming for a different type of contractual effect entirely. To use a word that is ambivalent as between (say) an obligation and a discretion will make it uncertain which of the two is intended, as happened in *Mamedoil-Jetoil Greek Petroleum Co v Okta Crude Oil Refinery*,[16] where 'wants to manipulate' ('manipulate' in the sense of 'handle') was used instead of 'shall manipulate' or 'may manipulate'.

Negative obligations: use 'shall not'

6.6 A negative obligation (a promise not to carry out act X) could be expressed in various ways. A few examples are:

> A shall not do X
>
> A must not do X
>
> A may not do X
>
> A shall refrain from doing X

[14] (1888) 38 Ch 56 (Court of Appeal); 14 AC 698 (HL).

[15] Lord Herschell in House of Lords did not mince his words when he discussed the quality of the drafting: 'My Lords, it has been my lot to attempt to construe many Acts of Parliament which were obscurely worded, but I do not think I ever met with one upon which it was more impossible to put a satisfactory construction than the statute with which we have to deal in the present case. If the object had been to render it as difficult of construction as possible, success could hardly have been more complete.' For a more recent example of the court focussing on the difference between obligatory and permissive language, see *Ener-G Holdings Ltd v Hormell* [2012] EWCA Civ 1059 at [27] (Lord Neuberger MR).

[16] [2001] EWCA Civ 406 at [41] (Rix LJ).

A is prohibited (or forbidden) from doing X

A promises (or undertakes) not to do X.

Which of these should the drafter choose? Economy of expression is itself a virtue, which is enough to make the last three examples unattractive unless all the first three shorter versions are disqualified for some reason. That leads us to consider 'shall not', 'must not' and 'may not'.

To eliminate first the most unsuitable candidate, *'A may not do X'* is ambiguous. The ambiguity lies in the uncertainty of what grammarians call the 'scope' of the negative represented by *not*.

The negative could have scope over (or in less technical terms govern) the whole of the rest of the sentence, so that the proposition that is negatived is 'A may do X'. If that is the reading, it does reflect a negative obligation. The positive statement 'A may do X' means that A is allowed to do X: if that is negatived in its entirety, the meaning is that A is not allowed to do X.

But it is a grammatically feasible reading of 'A may not do X' that the negative has scope over only the words 'do X'. On this reading, the permission granted by 'may' remains a positive one: what A is allowed to do is not to do X. In other words, it has the right not to do X if it so chooses not to, but impliedly could take the opposite choice and do X after all. So the meaning is very different from the 'negative obligation' reading.

It follows that 'A may not do X' is ambiguous. And word order cannot rescue the ambiguity as it sometimes can with other language. With the two sentences 'A is not permitted to do X' and 'A is permitted not to do X', the word content is identical, but the word order contrasts so as to allow two rival meanings to be signalled. But 'may' does not allow this contrast: we cannot say 'A not may do X'.

The ambiguity found with 'A may not do X' is not encountered with modal verbs other than 'may'. 'A cannot do X' has a clear meaning (negative obligation: the negative has scope over the whole of the positive equivalent 'A can do X'). And 'A can not do X' is also clear (A can decide not to do X if it does not want to). There is no risk of ambiguity because the two are spelled differently. So no ambiguity arises.

But ambiguity is hardwired into the grammar of 'may'. This means that out of the possible candidates for a modal verb to express a negative obligation, 'may' as in 'A may not do X' is the least suitable for the job.

'Must not' does not exhibit the ambiguity of 'may not'. 'A must not do X' is unambiguous in imposing a negative obligation. If we want to find the equivalent to 'A may not do X' in the narrow-scope-of-the-negative sense (A is permitted to refrain from doing X if it chooses), we cannot use 'must' to do it: we have instead to reach for another modal verb and say instead 'A *need* not do X'.

So 'must not' does not suffer from the same ambiguity as 'may not'. What about 'shall not'? Any possible ambiguity with 'shall not' is not as stark as with 'may not'.

It is, admittedly, possible to see a faint possible difference between two possible meanings of, say,

> I shall not see the Taj Mahal again.

One meaning has 'shall' as a simple marker of futurity: perhaps the speaker is getting too old to travel, and is just accepting that he or she has seen it for the last time. The other accords 'shall' a more forceful expression of determination: I went there once, but it didn't impress me enough to want to go back.

But these shades of meaning are confined to first person utterances where the subject is 'I' or 'we', and do not taint contractual drafting, which is usually[17] in the third person. 'Shall not' in a contract is no less clear than 'must not' in imposing a negative obligation.

That leaves the drafter free to choose between 'shall not' and 'must not' in expressing negative obligations. And for the same reasons that suggest that 'shall' is to be preferred to 'must' in positive obligations,[18] 'shall not' seems the better choice. The additional marginal point is that if 'shall' is chosen for positive obligations and 'must not' for negative ones, a mischievous argument could be raised to the effect that the two different modal verbs must have been chosen with some subtly different nuance in mind, which is not the case. A negative obligation and a positive one are intended as exact opposites.

'Permissive language': use 'may'

6.7 The modal verb 'may' offers the drafter a straightforward way of framing permissive language. It is free from the ambiguity that makes the negative form 'may not' unsuitable for either a negative obligation[19] or sanctioned omission.[20] In normal speech 'may' can carry a meaning other than the grant of permission: a speaker who says 'the sun may shine tomorrow' is not granting it permission to do so. The modality conveyed by 'may' in such an utterance is that the speaker is distancing himself or herself from the firm prediction of 'the sun will shine tomorrow' and is acknowledging that tomorrow might instead be cloudy.

But a contract does not deal in predictions of varying levels of firmness. It has the narrower purpose of recording the parties' mutual obligations, to which,

17 Though not always: see **11.4** below.
18 See **6.3** above.
19 See **6.6** above.
20 See **6.8** below.

subject to the satisfaction of any relevant conditions,[21] they are unequivocally bound. So 'may' in a contract will naturally be taken as permissive, and there is no reason for the drafter to shun it. 'May' is sharply distinguishable from the modal verbs 'shall', 'will' and 'must' that are used to denote obligations: a court will not readily find that 'may' has a compulsory meaning.[22]

Lawyers' prolixity sometimes tempts them into other expressions to confer permission. Examples are 'shall be entitled to',[23] 'shall be permitted to', and 'shall have the right to'. None of these achieves any more than a simple 'may', which is therefore recommended.

Drafters should, however, recognise that any formulation, whether or not using 'may', may not give free rein to the party to whom the latitude to act is expressed to be accorded. A body of case law suggests that contractual discretions may sometimes – indeed, often – be subject to an implied term to the effect that they must be exercised in a rational manner rather than 'arbitrarily, capriciously or in an irrational manner'.[24] The test is one similar to that which applies, as a matter of public law, to determine whether a public body's decision-making process is subject to judicial review: what lawyers refer to as *Wednesbury* unreasonableness.[25]

Some cases suggest that rationality (in this sense) is demanded whenever a party is given responsibility to one party for making an assessment or exercising a judgement on a matter which materially affects the other party's interests. Arguably that is to put the point too generally. There must surely be cases where the discretion given to a party is understood on both sides to be one which the party is entitled to take in its own interest, as irrationally as it cares to. An example would be the right of an optionholder to exercise an option to acquire a painting, even if an independent art expert might advise the buyer that it was overpaying for it; or the right of a party to exercise a free termination right to bring a commercial contract to an end, even if any business adviser would have advised the terminating party that it was throwing

21 See generally Chapter 9 below.

22 *Ener-G Holdings Plc v Hormell* [2012] EWCA Civ 1059 at [27] (Lord Neuberger MR) and [62] (Gross LJ), though Longmore LJ was less convinced ([45])); see also *Zayo Group International Ltd v Ainger* [2017] EWHC 2542 at [81] (Simon Bryan QC). In *OCM Maritime Nile LLC v Courage Shipping Co* [2022] EWHC 452 (Comm), the drafter emphasised the point by adding, after 'may at their option', some extra language: 'but with no obligation to do so'. Unsurprisingly, this was held to connote a discretion: see [131] (Sir Andrew Smith), his judgment on this point explicitly endorsed by the Court of Appeal: [2022] EWCA Civ 1091 at [25] (Males LJ).

23 Or, eccentrically, 'should be entitled to' as in *Towergate Financial (Group) Ltd v Hopkinson* [2018] EWCA Civ 2744: 'Each of the persons giving the indemnity ...should be entitled to require the [indemnitors]... to take [particular action].' 'Should' in a contract suggests a sense of moral obligation (rather like 'ought') rather than a straightforward obligation, which is what the drafter is (or should be) aiming to convey.

24 The formulation given by the Court of Appeal in *Abu Dhabi National Tanker Co v Product Star Shipping Ltd (The 'Product Star')* [1993] 1 Lloyd's Rep 397 at [404]. For a more recent discussion of the principle, see *Langage Energy Park Ltd v EP Langage Ltd* [2022] EWHC 432 (Comm).

25 Under the tests set out in *Associated Provincial Picture Houses Ltd v Wednesbury Corporation* (1948) 1 KB 223, discussed in *Braganza v BP Shipping Ltd* [2015] UKSC 17.

away a valuable opportunity for profit. That point was recognised in the Court of Appeal in *Compass Group UK and Ireland Ltd (t/a Medirest) v Mid Essex Hospital Services NHS Trust.*[26]

It follows that an implied term of this type is more likely to be found in a case where the party's discretion is to take a decision or make a determination within the framework of an ongoing contract than in a case where the party is given a more basic right. But where it exists, the implied term will apply however the discretion is framed: whether the drafter has used *may* or some other formulation and whether or not the drafting purports to give the party exercising the discretion *sole discretion* as to whether and how to exercise it.

As a basic matter, implied terms are not incorporated into contracts if they conflict with an express term.[27] It would be tempting to think that if a contract provides for a party to be given the right to determine a matter in its 'sole discretion', this express language would be enough to signify that the party has complete freedom to decide as it wishes. But this does not seem right. The true significance of 'sole discretion' appears to be that the party enjoying the discretion is not required to consult anyone else: it does not remove the party's duty to exercise the discretion rationally. Jackson LJ in the *Mid Essex* case[28] suggests that it is 'extremely difficult' to exclude an implied term requiring the party to avoid exercising its discretion arbitrarily, 'although I would not say it is utterly impossible to do so'.

It is obviously unattractive to provide expressly that a party is permitted to act capriciously or irrationally. A more promising method of excluding the implied term would be to state expressly that in exercising the discretion, the party in question is entitled to determine the matter 'exclusively in its own interests and without being required to take into account those of any other party'. Or perhaps, if that is also too inflammatory, an express clause could enumerate a specific list of considerations which it is acknowledged the party need not have regard to in exercising its discretion, whether they are factors that would otherwise be intrinsic to a rational exercise of the discretion or relate to the effects of it being exercised in a particular way. Though this type of language will still require the party with discretion to act rationally, it will have more freedom of manoeuvre than if the contract were silent on the point.

26 [2013] EWCA Civ 200: see [83] (Jackson LJ), suggesting that a 'simple decision whether or not to exercise an absolute contractual right' might be different from a right to exercise a discretion within a contractual framework. See also *Optimares SpA v Qatar Airways Group QCSC* [2022] EWHC 2461 from [61] (parties' contractual obligations to act 'in good faith in the performance of their respective responsibilities and obligations' not relevant to a right to terminate); and to the same effect *TAQA Bratani Ltd v Rockrose UKCS8 LLC* [2020] EWHC 58 (Comm).

27 'It is not possible to imply terms into a contract that are inconsistent with its express terms': the Court of Appeal in *Autoclenz Ltd v Belcher* [2009] EWCA Civ 1046 at [88] (Aikens LJ); endorsed in the Supreme Court [2011] UKSC 41 at [20] (Lord Clarke).

28 [2013] EWCA Civ 200 at [83].

Sanctioned omission: use 'need not'

6.8 What is in **6.4** above termed 'sanctioned omission' is the type of language that aims to relieve a party from some course of action which it would otherwise expressly or impliedly be obliged to follow. A party can be relieved of what would otherwise be an *express* obligation by limiting or restricting the express obligation in the first place, using words of limitation such as 'except' or 'other than':

> The Executive shall be responsible for the Business in all EU territories except Spain and Portugal.

But it is not so easy to make it clear that an *implied* obligation is to some extent overridden or excluded, precisely because the implied obligation does not appear on the face of the contract and so the drafter has no language in which to embed the exception.

In this situation the negative modal verb 'need not' is the neatest way to achieve the drafter's objective:

> In determining whether to appeal against any refusal of the planning permission, the Lessor need not consult the Lessee

makes it clear that, even if the Lessor might be argued *impliedly* to have an obligation to consult the Lessee, any such obligation is contractually overridden.

The formulation 'need not' does not suffer from the same ambiguity relating to the scope of the negative as does 'may not'.[29] 'A need not do X' is the negative counterpart of 'A must do X' or, in more conventional contractual language, 'A shall do X'. The negative in 'need not', in other words, has wide scope over the whole sentence. For a narrow scope meaning[30] two subtle but distinct changes have to be made: 'need' has to become 'needs' with an extra 's' and the form of the principal verb has to be in the full infinitive form with 'to' rather than a bare form:

> A needs not to do X.

In that form, the negative has narrow scope: it relates only to the doing of X, not the need to do X. The distinction is clear, and that makes 'need not' unambiguous. It also benefits from being more economical than the alternatives to which drafters unnecessarily resort, such as 'shall not be obliged to' or 'shall not be required to'. 'Need not' is therefore recommended for sanctioned omission.

[29] See **6.6** above.
[30] The equivalent of 'A may not do X' meaning 'A is permitted not to do X', in other words.

Required mode of behaviour: use 'must'

6.9 A contract may often need to stipulate how a discretion needs to be exercised for the exercise to be valid. For example, if a lease contains a break clause in favour of a tenant, it may set out what the tenant has to do to bring the lease to an end. And an option agreement may lay down a procedure for its exercise. What is being set out in such a case is not *obligatory* on the party whose behaviour is affected. It is rather that, unless the party acts in the manner set out, it will not lead to the contractual consequence at which the party is aiming.

For this type of contractual language, 'must' may be a better choice than 'shall':

> To terminate the lease, the Tenant must...
>
> To exercise the option, the holder must...

The reason for this recommendation is that 'shall', being the word recommended for use to signify obligation, may suggest that what is intended merely as a stipulation as to how a *right* needs to be exercised disguises an *obligation* to act in that prescribed manner.

An argument along those lines persuaded the New Zealand Court of Appeal in *The Melanesian Mission Trust Board v Australian Mutual Provident Society*.[31] Although the Privy Council reversed this finding, it serves as a warning that it is better to make clear the distinction between obligations and stipulations that lack that force. For that reason, 'must' deserves to be preferred when setting out a required mode of behaviour.

Aspirational language: use 'shall'

6.10 Sometimes, as **6.4** above suggests, parties want to record in their contract something that relates to their relationship but which they cannot control. Common examples include the nature of the contractual relationship they have created, which they would like to be characterised in a particular way. Or the parties may want to clothe particular provisions of their agreement with some quality or other. For example, they may want to assert that a stipulated payment represents liquidated damages and so is not subject to the rule against penalties. But the true characterisation of the relationship, or the provision, is not within their power to determine: it is a matter of law, for the courts to determine if necessary.

[31] [1997] 2 EGLR 128.

In such cases, any language used by the parties will not be decisive. But neither will it be wholly ignored by a court.[32] What language should the drafter use to record the parties' intention?

Take as an example the case where the parties want to declare that their joint venture relationship does not amount to a partnership. Possible candidates for the relevant language include

1) The relationship created by this Agreement shall not be a partnership
2) The parties intend that the relationship created by this Agreement shall not be a partnership
3) The parties intend that the relationship created by this Agreement will not be a partnership
4) The parties intend the relationship created by this Agreement not to be a partnership
5) The parties do not intend the relationship created by this Agreement to be a partnership

Of these possibilities, 1) is simple, but lacks self-awareness. A drafter using it may need to point out to the parties that they cannot, by a simple statement, control the legal nature of the relationship they are creating. The other versions do not show the same level of hubris. Of course, clients may be attracted to 1) just because of its uncompromising assertiveness.

All of 2) to 5) more modestly and realistically acknowledge that they represent an aspiration, and are not determinative.

5) differs from the others in meaning, again because of the scope of the negative. In 'The parties do not intend the relationship to be a partnership', the negative has wide scope over 'intend'. What is being negatived, in other words, is the entirety of the corresponding positive sentence without 'not': 'The parties intend the relationship… to be a partnership.' But the negative sentence in the form of 5) leaves it open as to whether the parties have any positive intention in relation to the character of the relationship at all. In 4), by contrast, the negative does not have scope over 'intend': the parties do have an intention, and the intention is that the relationship should not be a partnership. The language of 4) is accordingly crisper and more focussed than 5).

4) means the same as 2) and 3), and there is little to choose between them. The drafter may like 2) because it retains the public, declaratory flavour of 'shall', and emphasises that the parties' intention is not merely a matter of how they would prefer, simply as between themselves, their relationship to be viewed. A different view is that, if 'shall' is the modal verb chosen in the

[32] *Antoniades v Villiers* [1988] EWCA Civ 3 at [11] (Bingham LJ).

contract to express contractual *obligation*, it serves only to confuse matters if the same word is used the rather different question of the parties' *aspirations*. The author's view, however, is that the distinction between aspiration and obligation is adequately marked by 'intend', and that 2) accordingly represents the most attractive choice.

Chapter 7

Grammar

Some aspects of English grammar are particular sources of ambiguity in drafting. One risk is that drafters do not make it clear how far modifying language extends, often but not always when expressions are linked by a coordinating conjunctions like 'and' and 'or'. This risk is, when identified, easily fixed: so is the other common problem which arises when the antecedent of an expression is unclear. Drafters should prefer the active voice to the passive, and, because plural drafting creates some particular uncertainties, the singular to the plural.

BE ALERT TO GRAMMATICAL RULES WHEN DRAFTING CONTRACTS

7.1 Contract drafting is designed to enshrine as clearly as possible the obligations that the parties bind themselves to fulfil. That makes contract language different from the language used in everyday conversation. Normally, speakers do not have to be concerned that their words could have legal consequences enforceable in a court. So they are neither preoccupied with accuracy nor anxious about ambiguity. If something a person *says* is unclear, the speaker's puzzled interlocutor can simply interrupt and ask for an explanation. That is not a process that can rescue an unclear written contract.

Nonetheless, contract language is a version of the English language, written in sentences that fall to be interpreted in essentially the same way as a listener would decode something uttered outside a contractual context.[1]

The meaning of any sentence, including a sentence contained in a contract, depends on its grammar. In particular, the meaning depends on the aspect of grammar that is termed 'syntax' – the way in which the words in the sentence are ordered so as to convey a particular meaning. Syntax is only one component of grammar, which also covers 'morphology', the rules governing how the individual words in the sentence are formed. But this work will use the term 'grammar' rather than the somewhat more rarefied 'syntax', for which 'grammar' is a readily understood shorthand.

Drafters are not usually professional grammarians. But they need to be aware of the effect of some grammatical rules and how they can affect meaning. This chapter identifies some of the grammatical errors that drafters most commonly make in practice and explains how they can be eliminated.

GRAMMAR ISSUE 1: 'UNCERTAIN MODIFIERS'

First, identify the problem

7.2 To understand the uncertain modifier problem and how it arises, it is easiest to start with an example drawn not from contract but ordinary experience. If diners read on a menu that their crab mayonnaise starter is accompanied by

> brown bread and butter

they are not expecting the butter, when the waiter brings it, to be brown. Indeed, they would be upset if it were. The reason for this is that common sense suggests to them that the adjective 'brown' is in this context confined to modifying or qualifying 'bread'. Linguistically, however, an adjective placed before the first of two nouns separated by 'and' can readily be taken as modifying both. If the diners read on and see at the bottom of the menu the restaurant's claim that

> all our dishes are prepared using local fruit and vegetables

1 Cases abound in which judges discuss the need to start by considering the 'natural and ordinary meaning' of the words used in the contract: see, for example, *Bank of Credit and Commerce International SA (in liquidation) v Ali (no.1)* [2001] UKHL 8 at [8] (Lord Bingham). The process of contractual interpretation is of course a great deal more complicated than that: the relevant principles are discussed in detail in Sir Kim Lewison's imposing work *The Interpretation of Contracts,* now in its eighth edition (Sweet & Maxwell, 2024) and regularly referred to as authoritative in the courts.

they take the adjective 'local' to apply to both fruit and vegetables. They would feel hoodwinked if the vegetables turned out to have been shipped in from some faraway source.

The grammatical point is that identical drafting can be used to lead the reader to two different conclusions. The linguistic question is whether the modifying language (the adjectives 'brown' and 'local') are taken as qualifying only the expression they respectively appear next to in the sentence ('bread', 'fruit'), or both that expression and the more remote one ('butter', 'vegetables'). In this type of case, the adjective *always* modifies the noun it appears next to: the question is whether it also modifies the noun further away from it.

In *Cantor Fitzgerald & Co v YES Bank Ltd*,[2] Bright J asserted that in a simple case where the modifier is an adjective, the 'conventional understanding' is that an adjective that appears before the first of a list of nouns 'modifies all the nouns in the list (unless a discordant adjective or modifier breaks the pattern)'. *The Cambridge Grammar of the English Language*[3] is less definitive, confining itself to saying that such an interpretation is 'in general more likely'. For the drafter, the point is that the construction is potentially ambiguous: that is enough to raise a red flag.

In many cases, the context is enough to make it clear whether the modifying language should be read in the more limited sense (only the bread is brown, not the butter) or more widely (both the fruit and the vegetables are local). And, as pointed out in **7.1** above, a listener who is doubtful about the speaker's meaning can ask for clarification.

But in a contract, this type of linguistic ambiguity is dangerous. The reader, unlike the listener, cannot ask the parties to explain what they meant. Encouraged by their divergent financial interests, they may differ about the answer. And in any event, the parties do not themselves play different roles of a speaker and a listener: they are both, as it were, the speaker. The language in the contract has been used by them both. It is that feature which prompts the legal rule that the meaning of the contract language must be an objective one, to answer which the subjective intentions of either party are irrelevant (and evidence of them indeed inadmissible).[4]

Look out particularly for coordinations

7.3 As a matter of grammar, the 'uncertain modifier' issue arises most commonly where words or expressions appear as part of a 'coordination'. A coordination is the term awarded to two or more expressions that appear

2 [2023] EWHC 745 at [86].

3 Huddleston and Pullum, *The Cambridge Grammar of the English Language* (Cambridge University Press, 2016): see [1286].

4 See **2.1** above.

in a sentence and are of equal value to one another as a matter of language: in other words, neither is subordinate to the other. Typically, the expressions are separated (or could be) by a coordinating conjunction, such as 'and' or 'or'. More often than not, when the issue arises in contract drafting, the expressions that are in coordination are much more complex than the single words separated by the coordinating conjunctions in the 'bread and butter' and 'fruit and vegetables' examples given above.

When a coordination appears, all that is necessary to create a potential ambiguity is that some words of modification or qualification precede the first limb of the coordination or follow the second. So only two ingredients need to combine to provide an explosive mixture. Perhaps this explains why detonations are so common: what is certain is that drafters find the issue hard to identify. It causes disputes all the time. Two examples are discussed below.[5]

Example 1: Mid Essex[6]

7.4 Under an outsourcing agreement, an NHS trust appointed Compass to provide a variety of catering and cleaning services. One clause provided that:

> [t]he Trust and the Contractor will co-operate with each other in good faith *and* will take all reasonable action as is necessary for the efficient transmission of information and instructions and to enable the Trust… to derive the full benefit of the Contract.[7]

This wording imposes two separate obligations, each applying to both parties: an obligation to 'co-operate with each other in good faith' and an obligation to take 'all reasonable action as is necessary'. The obligations are, crucially, separated by the word 'and' that is italicised in the text – and are thus two parts of a coordination. Following the coordination are words of limitation or modification (the part of the drafting beginning with 'for the efficient transmission'), specifying the twin objectives of transmitting information and instructions, and of enabling the trust to derive the full benefit of the contract.

So the usual ingredients for ambiguity to arise – a coordination plus some modifying language – are both present.

In this case, the words of modification appear immediately *after* the two coordinated obligations and not, as does 'brown' in 'brown bread and butter',

5 And these examples are of course taken from cases that have reached the courts. In the author's experience, it is rare to read through a contract of any length, no matter how eminent the firm by which it has been drafted, without coming across examples. Although many are harmless, since context supplies the answer as to what the drafter must have meant, the best drafters root out all ambiguities of this type, even merely theoretical ones, so that the drafting is at a linguistic level unambiguous.

6 *Mid Essex Hospital Services NHS Trust v Compass Group UK and Ireland Limited (t/a Medirest)* [2013] EWCA Civ 200.

7 Emphasis added.

before them. But the linguistic question remains the same: does the modifying language relate only to the element in the coordination it appears next to, or to the more remote member of the coordination as well? In this context, the question amounts to asking: is the duty to 'co-operate with each other': (1) a limited one, relating only to the purposes specified in the modifying language, because that language applies to *both* limbs of the coordination; or (2) a free-standing unqualified obligation, because the words of modification apply only to the duty to 'take all reasonable action as is necessary'?

The result of the case is of less concern to drafters[8] than that the dispute arose in the first place, based on drafting that was flawed by ambiguity. The drafter failed to notice that the clause embodied an uncertain modifier, leaving open fertile grounds for dispute.[9]

The difficulty is not that the drafting is ungrammatical. It is perfectly grammatical. The difficulty is that the drafting is also *ambiguous.*

Example 2: Wood v Capita[10]

7.5 In this case, the same difficulty caused the drafting of a sale and purchase agreement to be disputed all the way to the Supreme Court. An indemnity clause provided:

> The Sellers undertake to pay to the Buyer an amount equal to the amount which would be required to indemnify the Buyer and each member of the Buyer's Group against all actions, proceedings, losses, claims, damages, costs, charges, expenses and liabilities suffered or incurred, *and* all fines, compensation or remedial action or payments imposed on or required to be made by the Company following and arising out of claims or complaints registered with the FSA, the Financial Services Ombudsman or any other Authority against the Company, the Sellers or any Relevant Person and which relate to the period prior to the Completion Date pertaining to any mis-selling or suspected mis-selling of any insurance or insurance related product or service.[11]

A close reading reveals the ambiguity. The two expressions that are in coordination are respectively

8 The Court of Appeal found that (1) was, as it turned out to have suited the trust to argue, the correct interpretation.

9 For very similar, and equally ambiguous wording, see *Jet2.com Ltd v Blackpool Airport Ltd* [2012] EWCA Civ 417: 'Jet2.com and BAL will co-operate together and use their best endeavours to promote Jet2,com's low cost services from [Blackpool Airport]'. Was there a free-standing general obligation to co-operate, or only an obligation insofar as related to the promotion of the specified services? That this ambiguity did not, as it happened, form the focus of the parties' dispute does not make the drafting any less risky.

10 *Wood v Capita Insurance Services Ltd* [2017] UKSC 24.

11 Emphasis added.

> all actions, proceedings, losses, claims, damages, costs, charges, expenses and liabilities suffered or incurred

and

> all fines, compensation or remedial action or payments imposed on or required to be made by the Company.

These two expressions are separated by the coordinating conjunction 'and' which is italicised in the full quote above. So the first usual ingredient of the uncertain modifiers problem (a coordination) is present. The remaining ingredient is some modifying language that appears next to one of the two coordinated expressions. Here it takes the form of the language at the end of the second expression: the whole language of the rest of the clause from

> following and arising out of claims or complaints registered with the FSA.

Both ingredients being present, the language is automatically ambiguous. It is unclear whether the modifying language attaches only to the 'fines, compensation or remedial action or payments' which it immediately follows, or to the 'actions, proceedings…and liabilities suffered or incurred' as well.

But uncertain modifiers can lurk even where there is no coordination

7.6 Though the uncertain modifier issue arises most commonly with two expressions that appear in coordination, it can arise in other contexts too. In *Youell v Bland Welch & Co Ltd*[12] a 131-word reinsurance clause provided as follows:

> The reinsured shall cede to the reinsurers and the reinsurers shall accept by way of reinsurance of the reinsured their proportion of the reinsured's liability in respect of risks attaching *for periods as original (up to but not exceeding 48 months)* covering the interests of hull, machinery (including protection and indemnity and/or running down closure and other risks normally covered under Institute Builders Risk Clauses or similar clauses) materials, suppliers and everything intended for and/or connected therewith plus any associated contingent interests written separately (such as, but not limited to escalation insurances, loans and equity interest insurances and the like) in respect of vessels (as defined below) whilst under construction, conversion et cetera as original and until handed over to and accepted by or on behalf of owners and/or as original.[13]

12 [1990] 2 Lloyd's Rep 431.
13 Emphasis added.

Here the modifying language whose scope was in dispute was that italicised above:

> for periods as original (up to but not exceeding 48 months).

Those words appear immediately after

> the reinsured's liability in respect of risks attaching.

If those are the words that are modified, the effect is that the modifying expression defines the risks that are being reinsured: it is only those short-term risks that are the subject of the reinsurance. But it is linguistically feasible that the modifying expression does not relate to 'the reinsured's liability in respect of risks attaching' but the earlier words

> the reinsurers shall accept by way of reinsurance.

On that reading, the modifying expression delimits the period for which the reinsurers agree to be on risk, so that they go off risk after four years.

The grammatical point here is that the two candidates for the language qualified by the modifying expression are *not* expressions in coordination, separated by a coordinating conjunction like 'and' or 'or'. They are respectively the object of the verb and the verb itself. And the question is not, as it is when coordinations feature in this problem, whether the modifying words qualify both the expressions or only the one next door to them. It is clear that they qualify only one expression; but it is not clear which.

For a similar example of an uncertain modifier where no coordination appears, see *Britvic PLC v Britvic Pensions Ltd.*[14] The drafting of a pension trust deed provided for an annual rate of increase in pensions that (simplified) amounted to:

> The rate of increase is the percentage increased by RPI, but subject to a maximum of 5% (or any other rate decided by the employer).

It was linguistically unclear whether the employer's right to decide on an 'other rate' related to the 5% cap or to the rate of increase itself (although that was not the way the question was framed in the courts).

Be vigilant: the uncertain modifier problem is ubiquitous

7.7 Even experienced drafters can overlook uncertain modifiers, sometimes even in circumstances where they are themselves the party whose interests are affected. In *Blacklion Law LLP v Amira Nature Foods Ltd*[15] a lawyer acting for a company planning a bond issue drafted a retainer relating to the firm's fee entitlement as follows:

14 [2021] EWCA Civ 867.
15 [2022] EWHC 1500 (Ch).

> We have agreed that the Firm will charge the Company a fixed fee of £300,000…for the Services… in connection with this Matter, subject to the completion of the Matter by 31 May 2017.

But what did the words at the end 'subject to completion of the Matter by 31 May 2017' qualify? Did they relate to *everything* that came before, so that if the completion did not happen by that date, no fee would be payable *at all*? Or did they just relate to the fixed nature of the fee payable for work up to 31 May – so that if the completion happened after that date, an extra level of fee would be payable for any post-May work? The language was ambiguous, and the failure to spot the uncertain modifier risked costing the law firm that drafted it £300,000.[16]

Drafters find it so difficult to eliminate uncertain modifiers that it can reveal itself in standard forms that have been used countless times. In the midst of a clause dealing with the giving of notices, a standard form issued by GAFTA[17] provided:

> In case of resales/repurchases all notices shall be served without delay by sellers on their respective buyers or vice versa, and any notice received after 1600 hours on a business day shall be deemed to have been received on the business day following.

The modifying language 'In case of resales/repurchases' clearly applied to the requirement to serve notices without delay generally – the words down to the comma. But did it also apply to the following language relating to notices received after 1600 hours, so that the 'deemed receipt on the following day' effect of that following language applied only to notices relating to sales and repurchases? Only by answering that question could one establish whether the 'deemed receipt the following day' language applied to *all* notices, or only those relevant to resales and repurchases. The drafting had not made it clear: a classic 'uncertain modifier' problem. That a linguistic ambiguity like this can appear in a trade body's standard form used thousands of times without anybody noticing is testament to the ubiquity of the problem, or perhaps the difficulty most lawyers seem to have in spotting it.

This third example illustrates that, in a contractual context as also in 'brown bread and butter', the modifying language (here 'in case of resales/ repurchases') can appear not only *after* the language it modifies (as in both *Mid Essex* and *Wood v Capita*), but also *before* that language. The grammatical issue is identical, whatever the respective position of the modifying language and the expression or expressions that language modifies.

16 The decision was that the law firm did have an entitlement to the £300,000, but the court could only reach that finding on the basis of the context: the language was not clear in itself.

17 The Grain and Feed Trade Association. In the case where the meaning of the language was disputed (*Soufflet Negoce SA v Fedcominvest Europe SARL* [2014] EWHC 2405 (Comm)), Eder J remarked that the clause in question 'appears in numerous GAFTA standard forms'.

Always consider whether it is clear how far modifying language extends

7.8 The above discussion illustrates that the problem with uncertain modifiers, though it arises most prominently in the context of coordinations, can arise in other contexts as well. How can drafters, or lawyers reviewing drafts prepared by others, best learn to identify the issue?

In the author's view, knowing that the problem *can* exist amounts to half the battle. If a drafter begins to view drafting in grammatically analytic terms, it becomes easier to isolate words of qualification and ask the question: is it clear how far these words extend? Eventually, with practice, it becomes second nature to perform a mental check to see if the problem arises. Focussing on the coordinating conjunctions 'and' and 'or' in the first instance is another possibility, though not perhaps as reliable since, as *Youell v Bland Welch*[18] shows, the problem can arise even where no coordination exists.

Draft in shorter units to help diagnose the issue

7.9 Dense and unpunctuated drafting, with clauses that run on for many lines without any sort of break, is unattractive for various reasons.[19] Prominent among those reasons is that a slab of drafting tends to obscure the existence of uncertain modifiers. It is no surprise that, for example, the critical sentence in *Wood v Capita*[20] ran to 119 words and that in *Youell v Bland Welch*[21] to 131 words.[22] It follows that a drafting style that divides the drafting up into shorter units helps readers, and indeed drafters themselves, diagnose whether an uncertain modifier problem exists.

But drafting in shorter units is no panacea. An uncertain modifier can lurk in even the shortest piece of drafting. An example is *BP International Ltd v Target Shipping Ltd*,[23] which involved a dispute over the amount of 'overage' (the amount in excess of the stated rate of charterhire) payable under a charterparty). The drafting provided laconically:

> Overage 50PCT applicable for Euromed discharge only.

[18] [1990] 2 Lloyd's Rep 431.
[19] See **1.28** above.
[20] [2017] UKSC 24.
[21] [1990] 2 Lloyd's Rep 431.
[22] Readers who need any more convincing of this point could do worse than read the drafting in *Rhodia International Holdings Ltd v Huntsman International LLC* [2007] EWHC 292 (Comm), where the drafting of the critical clause containing just this type of ambiguity ran to 260 words (see **1.28** above).
[23] [2013] EWCA Civ 196.

The modifying language here was the single word 'only', a word notorious for conveying different meanings according to its position in a sentence.[24] In this context, the question was whether the position of 'only' meant that: (a) it was only in relation to a 'Euromed discharge'[25] that any overage was payable (so that if discharge were for example at a port in the US, no overage was payable); or (b) the rate at which overage was fixed was 50% for a Euromed discharge, but without prejudice to overage being payable at other rates for discharge at ports elsewhere, based on other provisions in the charterparty. The judge in the High Court[26] posed the question as:

> does the word 'only' qualify simply 'overage' or does it qualify 'overage 50 PCT'?

The drafter had not made this clear, and to have done so would have needed to do more than simply repositioning 'only'. Language such as the following would have been necessary:

> Overage: only for Euromed discharge, and if so at the rate of 50%

or

> Overage: at 50% for Euromed discharge, and otherwise at any rates otherwise applicable under other provisions of this agreement.

The diagnostic lesson from the case is that to eradicate all uncertain modifiers from drafting is a task demanding constant vigilance.

To draft in shorter units is not only to diagnose, but often also to cure, the issue

7.10 The drafter who breaks drafting into shorter units – lettered or numbered subparagraphs, properly punctuated – achieves a remarkable double benefit. It becomes easier for the drafter or another reader to see whether an uncertain modifier problem exists. And it reduces the chances that it does, because it is by breaking down drafting into shorter components that the drafter can make it clear how far the modifying language extends.

24 The classic example is 'My brother broke his leg', where the list of various meanings that depend on where 'only' is located begins with the alternative meanings of 'Only my brother broke his leg' (nobody else did); 'My only brother broke his leg' (I don't have any other brothers); 'My brother only broke his leg' (all things considered, he got off lightly). The usual rule is that 'only' most naturally qualifies the word it appears immediately before: as can be seen, the drafter in *BP v Target Shipping* decided to ignore that rule and place 'only' right at the end instead.

25 A discharge at a port on the European coast of the Mediterranean, in other words.

26 Andrew Smith J at [2012] EWHC 1590 (Comm): another example of a very brief provision giving rise to a lengthy (seven day) hearing in the High Court, and a subsequent Court of Appeal hearing, because a few words were botched.

To illustrate this phenomenon, take the *Mid Essex* case[27] discussed in **7.4** above. When the Court of Appeal considered the dispute, they illustrated the two possible meanings by setting out[28] two alternative versions:

> The Trust and the Contractor:
>
> (1) will co-operate with each other in good faith; and
>
> (2) will take all reasonable action as is necessary:
>
> (a) for the efficient transmission of information and instructions; and
>
> (b) to enable the Trust... to derive the full benefit of the Contract

and

> The Trust and the Contractor will co-operate with each other in good faith and will take all reasonable action as is necessary:
>
> (1) for the efficient transmission of information and instructions; and
>
> (2) to enable the Trust... to derive the full benefit of the Contract.

The court used these two versions to illustrate the two rival contentions as to what the original version, lacking the sub-division into numbered and lettered sub-paragraphs, might mean. That was the task the court was faced with. But the point that obviously follows is that if the drafter had thought to do the same, the meaning would have been clear without resort to a court.

It follows that prominent among the benefits of breaking slablike drafting down into more manageable units is the benign consequence that it makes an uncertain modifier problem less likely.

GRAMMAR ISSUE 2: UNCERTAIN ANTECEDENTS

Identify the issue: not always associated with pronouns

7.11 Just as dangerous for the drafter as uncertain *modifiers* is the ambiguity that arises with uncertain *antecedents*. Antecedents arise in the area of grammar termed 'anaphora': the phenomenon in which one piece of language (the anaphor) is interpreted by reference to another piece of language (the antecedent).

The phenomenon is most commonly seen in ordinary speech with *pronouns*. If a speaker says

> John has just messaged to say he has caught the 7.30 train

[27] [2013] EWCA Civ 200.
[28] ibid at [97]–[98] (Jackson LJ).

the pronoun 'he' is the anaphor which the listener interprets by identifying (in the most obvious interpretation of the utterance) 'John' as the antecedent: John was messaging about himself.

The speaker relies on the listener recognising the antecedent and thus what the pronoun itself means. Normally this causes no problems. But if there are two or more possible candidates to rank as antecedent, ambiguity can arise. For example, if the same sentence had been uttered in the context of a conversation

> Speaker A: I wonder if Alan is going to attend the meeting
>
> Speaker B: John has just messaged to say he has just caught the 7.30 train

A is instead likely to take B to be referring to Alan, not John, as 'he'.

The ambiguity can arise quite apart from context. So a sentence in the form

> I was worried that the dogs might eat the mouldy biscuits, so I put them in the next room just in case

is *inherently* ambiguous as to whether the speaker put the dogs next door, or the biscuits.

In conversation, a listener can seek clarity by asking the speaker, 'What do you mean?' But that is not an available method of clarifying a written contract.

If a pronoun in a contract has an uncertain antecedent, a dispute can follow. An example is *Standing v Power*.[29] Pre-emption provisions in the articles of association of a private company[30] required a proposing transferor of shares to offer them

> to the members (other than the proposing transferor) as nearly as may be in proportion to the number of shares held by them respectively.

But to decide what this meant involved establishing what was the antecedent of 'them'. Was it the 'members' (as a whole)? If so, the proposing transferor, who intended to sell his entire 85% stake to a third party, needed to offer only 15% of that 85% stake to the minority shareholder. Or was the antecedent of 'them' the longer phrase 'the members (other than the proposing transferor)'? If so, the proposing transferor had to offer his whole 85% stake to the minority holder.

The problem is, however, not confined to pronouns. Any expression that refers to something referred to earlier needs to identify its antecedent clearly: if it does not, an ambiguity arises which can lead to a dispute, as the case law demonstrates.

29 [2021] EWHC 1744.
30 The company in question owned, indirectly, Swindon Town FC.

Example 1: Rainy Sky[31]

7.12 In this case, the word which triggered the antecedent hunt was 'such'. Lawyers are fond of 'such', but tend to overuse it: see, for example, the Scottish case of *Lagan Construction Group Ltd (in administration) v Scot Roads Partnership Project Ltd.*[32]

In *Rainy Sky*, a bank agreed in favour of a shipyard's customer to pay to the customer

> all such sums due to you under

the contract between the customer and the shipyard. 'Such' is a word that naturally demands that a reader look back to identify its antecedent.[33] and in this context presupposed an earlier mention of the 'sums' that 'all such sums' was intended to refer back to. The *Rainy Sky* language, therefore, necessarily required a reader to look back through the contract to identify what those 'sums' were. In grammatical terms: what was the antecedent of 'such sums'?

The difficulty was that more than one candidate could plausibly be argued to be the intended antecedent of 'such sums'. And whilst one candidate included pre-delivery instalments paid by the customer in circumstances where the shipyard later became insolvent, the other did not. Needless to say, an insolvency of the yard was exactly what had happened, and a dispute was triggered.

Grammatically, it is more common for an expression to refer to a nearer antecedent than a more remote one: to an antecedent which, in other words, a reader going backwards through the text from the anaphor encounters first. But unlike the position with co-ordinations, where the modifying language always relates to the closer expression,[34] there is no grammatical rule to this effect with antecedents. That meant that it was plausible for the bank in *Rainy Sky* to argue that the phrase 'all such sums' related to a more remote antecedent, with the consequence that they did not have to pay out under the bonds in the circumstances that had arisen. And they succeeded in persuading the Court of Appeal that the contract should be interpreted that way.

The Supreme Court preferred the alternative view, but only because they considered that it was more likely to accord with the commercial understanding. The drafting issue was therefore that by using the term 'such

31 *Rainy Sky SA v Kookmin Bank* [2011] UKSC 50.

32 [2023] CSIH 28 at [9] (reference to 'such Contracting Company' naturally suggesting to the first instance judge that its evident antecedent, which was 'Contractor' rather than 'Contracting Company', had been included by mistake) (Lord Carloway).

33 *Dassault Aviation SA v Mitsui Sumitomo Insurance Co Ltd.* [2024] EWCA Civ 5 at [30] (Sir Geoffrey Vos MR).

34 So that the ambiguity is generally confined to whether the modifying language also refers to the more remote language as well: see **7.4** above.

sums' without making it clear which antecedent was intended, the drafter had failed in the crucial task of eliminating ambiguity from the drafting.

Example 2: Orr Ewing[35]

7.13 In this case, the House of Lords had to contend with a similar issue, this time in the context of a partnership deed drafted in Scotland. This time the expression posing the question: which antecedent? was 'thereon'. The drafter had provided for repayments of partnership capital to be paid to outgoing partners in instalments, together with interest 'thereon'. But the drafting did not make it clear whether, in the case of any particular instalment, the interest payable related just to that instalment, or the whole amount of the balance yet to be repaid to the outgoing partner. Lord Bramwell remarked:[36]

> Now a difficulty is raised upon the grammatical rule that the word 'thereon' must be taken to refer to the last antecedent...you do not come to the antecedent which the appellants are so anxious to rely upon...until you have passed over four other antecedents. That being the case, if you may pass over four antecedents on account of the good sense of the thing, I cannot see why you may not pass over a fifth.

An uncertain antecedent can follow the anaphor as well as preceding it

7.14 It is most common for the antecedent to appear *before* the anaphor. In a contract, language like 'such' and 'thereon' (the words used in the two cases discussed immediately above) are of that type, and others are frequently used by drafters ('abovementioned', 'referred to above' and 'referred to earlier' for example).

However, the uncertain antecedent may also *follow* the anaphor rather than preceding it ('hereunder', 'referred to below', 'as mentioned below', 'as hereinafter mentioned' and the like).[37] Although the word 'antecedent' derives from the Latin for to 'go before', and most antecedents *do* come before their anaphor, grammarians still refer to post-anaphor examples as 'antecedents'.

Drafters who want to diagnose an uncertain antecedent problem need to look out for anaphors – words or expressions that demand an antecedent to interpret them – and ask themselves: does the anaphor have as a possible

35 *John Orr Ewing & Co v John Orr Ewing* (1882) Scottish Law Reporter vol XX 240.
36 ibid at [244].
37 The old-fashioned and legalistic language appears to clothe the drafting in respectability, but in reality, the emperor has no clothes.

antecedent only the one that is intended? Or could it be argued that the anaphor has another, unintended, antecedent? If the answer to the second question is yes, the drafter has more work to do to address the problem.[38]

As with uncertain modifiers, it is harder to diagnose that there is a problem if the drafting is in long sentences, not broken up into separate shorter units, or is unpunctuated, or both. In the *Orr Ewing* case,[39] none of the four sentences quoted in the part of the drafting cited in the House of Lords was shorter than 115 words, and one weighed in at 209 words. None of the sentences was divided into shorter sub-paragraphs. Within these heavyweight sentences, it is harder for the drafter or any other reader to recognise that a single word like 'thereon' may be an anaphor suffering from an uncertain antecedent problem. It is theoretically possible for sentences of this length to be framed without lapsing into ambiguity of the type under discussion here. But drafters who adopt this style are tempting fate.

Cure the issue by adequately specific drafting

7.15 Whether the antecedent lies before or after the anaphor whose meaning it determines, to eliminate potential ambiguity the drafter needs to take steps to make clear that the intended antecedent is the one the anaphor refers to. In *Rainy Sky*,[40] for example, the position would have been clear if the language dealing with the 'sums' had referred explicitly to either one of the two candidates for 'such sums', which were as it happens either 'the sums referred to earlier in this sub-paragraph' or 'the sums referred to in sub-paragraph (2) above'. The drafter is therefore recommended to be explicit and detailed when referring to an antecedent.

As with uncertain modifiers, the technique recommended to help diagnosis (draft in shorter units, avoiding slabs) itself makes the cure easier. It is much easier to be clear about an antecedent if drafting is sub-divided: a reference to a short numbered or lettered subparagraph is bound to be more focussed than a reference to a lengthy, undivided piece of drafting.[41]

The solution to the drafting problem is therefore straightforward, and well within the abilities of most drafters: the challenge is not to effect the cure, but to carry out the diagnosis.

Drafting that is careful to identify the antecedent of an anaphor is attractively resilient to challenge. For example, take *Palladian Partners LP v The Republic*

[38] Sometimes the maladroit drafter suggests that an anaphor has an antecedent but fails to provide one, as noted in the High Court in *The Prudential Assurance Co Ltd v Ayres* [2007] EWHC 775 (Ch) at [21] (reference to 'such default' when no 'default' had previously been referred to at all (Lindsay J)).

[39] Scottish Law Reporter vol XX 240.

[40] *Rainy Sky SA v Kookmin Bank* [2011] UKSC 50.

[41] Though the drafter should also be careful with cross-referencing: see **1.27** above.

of Argentina.[42] In that case, the drafter faced the daunting task of drafting the conditions attaching to payments under sovereign bonds issued by Argentina that were linked to the country's GDP. The drafting had to cope with what would happen if the country's reported GDP figures were rebased (measured by reference to prices in a different reference year from previously published figures). The drafting (slightly simplified) took the form

> The Base Case GDP for *each* Reference Year shall be adjusted by multiplying the Base Case GDP for *such* Reference Year [by a factor][43]

with the antecedent for 'such Reference Year' therefore clearly being identifiable as the Reference Year whose Base Case GDP was being adjusted. It was held that the drafting was so clear in this respect that no other reading was possible.[44]

OTHER GRAMMAR ISSUES

Distinguish between the active and the passive voice

7.16 Teachers of English often recommend using the active voice rather than the passive voice for ordinary English prose. They say, correctly, that the active voice tends to come across more directly and vividly to the reader. A contract drafter is not centrally concerned with matters of literary style. The drafter's overriding concern is to be completely clear. Drafting can be clear in either the active voice or the passive voice. Equally, inexpert drafting in the active voice can be just as unclear as its passive equivalent.

But the drafter still has to choose whether to draft in the active or the passive voice, and should not assume that it does not matter which is chosen.

The active voice cannot suppress who does the action

7.17 The active voice has the benefit, for a drafter, of ensuring that the person who owes a contractual obligation is identified. Compare the active

> The Seller shall deliver the application to the regulator

with its passive equivalent

> The application shall be delivered to the regulator by the Seller.

These two formulations mean exactly the same thing. They are distinguishable only at a stylistic level: a teacher of English might argue that the active version

42 [2023] EWHC 711 (Comm).
43 Emphasis added.
44 [2023] EWHC 711 at [183]–[184] (Picken J).

creates a more immediately vivid picture in the reader's mind, by focussing on the actor performing the verb rather than the item to which the action relates.

But if the final few words are removed, the passive version can be rendered without reference to the actor at all:

> The application shall be delivered to the regulator.

This grammatical usage is termed in what follows the 'unattributed passive': it does not attribute responsibility for the action described. It makes for unsatisfactory drafting, because the identity of who has to carry out the obligation is left open. Often context will make this obvious. But to rely on context is a hallmark of substandard drafting: everything should be clear explicitly, without recourse to context. A contract exists to record enforceable promises: if it fails to make clear who owes the obligation it sets out and leaves that vital piece of information to be inferred, it is fundamentally flawed.

If one tries to replicate the lack of clarity in the active voice, it is impossible. The grammar of the English language does not allow an active verb to appear without a subject:

> [...] shall deliver the application to the regulator

demands that the gap be filled in for it to be meaningful.

It follows that while the passive voice *allows* clarity about who owes the obligation, the active voice *requires* it. On those grounds alone, the drafter is recommended, all other things being equal, to favour the active voice in contractual drafting. Whether all other things are equal is the subject of the following paragraph.

Expressions in the unattributed passive are wider than expressions in the active voice

7.18 The grammar of the English language entails an expression couched in the unattributed passive being necessarily wider than an expression, whether in the active voice or the passive, where the identity of the person doing the action of the verb is specified. In other words

> The application shall be delivered to the regulator

is wider than either the active version

> X shall deliver the application to the regulator

or a passive version which does attribute the action

> the application shall be delivered to the regulator by X.

The version in the unattributed passive is wider because, unlike the other two, it admits of the possibility that Y or Z may deliver the application instead.

It follows that where an expression is designed to act as a contractual trigger, the trigger is activated in a wider set of circumstances if it is expressed in the unattributed passive than if the actor is specified.

As an example, take *Milton Furniture Ltd v Brit Insurance Ltd.*[45] A condition of insurance cover was that certain security protections

> shall not be withdrawn or varied to the detriment of the interests of Underwriters without their consent.

Notably, the condition was not framed in the active voice: it did not say that the insured company Milton should not itself withdraw or vary the protections. The drafting took the form of an unattributed passive: that the protections should 'not be withdrawn or varied'. So the contractual trigger operated, and cover was lost, even where (as happened) it was a third party, rather than Milton, who withdrew the protections. If the wording had been couched in the active voice ('Milton shall not withdraw or vary'), Milton would have had a viable argument that the contractual trigger did not operate and that their cover was intact.[46] But as it was, they were held not to be covered.

Another case that brings home, in a completely different context, the breadth of language couched in the unattributed passive is *Dorchester Project Management Ltd v BNP Paribas Real Estate Advisory & Property Management Ltd.*[47] In that case, two parties entered into a confidentiality agreement in the context of a property development proposal. The contract provided that one party, BNPPRE, was to be responsible to the other, Dorchester

> for any unauthorised disclosure, whether by it or any third Party to whom disclosure is made.

Notably, the form of the language 'to whom disclosure is made' was an unattributed passive. It did not say, in the active voice, 'to whom BNPPRE discloses the information'. Accordingly, when a third party to whom the information had been passed went on to disclose it, BNNPRE was responsible for the disclosure, even though it was Dorchester itself – the party taking legal action against BNNPRE – that had made the disclosure to the third party in question.

There can be few starker illustrations of the sometimes unexpectedly wide import of the unattributed passive voice.

Singular and plural drafting: generally prefer to draft in the singular

7.19 A further choice facing drafters is whether to draft in the singular or the plural. It must be rare for an agreement to offer no such choice, perhaps

45 [2015] EWCA Civ 671.
46 ibid at [61] (Gloster LJ).
47 [2013] EWCA Civ 176.

only in a case where a single obligor owes a single obligation to provide a single item of goods or a single service to single counterparty.

For the reasons discussed below, drafters are recommended to prefer drafting in the singular. To do so generally leads to a clearer result.[48]

Inconsistency between singular and plural often betrays muddled thinking on the drafter's part. And, even if it does not cause a dispute, the inconsistency contributes to the sense that the drafting is not fully to be trusted.

For example, in *Al Sanea v Saad Investments Co Ltd*[49] a put option was granted over a substantial block of shares in a quoted company. The block of shares was referred to as 'the Shares'. But the drafter seems to have been uncertain whether the asset referred to as 'the Shares' was conceptually singular (the block) or plural (the shares that made up the block). So the option was expressed as a right

> 'to sell… all or any part of the Shares'

The words 'part of' suggest of course that 'the Shares' was conceptually a single asset. But later the notice exercising the put option was required

> to specify the number of Shares being sold

which switched back to a (more conventional) recognition that each Share represented a single asset. The confusion was symptomatic of the drafter's lack of conceptual control, which duly led to another part of the drafting being unclear enough to lead to a dispute.

In *Pink Floyd Music Ltd v EMI Records Ltd*,[50] a provision aimed at making clear the royalties on the exploitation of recordings provided:

> [EMI's] receipts shall be calculated at the so-called 'source' so that they shall incorporate the receipt of EMI's licensees sub-licensees affiliates or any third party obtaining rights in this respect directly or indirectly from [EMI].

Why did the drafter provide for EMI's 'receipts' (plural) to incorporate the 'receipt' (singular) of licensees? The difference initially suggests that some distinction was intended: perhaps on its second appearance the word 'receipt' is being used as an abstract noun referring to the process of receiving rather than the amounts received. But on examination that seems to be a red herring, and the likely explanation is that the drafter did not notice the disparity between two terms intended to mean the same thing, or was too lazy to fix it. Neither explanation is encouraging for any reader hoping to find the agreement coherent in other respects.

48 Though see **4.9** above for the awkwardness that results if an essentially plural concept is defined by a singular expression.
49 [2012] EWCA Civ 313.
50 [2010] EWCA Civ 1429.

As a final example, consider the following from a document appointing a party called a 'Servicer' under a financing arrangement.[51] It was expressed as a condition precedent to a termination right that:

> the Servicer... shall have notified each of the Rating Agencies in writing of the identity of the successor Servicer... and the Rating Agencies shall have confirmed that the appointment of the successor Servicer... will not result in an Adverse Rating Event.

The two references to 'Rating Agencies' are different. The first reference is to 'each of the Rating Agencies' (there were three of them) and plainly envisages each of the three receiving a separate notification. But the other reference is not to 'each of the Rating Agencies' (singular) but to 'the Rating Agencies' (plural). The difference plainly provides room for an argument that the confirmation they were required to give to satisfy the condition was a joint confirmation. But that is at odds with what the Rating Agencies had to give a confirmation of, namely that the appointment of a successor Servicer or Special Servicer would not give rise to an Adverse Rating Event. An Adverse Rating Event was (broadly) a ratings downgrade. And ratings are awarded not by ratings agencies jointly but separately.[52] So the plural, with its suggestion of a joint confirmation, was simply misleading.

Do not assume that boilerplate language will resolve a singular/plural problem

7.20 It is common to see generally applicable language that looks as if it is intended to make irrelevant any decision the drafter might make to choose between singular and plural forms in the drafting of specific provisions. The language is along the lines of

> Words in the singular shall include the plural and vice versa.[53]

But general language like this type will not hold sway if, in any specific provision, the drafting makes it clear that a distinction between singular and plural is to be respected. In *Decision Inc Holdings Proprietary Ltd v Garbett*,[54] for example, general language of this type was not enough to validate a warranty notice which did not specify, as the provision referring to notices demanded,

51 The drafting is taken from *US Bank Trustees Ltd v Titan Europe 2007-1 (NHP) Ltd* [2014] EWHC 1189 (Ch). The argument identified above was not advanced: this illustrates a common feature of disputed drafting, namely that it is common for documents to contain many more errors and uncertainties than are actually disputed.

52 The judge said (generously) that it was 'obvious, and common ground, that any confirmation from a particular Rating Agency is only required to relate to its own rating, and not to the rating of any of the other agencies' (ibid at [90]).

53 Sometimes the words 'Except as the context otherwise requires' also appear, which tend to provoke a further level of uncertainty in applying the language to any particular case where it might be relevant: see also **4.1** above.

54 [2023] EWCA Civ 1284.

the amount of any particular 'Claim' (singular) that a purchaser might bring. It was not enough for the purchaser to refer to an amount attributable to all Claims (plural), relying on the general 'singular includes the plural' language to validate the notice.

So in formulating any particular provision, a drafter should constantly bear in mind whether a singular or plural form of language is appropriate, whether or not any such general language appears.

Drafting in the plural raises questions of joint and separate obligations, and joint and several liability

7.21 If a joint venture agreement involving four equal shareholders A, B, C and D provides:

> The Shareholders shall subscribe £100,000 for shares in JVCo on 31 March

or for that matter

> A, B, C and D shall subscribe £100,000 for shares in JVCo on 31 March

the reader is left uncertain of the intended effect. Is the total amount to be subscribed £100,000, or is it £400,000, in other words £100,000 per shareholder?

The difficulty arises because it is uncertain whether the shareholders are being viewed as a group, or individually.

It does not help here to use the word 'all':

> All the Shareholders shall subscribe £100,000 for shares in JVCo on 31 March

can equally be interpreted as leading to either the £100,000 or £400,000 result.[55]

A grammarian would describe the difference between the rival meanings as depending on whether or not 'the Shareholders' was intended to be understood *distributively*. A distributive reading is one that looks at each Shareholder separately: the alternative, non-distributive, reading looks at them together. In the distributive reading, the obligation to subscribe £100,000 applies separately to A, to B, to C and to D, leading to the £400,000 answer. The non-distributive reading views the group of A, B, C and D as

[55] And if there are only two shareholders, 'both' instead of 'all' is still unsatisfactory: although the more natural reading is that they are being viewed separately, that is not necessarily its meaning: 'both the Shareholders will appoint an appropriate company doctor to rescue JVCo if it risks becoming insolvent', for example, suggests a common effort, with one doctor rather than two being appointed.

together owing the obligation to subscribe £100,000 (and there is only one such amount due).

This contrast operates at the level of describing the contractual *task*. A separate distinction operates at the level of determining *liability* if the task is not performed: in the above example, how and against whom could JVCo enforce the contractual obligation to subscribe for shares? This question is bound up with the concepts of joint and several liability.

In the example given, there are four possibilities:

(a) the contractual task is viewed distributively, so that each of A, B, C and D, viewed separately, promises to subscribe £100,000 (meaning therefore that JVCo is entitled to £400,000 in total). None of A, B, C and D is responsible for the failure of any of the others to meet its promise;

(b) the contractual task is viewed distributively, so that again, each of A, B, C and D separately promises to subscribe £100,000 and JVCo is entitled to £400,000. But the parties wish the arrangement to have the effect that if any of the subscribers defaults, JVCo can require the others to make up the missing £100,000;

(c) the contractual task is viewed jointly, so that there is a single obligation to subscribe £100,000 to JVCo, owed collectively by A, B, C and D (so they have 'joint liability'): the consequence of joint liability is that if JVCo wishes to enforce the promise, it should take proceedings against all four subscribers;

(d) the contractual task is viewed jointly, but the liability to meet it is 'joint and several': the significance of the liability being several as well as joint is that JVCo can pursue any one of the subscribers alone to enforce the single obligation to subscribe £100,000.

Although (b) above imposes what might in a general sense be termed 'joint liability', the arrangement does not truly amount to joint liability, because there are separate promises on the part of each of the subscribers. The analysis is more that each of the subscribers, as well as making its own promise, is a member of three different sets of co-guarantors of the others' promises.

In the examples given above, the obligation to subscribe £100,000 is a single concept. The question whether the reference to the Shareholders is read distributively or non-distributively affects the number of times the JVCo receives its £100,000 subscription.

It follows from the above that drafters should be alert to the dangers of potential ambiguities where the obligors are plural and either making identical promises or a joint one. Drafting tends to be clearer if the drafter drafts in the singular rather than the plural. The word 'each' forces a singular reading:

> Each Shareholder shall subscribe £100,000 for shares in JVCo on 31 March

and

> Each of A, B, C and D shall subscribe £100,000 for shares in JVCo on 31 March

are both wholly clear in imposing the meaning referred to in (a) above (four separate identical obligations). Additional language is of course needed to impose the level of guaranteed performance suggested in (b).

If by contrast a single obligation is intended, it is best to add some different language to make it clear that a single obligation is created:

> A, B, C and D shall between them subscribe £100,000 for shares in JVCo on 31 March

with a specific acknowledgement as to whether the liability for that promise is joint only, or joint and several.

Prefer singular drafting in other cases too

7.22 The solution of drafting in the singular also works, grammatically speaking, if the group is the *object* of the action, whether direct:

> JVCo shall nominate each of A, B, C and D as its agent to receive any notice under clause 9.3 of the Supply Contract

or indirect

> JVCo shall deliver a copy of its accounts to each Shareholder within 7 days of their being approved by the JVCo Board.

Sometimes, in these cases, the plural is genuinely misleading. In one case, each of a series of charterparties contained a clause providing for commission to be paid to brokers in the following terms:

> A commission of 2 per cent for equal division is payable by the vessel and owners to Messrs Ifchor SA Lausanne and Messrs Cleaves and Company Ltd, London on hire earned and paid under this Charter, and also upon any continuation or extension of this charter.[56]

Here the words 'for equal division', to the drafter's credit, closed off an uncertainty that would have arisen had they been omitted: should the reference to Ifchor and Cleaves be read distributively so that they were *both* entitled to receive 2%, meaning that the total commission was 4%?

But the drafting, being in the plural, was still awkward. The judge said:

[56] *Nisshin Shipping Co Ltd v Cleaves & Co Ltd* [2003] EWHC 2602 (Comm).

> It is in substance exactly the same as if the clause had provided that there was to be a commission of 2 per cent of which 1 per cent was to be paid to Ifchor and 1 per cent to Cleaves.

But clearer drafting would have dealt with Ifchor's entitlement and Cleaves's separately. It would then have been clearer, though nobody thought about the point at the time, that Cleaves had a right to enforce the payment of its commission directly under the terms of the Contracts (Rights of Third Parties) Act 1999. So this was another case where drafting in the singular rather than the plural would have made more sense.

Remember the special trap with plural obligors and plural obligations

7.23 A different version of the same issue arises when not only are the obligors plural, but the obligation itself is a plural one. Drafting such as

> If the court refuses the application, A and B shall lodge an appeal and pay £250,000 into court

can again involve 'A and B' being read either distributively or non-distributively. On the distributive reading, A is responsible for lodging an appeal and for paying the £250,000 into court; and B is also responsible for lodging an appeal and for paying £250,000 into court. The non-distributive reading has A responsible for the appeal and B responsible for the payment into court.

To make it clear that the latter effect is intended, the drafter can reach for the word 'respectively':

> If the court refuses the application, A and B shall respectively lodge an appeal and pay £250,000 into court

though the simpler course in a straightforward case like this[57] is to deal with the obligors separately:

> If the court refuses the application,
>
> (a) A shall lodge an appeal; and
>
> (b) B shall pay £250,000 into court.

But if drafting in the singular, pay close attention to the right form of words

7.24 Though the drafter is recommended normally to use the singular rather than the plural, it is always crucial to consider whether the form of

[57] Showing the attraction of drafting in the singular rather than the plural.

the singular drafting achieves the drafting objective. An illustrative case is *Drax Energy Solutions Ltd v Wipro Ltd.*[58] A clause limiting liability under an agreement for the provision of software services capped the amount of the supplier's 'total liability' by reference to the charges paid in the

> preceding twelve months from the date the claim first arose.

The use of the singular 'the claim' influenced the court to hold that that the clause envisaged a single overall cap, no matter how many times the supplier might breach the agreement in no matter how many different ways.[59] This may have been the parties' intention: of course the supplier argued that, on an objective interpretation, it was. But the drafting point is that the use of the simple singular 'the claim' was fatal to the customer's argument that the cap should apply separately to the various instances of breach that it argued should ground a plurality of claims. If separate caps had been intended, singular drafting could still have achieved the objective: 'each claim' (instead of 'the claim') is still singular, but would have made it clear that the cap could apply more than once. The moral is not so much to abandon singular drafting as the default rule as to consider carefully the correct form of the singular to use.

Adjectives and adverbs

7.25 Adjectives narrow the scope of the nouns they describe. The category of a 'bus' (a noun on its own) is wider than the category of a 'red bus' (adjective plus noun). A yellow bus is a bus, but is not a red bus. So any adjective used to modify a noun in a contract will narrow the category to which the contractual provision applies. In *YJL London Ltd v Roswin Estates LLP*[60] the defined concept of a 'Final Account Statement' did not embrace a *provisional* account statement which could subsequently be amended: the adjective 'Final' narrowed the category of 'Account Statements' to which the provision applied.[61] Drafters should ask themselves whether that narrowing effect is what they want to achieve.

Adverbs in contracts raise other issues. Grammatically, they do not qualify nouns, but other parts of speech (often adjectives). An idea may be a 'bad idea', or a 'thoroughly bad idea', but not a 'thoroughly idea'.

Some adverbs are accepted as capable of operating detached from any moorings. In 'Disappointingly, the tickets did not arrive on time', the adverb 'disappointingly' is an adjunct which stands apart from the rest of the sentence

58 [2023] EWHC 1342 (TCC).

59 ibid at [57] (Waksman J).

60 [2009] EWHC 3174 (TCC).

61 See also the High Court judgment in *ABC Electrification Ltd v Network Rail Ltd* [2019] EWHC 1769 (TCC) (accepted that 'default', if it had been qualified by an adjective such as 'wilful', 'deliberate', 'serious' or 'persistent', would have been narrower than 'default' on its own (a conclusion not challenged on appeal [2020] EWCA Civ 1645)).

and provides a commentary on it, as it were from the outside. Not all adverbs qualify for this adjunct use. We cannot for example say 'Thoroughly, this was a bad idea': 'thoroughly' is not an adverb that English speakers use in that way,

Conventionally, drafters use adverbs to qualify particular words, not as adjuncts. So for example, in *Porton Capital Technology Funds v 3M UK Holdings Ltd*,[62] a party undertook an obligation to ensure that certain products were 'actively marketed' and a regulatory approval 'diligently sought'. It was plain that the adverbs 'actively' referred to the manner of the marketing and 'diligently' to the manner of seeking approval: no other interpretation would be arguable. And in that role, they behave like adjectives, narrowing the concept to which they apply. Products could be 'marketed' in a way that would not amount to their being '*actively* marketed' if the marketing were infrequent or half-hearted, for example.

Drafters would not normally have any reason to use an adverb as an adjunct in the manner of 'Disappointingly, the tickets did not arrive on time'. An adverb used in such a way frames the sentence in which it appears by expressing the speaker's or writer's view of it. But a contract is expressed neutrally, without any external commentary on the material it contains. So a drafter will not need to use an adverb in that manner.

Sometimes, however, drafters use an adverb in a way that neither qualifies a particular word nor stands as an adjunct to a sentence as a whole. In a loan contract, for example, a borrower may be required to provide security 'in a form reasonably satisfactory to a lender'. What, in that expression, does 'reasonably' qualify?

The first possibility is that it qualifies the adjective 'satisfactory'. Used in that way, 'reasonably' would normally suggest how far along a scale between, say, 'completely satisfactory' and 'not at all satisfactory' (wholly unsatisfactory) the recipient must find the security. That is how 'reasonably' is interpreted when a student is told that an essay is 'reasonably good': it is neither an excellent piece of work nor a hopeless one, but somewhere in the middle. But that does not seem convincing in the 'security reasonably satisfactory to the lender' example. The test which the drafter is trying to apply is not that the lender needs to evaluate the security as reaching a point on a scale.

Nor, however, is the adverb 'reasonably' somehow an adjunct providing a commentary on the expression as a whole. It does not appear in the trademark position at the front of the clause it qualifies (as does 'disappointingly' in the example relating to the non-arrival of the tickets). And in any event 'reasonably' (like 'thoroughly') is not within the class of adverbs that is used as an adjunct to provide commentary.

62 [2011] EWHC 2895 (Comm).

So what is the adverb 'reasonably' qualifying? In a contractual context, the drafter is intending the word to relate to whether the lender is acting reasonably in accepting or rejecting the security. In other words

> security in a form reasonably satisfactory to the lender

is shorthand, equivalent to

> security in a form satisfactory to the lender, who will act reasonably in evaluating it.

That a court would adopt this meaning is clear from, for example, *M/V Pacific Pearl Co Ltd v Osios David Shipping Inc*,[63] in which Males LJ, giving a judgment with which the whole court agreed, implicitly accepted that this was what 'reasonably satisfactory to the other' meant.

This decision is plainly consistent with the general objective approach to the interpretation of contracts. It would be bizarre for a court to enquire into (say) one party's subjective assessment of how far along a scale of satisfactoriness the security offered by the other falls. Nonetheless drafters should recognise that in using 'reasonably' in this shorthand way, they are acting outside normal grammatical rules. Prudent drafters are recommended to adopt a more conventional approach and spell out explicitly what the adverb qualifies:

> security in a form satisfactory to the lender, who will act reasonably in evaluating it

is, it is submitted, preferable drafting.

63 [2022] EWCA Civ 798.

Chapter 8

'And' and 'or'

The simple words 'and' and 'or', though superficially straightforward, can cause the drafter problems. It is too simplistic to regard 'and' as carrying a conjunctive meaning and 'or' a disjunctive one: disjunction is itself a concept with two meanings. The drafter needs to be alert to some particular cases where 'and' and 'or' frequently cause problems, including where the two words appear together. To omit both 'and' and 'or' is itself, however, dangerous. The use of 'and/or' is not recommended.

THE GRAMMAR OF 'AND' AND 'OR'

Do not assume that 'and' and' 'or' are straightforward

8.1 At first sight, the two simple words 'and' and 'or' seem to be straightforward and non-ambiguous. They are both in a grammatical sense coordinations: words which in ordinary language serve to separate words or groups of words which have an equal status within the sentence. In other words, in a sentence like

> The ship was ready and the crew were eager to depart

there is no grammatical hierarchy between the two parts of the sentence separated by 'and': the reader is not led to see either the ship or the crew as more important than the other. Similarly with 'or': in

> The summit will be held in New York or London

there is no difference in the importance the speaker is attaching to the two locations.[1]

The conventional explanation of the difference between 'and' and 'or'

8.2 The reason that 'and' and 'or' are at first sight non-ambiguous is that although they are both coordinations, any user of the language knows that they have different meanings. This is sometimes (including by judges)[2] described by saying that 'and' is used conjunctively whereas 'or' is used disjunctively.

What is meant by 'and' being used 'conjunctively'

8.3 To say that 'and' is used conjunctively is to say that 'and' signifies that both words or expressions separated by 'and' are to be considered together. Grammatically this is clearly the case if 'and' separates clauses:

> At completion, the Seller shall transfer the Shares to the Buyer and the Buyer shall pay the Seller the Price.

[1] Contrast a sentence like 'Though a few critics disagree about its exact status, *Citizen Kane* is a cinematic masterpiece.' In this sentence, the main clause is the second one: '*Citizen Kane* is a cinematic masterpiece'. The introductory clause beginning with 'though' is subordinate. This is easily seen if one imagines the two parts of the sentence as separate sentences. The main clause '*Citizen Kane* is a cinematic masterpiece' is fully grammatical. But the introductory clause 'Though a few critics disagree about its exact status' falls over without the main clause to support it, and cannot in conventional grammar constitute a separate sentence.

[2] For example in *Attorney General for Bahamas v The Royal Trust Company* [1986] 1 WLR 1001 (PC) (Lord Oliver).

Both obligations are to be performed, by the Seller and the Buyer respectively. And this conjunctive sense of 'and' is equally clear if 'and' functions at a less exalted place in the sentence, separating not clauses but simple words or expressions within a clause:

> The Seller shall deliver the Accounts and the Tax Computations to the Buyer.

The obligation clearly requires both items to be delivered.

The function of 'and' is therefore to yoke together the two bits of language it separates. In a contract, if they are obligations, both of them fall to be performed: if they are two noun phrases, the object of a verb like 'deliver', both are equally to be delivered.[3]

By contrast, 'or' is generally said to be used 'disjunctively'

8.4 To say that 'or' is used disjunctively is to say that the words or expressions it separates are not viewed together but separately. If a speaker says

> They will catch the last train or come by taxi

it is plain that the two modes of transport are not being considered together, but as alternatives.

If someone uses 'and' in a similar sentence and says

> They will go by train and taxi

the speaker is signifying something else, most probably that the journey is one where the nearest station is far enough away from the destination that 'they' need a taxi for the final leg. So 'or' plainly carries a meaning in contrast to 'and'.

As with 'and', 'or' can be used within a clause as well as to separate two clauses:

> The dispute shall be referred either to mediation or arbitration

and, as also with 'and', with different parts of speech.[4]

But this is an oversimplified account

8.5 However, in normal speech, the use of 'and' and 'or' is a little more complicated. And because contract language is interpreted against the

[3] The examples could be multiplied with 'and' separating other parts of speech: for example verbs ('The Company shall prepare and submit an application for planning consent') or adjectives ('The Consultant shall submit accurate and complete records of his findings').

[4] Such as, again, verbs ('The chairman refused to confirm or deny that a renewed bid for the Company had been received') or adjectives ('The disclosure letter appears to contain a number of deliberate or reckless misstatements').

background of how language is generally used and understood, the contract drafter needs to understand the subtleties of ordinary usage if ambiguity in contracts is to be avoided.

'And' can readily be used to convey a disjunctive result

8.6 If a speaker says

> If you want to go vegetarian, you can have the mushroom risotto, the aubergine tart and the vegetable curry

the meaning is understood, despite the use of 'and', as disjunctive: the listener is expected to choose one of the dishes from the list, not all of them.

In interpreting drafting, judges have sometimes come to the same conclusion: that in a particular context, 'and' does not bear its normal conjunctive meaning but is being used disjunctively. Often the context is that a list is being presented from which someone must make a selection. Some of the cases involve trust deeds where the trustees are given power to use the trust property to benefit particular objects or purposes. An example is the drafting in *Attorney General for New Zealand v Brown*,[5] where trustees of a will trust were directed to hold trust property

> for such charitable benevolent religious and educational institutions…as they…shall select.

If the adjectives here were regarded conjunctively, the meaning would be that only an institution that displayed all four characteristics could benefit. But the court held that this was not so. 'And' was, the court held, being used disjunctively, which led to the trust failing as a charitable gift because (for example) not all benevolent institutions were necessarily charitable, so the trust funds could be applied for non-charitable purposes.[6]

In that case Lord Buckmaster said explicitly that

> 'and' must be regarded as 'or'.

But this is, with respect, a misleading way of putting it. A better analysis is provided by Sargant J in *Re Eades*,[7] quoted in *Attorney General for Bahamas v Royal Trust Company*:[8]

5 [1917] AC 393.

6 The alert reader will identify that an additional linguistic possibility sees 'charitable' as an adjective qualifying a disjunctive list of three. If that were correct, the trustees could benefit any 'charitable benevolent institution', any 'charitable religious institution' or any 'charitable educational' institution they selected. This would be a sort of halfway house falling between a fully conjunctive and a fully disjunctive reading; but it did not attract their Lordships.

7 [1920] 2 Ch 353.

8 [1986] 1 WLR 1001 (PC).

> Such a construction... is sometimes referred to as a disjunctive construction, and as involving the change of the word 'and' into 'or'. This is a short and compendious way of expressing the result of the construction, but I doubt whether it indicates accurately the mental conception by which the result is reached. That conception is one, I think, which regards the word 'and' as used conjunctively and by way of addition, for the purpose of enlarging the number of objects within the area of selection; and it does not appear to be a false mental conception, or one really at variance with the ordinary use of language, merely because it involves in the result that the qualifications for selection are alternative or disjunctive.

This is the same issue that arises in ordinary speech in examples like

> The British Lions selectors should pick the best English, Scottish, Welsh and Irish players for their squad.

Each player has only one nationality, so 'and' here is necessarily being used disjunctively. The speaker is not suggesting that the selectors spend their time in a fruitless search for players who can each somehow claim to come from all four countries. But in this type of case, it is easy to see that the categories are mutually exclusive.

It was the feature that the categories were capable of overlapping in the case of

> for such charitable benevolent religious and educational institutions...as they...shall select

that caused the uncertainty in the *Brown* case.[9] And that case shows that 'and' can seemingly be used with a disjunctive result.

Are there cases which operate the other way round: where 'or' has a conjunctive meaning?

8.7 The case most usually cited in favour of this question being answered 'yes' is *Federal Steam Navigation Co. v Department of Trade.*[10] The language under consideration appeared in a statute rather than a contract, and was as follows:

> If any oil to which this section applies is discharged from a British ship, the owner or master of the ship shall... be guilty of an offence.

The House of Lords concluded that this language did not preclude *both* the owner *and* the master being separately guilty of an offence by reason of the same discharge.

[9] ibid.
[10] [1974] 2 All ER 97.

This case certainly demonstrates that the use of 'or' does not automatically signify exclusivity. But it does not follow that 'or' is being used *conjunctively*. A truly conjunctive reading would suggest that the owner and the master, viewed together, were guilty of the offence. But criminal liability is generally ascribed to individuals, not to groups of individuals.[11] Even with the offence of statutory conspiracy, which necessarily involves an agreement between two or more persons, liability is separately ascribed to each party to the conspiracy.[12]

An often unappreciated point: there are two types of disjunction

8.8 When it is said that 'or' sometimes means 'and', this disguises the true issue. The true contrast is not between 'or' being used sometimes disjunctively and sometimes conjunctively. Rather, the contrast is between two types of disjunction, a distinction recognised by logicians: between inclusive and exclusive disjunction.

An *inclusive* disjunction of A and B does not require that B is excluded if A applies. By contrast, an *exclusive* disjunction *does* require that B is excluded.

If a speaker says

> Either the fridge is leaking or Emma's dropped some ice cubes on the floor again

the context in which this is uttered is likely to be that, having found a puddle by the fridge, the speaker is offering what seems the most plausible explanation. The speaker may *imply* that the explanations are alternative, in that either on its own would account for the puddle. But although the word 'or' is used, the speaker is not ruling out the possibility that both explanations are true: (a) there is a leak, but also (b) Emma's dropped some ice cubes again. So this an example of inclusive disjunction: one limb does not exclude the other.

Contrast a sentence like

> Either someone's taken the keys this morning or I didn't put them back when I came in last night.

Again, two explanations are being offered for the phenomenon the speaker is reacting to, in this case that the keys are not on the hook where the speaker expected to find them. But the two explanations are mutually exclusive. If someone's taken the keys this morning, the speaker must necessarily have put them back last night. And if the speaker didn't put them back, nobody

[11] 'Generally' because exceptionally, it may be that groups of individuals, even if lacking separate legal personality (such as for example an unincorporated association), may be guilty of an offence: *R v L* [2008] EWCA Crim 1970.

[12] Criminal Law Act 1977, s 1(1) (as amended by the Criminal Attempts Act 1981).

can have taken them this morning. This is therefore an example of exclusive disjunction.

In ordinary speech, 'or' is often used to convey an inclusive disjunction. A speaker who says

> You can get the latest weather forecast from BBC Weather or the Met Office

does not imply that anyone who wants to compare what they say is somehow prevented from looking at both. And this is the explanation for the decision in the *Federal Steam Navigation Company* case[13] discussed above: when the statute said that 'the owner or master' was guilty of an offence, the statutory intention was inclusive disjunction (if the master was charged, it did not mean that the owner could not also be charged).

All this may not seem to matter much in ordinary speech. But when it comes to drafting contracts, it is important to be completely clear, including as to whether a disjunction is intended to be understood in an inclusive or exclusive sense.

The grammar of 'and' and 'or': a summary the discussion so far

8.9 'And' and 'or' have distinct meanings in ordinary speech:

(a) 'and' is always in itself conjunctive, but it can lead to a disjunctive result if it is used to join items in a list when the context suggests that only one of the list needs to be relevant;

(b) 'or' is always in itself disjunctive, but the disjunction it creates is capable of being understood in either an inclusive or an exclusive sense: the drafter needs to be confident that it is clear which of the two is intended.

PRACTICAL CONSEQUENCES FOR THE DRAFTER

'And': identify the straightforward cases

8.10 Unless the drafting falls within one of the danger areas identified below, it should generally be safe to use 'and' to express a straightforward conjunctive meaning. If a contract provides that

> A shall do X and Y

or

> A shall do X and B shall do Y

13 [1974] 2 All ER 97.

there is no doubt as to the conjunctive result that flows from the use of 'and'. In the first example, A has two contractual tasks to perform; and in the second, there are two contractual tasks to perform, each with a different obligor.

If the drafter wants to emphasise the conjunctive feature, the word 'both'[14] intensifies the effect if there are two items joined by 'and':

> A shall do both X and Y.

But with more than two items in the list, it is best to go further. 'Each of' can be used together with 'and' to make the position clear:

> A shall do each of X, Y and Z.

And 'all of the following', followed by a colon to introduce a list, demonstrates yet more strongly a conjunctive intention:

> A shall do all of the following:
>
> (a) M;
>
> (b) N;
>
> (c) O; and
>
> (d) P.

Any of these clearly indicates that the meaning is conjunctive.

But recognise when to use 'and' is to risk uncertainty

8.11 As noted above, doubts arise where an overlapping list of categories arises. It can then be unclear whether *and* leads to a conjunctive or a disjunctive result. But the problem can easily be fixed. For example, the language in *Attorney General for New Zealand v Brown*[15] could be rendered in either of two ways. The conjunctive meaning can be captured by

> The trustees shall hold the trust property for such institutions as they shall select, each of which displays all of the following characteristics, namely that it is
>
> (a) charitable;
>
> (b) benevolent;
>
> (c) religious; and
>
> (d) educational

14 Alternative language like 'in addition', 'also', or 'as well' would also work.

15 [1917] AC 393: see **8.6** above.

with a plainly conjunctive meaning: any selected institution has to display all four characteristics.

Where the intention is to convey a disjunctive meaning, the drafter is better to stick to 'or':

> The trustees shall hold the trust property for such institutions as they shall select, each of which displays any one or more of the following characteristics, namely that it is
>
> (a) charitable;
>
> (b) benevolent;
>
> (c) religious; or
>
> (d) educational.

Here 'any one or more' forces a disjunctive interpretation (and an inclusive one at that: 'any one or more' has that effect).[16]

Two other areas where 'and' can cause uncertainty are dealt with elsewhere in this work. The first is when 'and' is used to separate a list of plural obligors (at its simplest, 'A and B shall do X'). Issues arising here are dealt with from **7.21** above. The second is when the drafting involves conditions and the question arises whether they are cumulative or alternative. This is dealt with in **9.20** below.

Similarly, identify when 'or' is unambiguous

8.12 Some contract examples involving 'or' are reasonably straightforward. For example,

> Any notice shall be validly delivered only if sent by email or recorded delivery

does not mean that the intention was to disqualify a cautious party who decided to send a notice by both methods. In other words, this is an inclusive disjunction. Though the two ways of giving notices are alternative (or expected to be alternative), they are not exclusive. To use 'and' would be to court trouble:

> Any notice shall be validly delivered only if sent by email and recorded delivery

16 The two alternative renditions would it appears each have given rise to problems in the actual case. The conjunctive version would have been so restrictive as to 'all but render the gift inoperative' (ibid at [397] (Lord Buckmaster); but the disjunctive reading (which is how the court interpreted the original wording) caused the gift to fail as a charitable gift: see **8.6** above. But if the drafting had been clear, somebody might have spotted this before the will was executed.

would give the wrong impression: it could easily[17] be taken to signify that only a double notice, sent in both formats, would suffice.

Similarly

A shall do X or Y

clearly involves a disjunctive result. It could not realistically be argued as imposing a simultaneous obligation on A to do both X *and* Y.

But recognise when 'or' is problematic

8.13 As discussed, 'or' is used for disjunctions in both inclusive and exclusive senses, and the task for the drafter is to make clear which sense is intended. In other words, though with

A shall do X or Y

A is not obliged to do both X and Y, would the doing of X preclude A from doing Y if it also wanted to? This might be regarded as a possible implication of the common reading of 'or' as representing an exclusive disjunction, similar to the meaning of examples like 'They will catch the last train or come by taxi.'[18]

Again, with only modest changes to the language, the position can be made clear:

A shall do X or Y (but not both)

or

A shall do X or Y (and, if it does one, may also do the other).

Language of this type is arguably better than simply using 'either', which stands in some ways in relation to 'or' in a similar position as 'both' does in relation to 'and'. But

A shall do either X or Y

does not really provide a clear answer the question whether the doing of X should be inferred to preclude A also doing Y. It might possibly be said to suggest an exclusive disjunction slightly more than the version without 'either': it suggests more of a binary choice.

Furthermore, just as with 'and', the drafting of conditions raises questions in relation to the use of 'or'. Often the question is which of the two it is better to use. That subject is dealt with in **9.20** below.

17 Indeed, that is its natural meaning.
18 See **8.4** above.

Beware using 'and' and 'or' together

8.14 The above discussion relates to how to choose between 'and' and 'or'. But a different issue arises where 'and' and 'or' both appear in the same piece of drafting. The issue is best illustrated by an example:

> To qualify for its borrowings to be released from the Parent Guarantee, a Subsidiary must have net assets of at least £5 million at the date of release or post-tax profits of at least £1 million for each of its last three financial years and an opinion from its auditors that its financial position in the current financial year has not materially deteriorated.

This is not only difficult to follow: worse, it is ambiguous. The question is whether the auditors' opinion is needed only if the Subsidiary is relying on the profits test to secure its release from the guarantee, or is also required if it is relying on the net assets test. That both are equally plausible readings is caused by the presence of both 'or' and 'and' in the sentence, with no way of telling which prevails over the other.

As often happens with contract drafting, the cure is straightforward once the problem has been diagnosed. A simple layout change, together with separately lettered or numbered subparagraphs, can make the position clear:

> To qualify for its borrowings to be released from the Parent Guarantee, a Subsidiary must have:
>
> (a) net assets of at least £5 million at the date of release; or
>
> (b) post-tax profits of at least £1 million for each of its last three financial years and an opinion from its auditors that its financial position in the current financial year has not materially deteriorated.

On this version, it is clear that the opinion is needed only alongside the net profits measure. Alternatively, to achieve the opposite result, the drafter could provide:

> To qualify for its borrowings to be released from the Parent Guarantee, a Subsidiary must have:
>
> (a) net assets of at least £5 million at the date of release or post-tax profits of at least £1 million for each of its last three financial years; and
>
> (b) an opinion from its auditors that its financial position in the current financial year has not materially deteriorated.

It would then be clear that the opinion is needed whichever of the two tests in (a) is relevant).

To make the position still clearer, a drafter could consider adding some intensifying words immediately before the colon: in the first version, 'either', and in the second, 'both'.

'And/or': better avoided

8.15 It is common to encounter 'and/or' in legal drafting. But its use is not recommended. Quite a number of judges have gone out of their way to rail against its use[19] and, although some of the scorn heaped on the expression is arguably excessive, the wise contract drafter avoids using it.

The reason 'and/or' is popular with drafters is probably that it seems comprehensive, and saves – or appears to save – the drafter having to choose between 'and' and 'or' (which as the discussion earlier in this chapter may demonstrate, can be a surprisingly demanding exercise).

'A and/or B' embraces 'A and B' and also 'A or B'. In that simple form, the expression does not place excessive demands on the reader. If the expression appears as a condition, for example ('if A and/or B'), the reader has to accommodate mentally only three possible sets of circumstances: A alone; B alone; and A and B together.

But the difficulties of interpretation quickly multiply if the drafter is tempted to use 'and/or' more than once in the same contractual sentence, for example 'A and/or B and/or C'. The reader is faced with a thicket of possible combinations which are close to impossible to hold in mind simultaneously. Worse still, among those combinations are

> A and B or C

and

> A or B and C

which, as explained in **8.14** above, are themselves inherently ambiguous because of the effect when 'and' and 'or' appear in the same sentence. The range of possible combinations increases exponentially with the number of appearances of 'and/or'. And if a list is expressed by 'A, B and/or C', the reader is presented with an additional difficulty of ascertaining (or guessing) whether the unexpressed connection between A and B is itself 'and/or'.

It is fair to note that in one case, *Stanton v Richardson*,[20] the House of Lords were not troubled by these issues. They held that a charterer of a vessel who had a right (and corresponding obligation) to load a vessel with language equivalent to 'A, B and/or C' could choose to make up the cargo with any of the categories in any combination:

> These words 'and' and 'or' are not without some significance, because they appear rather to show that this specification of different kinds of cargo was to be read either disjunctively or conjunctively, it might be all of one kind, or it might be a mixture of the two kinds mentioned.[21]

19 Entertainingly collected in *'Andorandororand'*, an essay by Sir Robert Megarry appearing in Garner, *A New Miscellany-at-Law* (Hart Publishing, 2005).
20 (1875) 3 Maritime Law Cases 23 (H/L).
21 ibid at [24] (Lord Cairns LC).

That Lord Cairns refers to *two* categories of cargo rather than three (despite the original drafting being in the form 'A, B and/or C') makes it difficult, however, to be completely confident about the reliability of his reasoning.

In any event, the safer course, in a simple case where A and B are the only two possibilities, is to express 'A and/or B' as 'A or B or both'. This makes clear the range of possible combinations, and does so in a way that makes it less likely that the drafter will overlook the confusing multiplier effect of repeating it. Where more than two possibilities are involved, more elaborate language may be necessary:

> If any of the circumstances respectively referred to in (a), (b), (c) and (d) below apply (whether alone or in combination with any one or more of the others), X shall do Y.
>
> Those circumstances are:
>
> (a)...;
>
> (b)...;
>
> (c)...; and
>
> (d)....

Do not dispense with both 'and' and 'or'

8.16 It is dangerous to try to streamline drafting by omitting 'and' *and* 'or' if the question can arise whether two items are to be considered together or separately (conjunctively or disjunctively).

In a company's employment handbook, two adjacent sentences read:

> Changes [to the employee's terms and conditions of employment] can only be made by a member of the Human Resources Department and must be communicated to you in writing. When the change affects a group of employees, notification may be by display on notice boards or Company Intranet.

But were the requirements in the two sentences cumulative or alternative? Were the sentences to be read conjunctively or disjunctively? When a change was announced over the company intranet but not by a member of Human Resources, was the change effective? The drafter had failed to make the position clear, and the interpretation had to be determined by the Court of Appeal. [22]

22 *Dresdner Kleinwort Benson v Attrill* [2013] EWCA Civ 394. In all the circumstances, the court preferred a disjunctive reading: [51] (Elias LJ).

Chapter 9

Conditions

'Condition' is a chameleon term: grammarians use it differently from lawyers (who do not themselves use it consistently), though the respective meanings overlap. Lawyers refer to different types of 'condition', but the confusion this causes means that the term 'condition' needs handling with care. True grammatical conditions are best framed explicitly using 'if' rather than any alternatives, and with care over the word order within the condition. The able drafter distinguishes between cumulative and alternative conditions, and between trigger conditions and state-of-affairs conditions. Conditional drafting invites the question of what is to happen if the condition is not fulfilled.

9.13 Avoid more elaborate expressions: use 'if' instead

9.14 Some expressions serve to mask conditions, and are more dangerous still

9.15 Do not use 'provided that': sometimes equivalent to 'if', but sometimes not

9.16 Conclusion: 'if' language is preferable, and should be used consistently

9.17 Be sensitive to how to order the 'if'-clause and the consequence

9.18 Use 'if…then' for clauses in which the 'if'-clause comes first

9.19 Reserve 'if' for 'if'-clauses

9.20 Cumulative and alternative conditions: consider whether to use 'and' or 'or'

9.21 Do not omit both 'and' and 'or' in a list of conditions

9.22 Do not repeat 'if' in cumulative conditions…

9.23 …or, though it is less dangerous, in alternative conditions either

OTHER ASPECTS OF CONDITIONAL DRAFTING

9.24 'If P, then Q' drafting provokes the question: what if P is not the case?

9.25 The normal negative implication: if not P, then not Q either

9.26 Draft explicitly to make clear whether the negative implication applies

9.27 The negative implication where the consequence of P is permissive: 'If P, A may do X'

9.28 The tense of conditions: do not use 'if…shall'

9.29 Distinguish between trigger conditions and state-of-affairs conditions

INITIAL ANALYSIS: WHAT DOES 'CONDITION' MEAN?

'Condition' is a word with more than one meaning

9.1 When English lawyers use the word 'condition' in relation to contracts, they use it with more than one meaning.[1] Nor do they always distinguish between the various meanings. This is dangerous: with contracts, being clear is everything.

In order to understand the drafting techniques for handling conditions – in whatever meaning – it is important first to understand the range of possible meanings of 'condition'.

A drafter can best approach this by considering what a *grammarian* would mean by the term 'condition'. The grammar of the English language underpins everything that a drafter does, and it is only with a grammatical understanding that a drafter can handle 'conditions' – in whatever sense – effectively.

The grammatical meaning of 'condition'

9.2 One dictionary definition of a 'condition' is that it is a 'prerequisite' or 'prior requirement'.[2] This definition is familiar to the grammarian, who usually thinks of a 'condition' in that sense. A conditional sentence is what could loosely be termed an 'if sentence':

> If there's time when I get home, I'm going to mow the grass before it gets dark.

The speaker's getting home in time is a 'condition' of the grass being mown: the mowing is 'conditional' on this happening. Another useful word to describe a 'condition' in this sense is a 'contingency': the mowing of the grass is 'contingent' on the speaker's getting home on time.

A conditional sentence necessarily falls into two parts. One part – the 'if' part of the sentence – contains the condition in the dictionary sense of the 'prerequisite' or 'prior requirement'. The other part sets out the consequence that follows if the 'if' part becomes true.

A grammarian uses two technical terms for these two parts of a conditional sentence. The part that expresses the condition (in the sentence above the words 'if there's time when I get home') is the protasis.[3] The part that contains

1 In *Total Gas Marketing Ltd v Arco British Ltd* [1998] UKHL 22 Lord Steyn observes that '[t]his is a source of recurring confusion. But the prospects of persuading lawyers to adopt a more rational terminology are bleak.' This entire chapter might therefore strike the reader as overambitious.

2 *The Chambers Dictionary* (13th edn, Chambers Harrap, 2011).

3 Pronounced prot-er-sis.

the consequence if the protasis is fulfilled ('I'm going to mow the grass before it gets dark') is the apodosis.[4] These terms will be unfamiliar to most users of this work, so the term 'if-clause' (with the 'if' in quotes) is generally used for the protasis, and the apodosis is labelled the 'consequence'.

'If there's time when I get home, I'm going to mow the grass before it gets dark' is a sentence which is of course non-contractual. The speaker is likely to say it as a declaration of intention, but without any legal consequences flowing if the speaker has a change of heart and, even though arriving home in time to do the mowing, decides to do something else instead.

But contracts also contain many sentences that are conditional sentences in this sense. Contracts exist to regulate the parties' future conduct. Although the future is inherently unknowable, the parties want to regulate their conduct in circumstances that they can foresee as likely, or at least as possible. So most contracts contain a large number of provisions that take an 'if'-clause/ consequence form:

> If P happens, then A shall do Q.

A grammarian (or indeed anyone who is not a lawyer) would agree that this is a conditional sentence. They would naturally label the 'if'-clause ('if P happens') as a condition (in a 'prerequisite' or 'prior requirement' sense): P's happening is the condition for A to have to do Q. The satisfaction of the condition or 'if'-clause triggers the obligation ('A shall do Q') contained in the consequence.

But lawyers use 'condition' more widely

9.3 Lawyers would certainly recognise the grammatical meaning of 'condition' and itself describe an 'if'-clause as a condition. But lawyers have taken that straightforward grammatical sense of the word 'condition' and developed it in two ways.

First, lawyers have come to use the term to refer not merely to the 'if'-clause part of a conditional sentence but to the *whole sentence*: the 'if'-clause and consequence together. And as discussed below, they have even allowed it to extend further: not merely to a contractual provision containing an 'if'-clause plus a consequence, but to one that does not, but is simply in the form 'A shall do Q'.

This quirk of lawyers' language has tended to make the term 'condition' cover a much wider field, at the expense of precision. Perhaps sensitive to the feeling that they of all people ought to use language carefully, lawyers have attempted to remedy matters by classifying what they call 'conditions' into

[4] Pronounced a-pod-er-sis.

various types, depending on their various characteristics. They distinguish 'conditions precedent' from 'conditions subsequent'; they also use the expressions 'promissory condition' and 'contingent condition'.

All these labels are more easily understood by the lawyers who use them than by their clients, to whom they probably come across as a rank example of legalese. Any self-respecting drafter would prefer to be understood than to be resented. To draft 'conditions' of all these types in all these senses in a way that the users of contracts can understand, a drafter must first disentangle the uses of the term, with a view to seeing if the concepts enshrined in the legalese can be rendered in simpler language.

Legal meaning A: any contractual provision

9.4 The first way in which lawyers have stretched the meaning of 'condition' is to use it to mean simply 'a term in a contract'.[5] Non-lawyers probably think of this as the legal meaning of the word 'condition'. They are used to rapid-fire media advertisements which tell them 'terms and conditions apply' to an offer.[6]

When used in this sense, a condition could mean *any* term in a contract.

Lawyers who use 'condition' in this sense have moved on in two ways from the 'prerequisite' or 'prior requirement' meaning. First, a condition in this 'term of a contract sense' need not contain a condition in the grammatical sense at all. In other words, it may take the form 'A shall do Q' without there being any element of conditionality in a grammatical sense ('if P happens') at all: A's obligation to do Q could be absolute, intended to bind A in all circumstances. Second, if a contract term *does* contain a grammatical condition (so that it takes the form 'if P happens, A shall do Q') the lawyer sees the *whole* of the provision as a 'condition', not just the 'if'-clause part ('if P happens').

Narrower legal meaning B: a provision whose breach gives the right to terminate

9.5 Having thus widened the meaning of 'condition' beyond its grammatical meaning, lawyers then proceed to narrow it again. One sub-meaning of 'condition' in the sense of an entire contractual term is that of a particularly important term of a contract, breach of which entitles the

5 *The Chambers Dictionary* (13th edn, Chambers Harrap, 2011) (this is the first of the specific legal meanings of the word to be given).

6 They may well, if they think of the point at all, assume that the legal drafter is using two similar words – 'terms' and 'conditions' – to cover the same concept – a redundant double to which lawyers seem to be attached, like 'all and any', 'final and conclusive', and 'perform and discharge': see **11.9** below.

innocent party to treat itself as discharged from any further obligation to perform under the contract. That was the connotation argued for in the House of Lords in *Schuler (L) AG v Wickman Machine Tool Sales Ltd*.[7]

'Conditions' in this sense are a subset of 'conditions' under legal meaning A. And, like 'conditions' in that sense, they need not contain a grammatical condition (an 'if'-clause) at all. For example, in *Schuler* the obligation in the provision in question (to send representatives to particular customers weekly to solicit orders) was not dependent on any contingency or trigger. Nor, if a 'condition' in this breach-entitles-termination sense *does* contain a contingency or trigger, is the sense of 'condition' restricted to that part of the term: the *whole* provision, not just the contingency, is the 'condition'.

The grammatical meaning and legal meaning B overlap

9.6 Legal meaning B and the grammarians' meaning are connected in one sense. Under legal meaning B, if the obligation contained in the 'condition' is breached, the innocent party is entitled to be released from the contract. This is itself a conditional concept similar to 'if P, then Q'. The very survival of the contract depends on the 'prerequisite' that the provision that is labelled a 'condition' is *not* breached. But the analogy only goes so far. The contractual position is not that a breach of a 'condition' in the legal meaning B sense automatically brings the contract to an end. Rather, breach gives the injured party the *right* to treat the contract at an end. But the party may choose to affirm the contract instead, and if so, it stays alive. The contract is accordingly not truly 'conditional' in the grammarian's sense: its existence does not depend entirely on the so-called 'condition' (the obligation not being breached) being observed.

It is less easy to see any overlap between legal meaning A and the grammarian's meaning, though it is possible that a phrase like 'terms and conditions' reflects the idea that some contractual terms may deserve the special title of 'conditions' in the meaning B sense.

At this point in the analysis, therefore, three meanings of condition have been distinguished:

1. the grammarian's meaning: a condition is only part of a sentence: an 'if'-clause that must be fulfilled if the apodosis or consequence is to follow;
2. legal meaning A: a condition is any term in the contract, which may or may not contain a 'condition' in the grammarian's meaning;
3. legal meaning B: a condition is a subset of conditions under legal meaning A, including only terms whose breach can lead to the contract being terminated.

7 [1974] AC 235.

Attention must now turn to some other lawyers' terms including the word 'condition'.

'Condition precedent': another term itself used inconsistently (but distinguishable from 'condition subsequent')

9.7 'Condition precedent' is a lawyers' term, as the odd word order (adjective following noun) suggests.[8] A cynic might wonder whether lawyers who use the term to parade their erudition might sometimes not know exactly what it meant. The cynic may be right: the term is itself ambiguous. But in both of its meanings, the *grammatical* meaning of 'condition' is to the fore.

In one sense, a 'condition precedent' means a 'condition' – in the grammarian's sense of a 'prerequisite' – that must be satisfied before a contract comes into existence in the first place. Unless the condition is satisfied, there is no contract *at all*. The condition precedent is tantamount to

> If P happens, then A and B agree as follows.

This can be labelled 'meaning 1' of the term 'condition precedent'.

But a 'condition' – still meaning a 'prerequisite' – with a less radical effect is also sometimes termed a 'condition precedent'. With a 'condition precedent' of this type, the contract *exists* whether or not the condition precedent is satisfied. But unless and until it is, a *particular* obligation or set of obligations does not spring up. The condition precedent is a prerequisite or contingency on which particular obligations, or sets of obligations, depend. The condition is effectively

> If P happens, A shall (in addition to its other obligations under this Agreement) do Q.

This can be termed 'meaning 2' of 'condition precedent'.

Whether a 'condition precedent' falls within meaning 1 or meaning 2, it is a 'condition' in the grammatical sense – a prerequisite or 'if'-clause going to (in the meaning 1 case) a contract coming into existence or (in a meaning 2 case) the specified obligations arising.

The term 'condition precedent' remains in very wide use among lawyers. It seems likely that the origin of the phrase lies in lawyers' attempts to distinguish that type of condition from a 'condition subsequent'.

The term 'condition subsequent' is mercifully less common in modern legal parlance. It refers to a term in a contract that brings a contract to an end (or brings a property right to an end) if it occurs. In that sense, it comes close to a

[8] Other examples are 'decree absolute', 'letters-patent' and 'court-martial'.

condition within legal meaning B (contractual term which, if breached, gives the innocent party the right to terminate). But a 'condition subsequent' is usually understood to bring the contract to an end *automatically* (if P happens, this contract shall automatically terminate), rather than (as with a 'condition' in legal meaning B) giving the innocent party a right to terminate, but also a right to affirm.

Lawyers tend, however, to use the term 'condition precedent'[9] loosely. They sometimes use it to refer not merely to the 'if'-clause that represents the contractual trigger ('if P happens') but the whole provision within which it is contained. A lawyer might for example often say that a contract 'contains' a condition precedent, or that clause Z 'is' a condition precedent, rather than that the contract is 'subject to the condition precedent provided for in clause Z'.

In other words, though the grammatical sense of 'prerequisite' is central to what a lawyer terms a 'condition precedent', lawyers are not disciplined enough to restrict the meaning of 'condition precedent' to the grammatical meaning.

Promissory conditions distinguished from contingent conditions

9.8 Another lawyers' classification distinguishes 'promissory conditions' from 'contingent conditions'. This distinction lies along a different axis, and interacts with the concepts described above. Again, lawyers use the terms as a label for entire contractual provisions, though (as with 'condition precedent') the focus is mostly on the 'if'-clause part of the provision that represents a 'condition' in a strict grammatical sense.

A 'promissory condition', as its name suggests, is one which one of the parties undertakes to bring about as part of the contract. Fulfilment of the condition is part of the party's contractual performance.

It follows that a 'promissory condition' can also amount to a 'condition' within legal meaning B above, depending on whether, if the party who undertakes the promise fails to fulfil it, the innocent party may treat the contract at an end.

It also follows that a 'promissory condition' *cannot* be a 'condition precedent' within meaning 1. A 'promissory condition' represents one party's obligation *under the contract*, and meaning 1 of 'condition precedent' implies that no contract *exists*.

[9] And 'condition subsequent' for that matter, when they refer to that type of 'condition'.

A 'promissory condition' could, however, be a condition precedent within meaning 2. A contract exists; one party is obliged to undertake the promissory condition; if it does so, other contractual obligations will spring up.

A 'contingent condition' is one that neither party undertakes, as part of the contract, to fulfil. Or, if a party does undertake to fulfil it, it does so as an obligation that is collateral to the main contract.

Since, as explained above, a 'condition precedent' within meaning 1 cannot be a 'promissory condition', it will always be a 'contingent condition'.

A 'condition precedent' within meaning 2 may be a 'contingent condition'. This would be the case if a contract has come into existence, but some obligations lie in abeyance pending fulfilment of a contingency which neither party has undertaken to bring about (perhaps because it is outside their power to do so).

The plurality of meanings of 'condition' causes confusion

9.9 *Aspen Insurance UK Ltd v Pectel Ltd*[10] illustrates the difficulties that can arise if the term 'condition' is used carelessly – in that case, in two different senses within the same insurance contract, predictably leading to a dispute.

Various contractual terms were included under a clause labelled 'Conditions'. Not all these imposed an obligation on the insured: for example, one of them simply provided for English law to be the governing law. The drafter was therefore using the label 'Conditions' to refer to the terms of the contract in a general sense: in the language used above, the drafter was using legal meaning A.

But the contract also provided that

> The liability of the Underwriters shall be conditional on [Pectel] ... observing the terms and conditions of this insurance.

This was held to be using the word 'conditional' in its grammatical sense, referring to a prerequisite or 'if'-clause. Pectel had not observed one of the 'conditions' requiring it to give immediate written notice of matters giving rise to a claim. So the insurers escaped liability, though only after a dispute in court partly attributable to the drafter's indiscriminate use of the concept of a 'condition'. Something that foreshadows the recommendations below is that the drafting would have been clearer if it had not used the word 'condition' at all, but had provided straightforwardly that 'unless' Pectel met its obligations, the insurers Aspen were *not* liable under the policy.

10 [2008] EWHC 2804 (Comm).

DRAFTING 'CONDITIONS': GENERAL RECOMMENDATIONS

Do not use the term 'condition' as a label to describe a contractual term

9.10 If a contractual term recording an obligation is referred to as a 'condition', it is unclear whether legal meaning A or legal meaning B is intended. In other words, it is unclear whether, if the obligation is breached, the innocent party has the right to terminate the contract, or merely a right in damages for the breach. Ambiguity of this type is toxic for contract drafting. Whichever meaning the drafter has in mind, it is arguable that the contract overall supports the other meaning.

The risks run both ways. A drafter who has legal meaning A in mind may label all contract provisions 'conditions', without wanting to signify that any breach by the drafter's own client will entitle the other side to treat the contract as discharged. But the other side may argue that this is the effect, because *'condition'* in the contract should be interpreted to bear legal meaning B.

By contrast, the drafter may *intend* legal meaning B, wanting to signify that drafter's own client would be entitled to treat the contract as discharged if the other side were in breach. But the other side may argue that meaning A applies, denying the drafter's client the remedy the drafter hoped to secure.

The parties themselves may well not understand that the term has two possible meanings, and that the contractual consequences may differ depending on which meaning prevails.

Accordingly, recommended practice is for the drafter not to use the shorthand 'condition' when referring to a contractual term at all.

Instead of using 'condition' when aiming at meaning A (in other words, to signify a contractual term generally), the drafter should use a less loaded term like 'obligation' or 'provision'.

But a drafter may *want* to signify meaning B: that an obligation is so important that its breach can allow the innocent party to treat itself as discharged. To achieve this, it is better to avoid the term 'condition' but instead use unambiguous and explicit language. Explicit drafting of this type carries another benefit: the parties can readily understand what it means. Drafting along these lines might be considered:

> [In the definitions section]
>
> A 'Primary Obligation' means an obligation arising under this Agreement which the Agreement expressly provides is to amount to a Primary Obligation.
>
> [separate clause]

If

(a) a party is under a duty to meet a Primary Obligation; and

(b) that party fails to meet the Primary Obligation in full at the time the Agreement requires it to be met,

the party to whom the duty to meet the Primary Obligation is owed may bring this Agreement to an end by [stipulated procedure].

And, to confer the relevant status on the obligation, something like (say):

A shall, as a Primary Obligation, keep B fully informed of any circumstances that could cause the Subsidiary to cease to be entitled to carry on its business of manufacturing components for nuclear submarines.

Be sparing with other uses of the term 'condition'

9.11 As pointed out above,[11] to call a provision a 'condition precedent' is not to specify its effect. It might be a condition precedent within meaning 1, so that until it is fulfilled, no contract exists. Or it might have meaning 2, signifying that a contract exists, but that various obligations under the contract depend on it being satisfied. To label a term a 'condition precedent' risks creating uncertainty as to which meaning is intended.

The other expressions using the term 'condition' described above ('condition subsequent', 'promissory condition', 'contingent condition') are also best avoided. They may be useful lawyers' jargon for classifying features of contractual drafting. But users of the contracts may not understand their legal significance, and it is better to use a label that the non-legal reader can understand. Rather than calling a contractual term a 'condition' in a doomed attempt to describe its effect, a drafter would be better to use more neutral language to describe it, and rely on the actual language of the drafting to make it clear what it is intended to mean.

In this work and in particular in the remainder of this chapter, 'condition' is used mainly in the grammatical sense discussed in **9.2** above and appears without the quotes used in the discussion above.

Use 'if'

9.12 The clue to how a drafter should proceed lies in recognising that, in any case which involves an 'if'-clause and a consequence, the drafter is trying to capture what a grammarian would happily label a conditional sentence. Such a sentence is in other words like an 'If P, then Q' sentence.

11 At **9.7**.

This points to how such a clause should be drafted. Like any other provision that embodies a grammatical condition, the solution is to use 'if'.

'If' is the clearest word to frame an if-clause:

> If P, then Q.

'If' is, at a practical level, all but unambiguous. Although 'if' can also be used in the sense of 'whether' ('I am not sure if I am going to be able to come'), 'if' in this sense is always preceded by some introductory words (in this example 'I am not sure') that signal that 'if' is being used in its special sense of 'whether'.[12]

Drafters are often tempted by simple alternatives to 'if', but they are not recommended:

> This liability and indemnity is subject to clause 6.1.3 and, where clause 6.3C.1 is applicable, excludes loss or damage to any property required to be insured thereunder.[13]

'Where' here is equivalent to 'if'; but it is a word of wider meaning, so the simpler 'if' is preferable.

> In the event that the Purchaser nominates a Designated Purchaser the Purchaser agrees to guarantee [certain obligations].[14]

'In the event that' never means anything other than 'if', and, when used, prompts an uncharitable thought that the drafter never uses one word when four will do.

In *Charter Reinsurance Co Ltd v Fagan*[15] the drafting of a reinsurance contract took the form:

> The reinsurer shall only be liable if and when the ultimate sum actually paid by the reinsured…exceeds £3,000,000.

In the Court of Appeal, Nourse LJ observed that the words 'and when' added nothing to 'if'.

12 In *WS Tankship II BV v The Kwangju Bank Ltd* [2011] EWHC 3103, Blair J comes close ([113]–[114]) to denying that 'if' imposes what he rather quaintly calls 'a liability on a contingency'. But this observation is better seen in the context of the question that Blair J was actually examining, namely whether a *guarantee* imposed a primary liability or merely a secondary one. In reaching his decision Blair J refers to (and in this respect follows) an earlier decision of Beatson J (*Meritz Fire & Marine Insurance Co Ltd v Jan de Nul NV* [2010] EWHC 3362 (Comm)). In that decision at [75], Beatson J acknowledges that 'if' connotes a condition: the only question is to identify exactly what it means.

13 The language appears in *The Co-operative Retail Services Ltd v Taylor Young Partnership* [2002] UKHL 17.

14 The language used in clause 2.9 of the agreement in dispute in *Rhodia International Holdings Ltd v Huntsman International LLC* [2007] EWHC 292 (Comm).

15 [1997] AC 313.

Avoid more elaborate expressions: use 'if' instead

9.13 Expressions like 'where' and 'in the event that', even if not as good as a simple 'if', are at least recognisable as signalling an 'if'-clause. Less satisfactory is drafting which is intended to create an 'if'-clause, but disguises this from the reader:

> This order is given on the understanding that the balance of the purchase price can be had on hire purchase terms over a period of two years.[16]

'On the understanding that' really means 'if': 'if' would have been clearer. Similar expressions include 'on the basis that', 'in circumstances where', and 'on the assumption that'.

Expressions like this may hint at a condition, but do not clearly signify one. In *Capita Business Services Ltd v IBM United Kingdom Ltd*,[17] for example, the drafting recorded that 'it is assumed that' a particular IT service would be operational by a stated date. The following sentence provided that 'as such'[18] IBM's obligations to provide services would cease 'at that date'. But it was unclear whether the cessation of IBM's obligations was truly conditional on the assumption proving correct. And when the parties disputed the question, it was held that 'it is assumed that' was *not* enough to signify a condition.

Drafters also sometimes express what could be framed as 'If P, then Q' with the reverse expression 'Q is conditional on P'. This disguises the feature that the drafting deals with only one of two possibilities, namely that Q happens. The missing question is a type of 'What if?' question:[19] what if Q does not happen? This was what happened in *Total Gas Marketing Ltd v Arco British Ltd and others*,[20] Lord Steyn commenting accurately that the consequence was that the relevant clause was 'structurally incomplete'.

A drafter who uses expressions of this type would do better simply to use 'if'.

If the drafter does not use 'if' or otherwise signal unambiguously that a consequence depends on an 'if'-clause, a judge may well find that the linkage is absent and the drafting does not achieve a condition. In *Bremer*

16 The language used in *G Scammell and Nephew Ltd v H C & J G Ouston* [1941] AC 251. Admittedly it was not the use of 'on the understanding that' that caused the contract to fail for the lack of certainty, but the failure to nail down any characteristics of what hire purchase terms might be acceptable. But an outsider reading the case suspects that the parties may have understood more readily that the contract depended on them agreeing HP terms if the drafting had made the conditionality clear – by using 'if'.

17 [2023] 2623 EWHC (Comm).

18 A piece of linking language here used loosely and with uncertain significance: see ibid at [72(i)] and [73(i)] (Foxton J).

19 See Chapter 13 below.

20 [1998] UKHL 22: see n 1 above. The sale of an interest in a gas field in the North Sea was expressed to be conditional on various conditions being fulfilled, among which was that the seller became party to an 'Allocation Agreement', which it never did.

Handelsgesellschaft mbH v Vanden Avenne-Izegem PVBA,[21] the House of Lords considered the effect of a GAFTA form providing for: (a) cancellation of a soya bean export contract in the event of an export embargo; and (b) the sellers to notify the buyers of any such embargo. But the cancellation in (a) was not expressed to be conditional on the giving of notice in (b), though the two appeared in adjacent sentences. The House of Lords held that there was no true condition: the form of the clause was the first of the reasons Lord Wilberforce advanced for his decision on the point.[22]

The same conclusion (no true conditionality) was reached in *Lidl Great Britain Ltd v Closed Circuit Cooling Ltd (trading as 3CL).*[23] Even vehement language to the effect that a notice requiring payment 'must' comply with certain requirements did not mean that the validity of the notice was conditional on compliance.

Similarly, in *Paribas Trust Corporation UK Limited v URO Property Holdings SA,*[24] the right to a payment of a substantial premium on an event triggering early redemption of a loan was held not to have been lost by the lender's failure to certify the amount of the premium in the contemplated time frame: the drafter had not put any 'if' language in the drafting.

Some expressions serve to mask conditions, and are more dangerous still

9.14 The expressions discussed above may be less clear than 'if'. But at least they suggest to an attentive reader that a grammatical condition is or may be what the drafting is intended to express. More dangerous are expressions which disguise a grammatical condition as something else.

One example is 'nominalisation' – the use of *nouns* (usually abstract nouns) to convey the meaning of drafting. Lawyers have a tendency to overuse abstract nouns. They (the nouns) are often polysyllabic and, while they give the drafter a reassuring feeling of gravitas, are hard for a reader to understand. In *Royal Bank of Scotland Plc v Highland Financial Partners Ltd*[25] a 'Termination Date' in an Interim Services Deed was expressed to occur

> on…the termination of the Mandate Letter pursuant to the terms thereof and which of such termination is provided in writing by [one party to another].

21 [1978] 2 Lloyds Rep 109.

22 'Without such words [ie words importing conditionality], the second sentence does not obtain condition status' (Lord Wilberforce ibid at [113]; see also [120] (Viscount Dilhorne), [128] (Lord Salmon) and [130] (Lord Russell of Killowen).

23 [2023] EWHC 2243 (TCC): see from [47] (Stephen Davies).

24 [2022] EWHC 3251 at [121] (Jacob J).

25 [2010] EWCA Civ 809.

The drafting is, on inspection, obviously ungrammatical. It was held that 'which' was a misprint for 'notice', and the clause applied as if 'notice' had appeared instead. The grammar of the provision, even with the error corrected, is strained. But the main thing the drafter got wrong was to wrap what was truly an 'if'-clause – the termination would be triggered *if* a notice was given – into the abstract noun 'termination'. The drafting would have been easier to follow, even retaining the otherwise antique flavour of the original drafting, if the 'Termination Date' had been expressed to occur

> if the Mandate Letter is terminated pursuant to the terms thereof and notice of such termination is provided in writing by [one party to another].

In that version, 'if the Mandate Letter is terminated' would obviously have been an 'if'-clause: the original nominalisation 'on the termination of the Mandate Letter' was not.[26]

For another example of a concealed 'if'-clause, consider *BJ Aviation v Pool Aviation Ltd*.[27] The disputed language was contained in a seven-year lease of a small airport granted by the landowner to an operator. The lease envisaged that it could be extended for a further seven years

> subject to the renegotiation of the rent payable in no less a sum than that which shall be payable under the terms of this Agreement.

What this really meant was that *if* the rent could be renegotiated (agreed) at a rate no lower than the existing rent, the lease would be extended. In other words, the extension was conditional on (would not happen without) an agreement on a revised rent. But if, as happened, no agreement could be reached, the extension would not happen. The conditionality of the drafting was suppressed by the formula 'subject to + abstract noun': a straightforward 'if'-clause ('if + verb') would have been clearer. If the drafter had adopted that clearer and obviously conditional drafting, it seems more likely that the parties (particularly the disappointed operator which had sought the extension) would have recognised that the agreement did then not address the 'What if?' question: what happens if we do not agree on a revised rent?[28]

If it is desirable to use 'if X' language in making it clear what consequences follow if 'X' occurs, it is just as desirable to use 'if not X' (or, as it would be more likely to be couched in actual drafting, 'if X does not happen') to express the equivalent negative condition.

26 Though this is of course only speculation, it seems likely that the simpler and more straightforward grammar of the 'if' version might have made it slightly more likely that the typographical error would have been identified and fixed as well.

27 [2002] EWCA Civ 163.

28 'Subject to' caused a similar difficulty in *Blacklion Law LLP v Amira Nature Foods Ltd* [2022] EWHC 1500 (Ch) (fixed fee stipulated in solicitors' retainer 'subject to the completion of' a transaction by a stated date; when the timetable slipped, arguable that the solicitors had agreed to forgo any right to fees at all: see also **13.8** below).

Expressions that are less explicit than 'if not X' or 'if X does not happen' can be unclear: for example the single word 'otherwise' that caused a dispute in *Al Mana Lifestyle Trading LLC v United Fidelity Company PSC.*[29] A sentence expressing a general principle as to what laws and jurisdiction applied to resolve contractual disputes was followed by a sentence beginning with the word 'otherwise'. All the judges in the Court of Appeal were prepared to find that 'otherwise' meant something equivalent to 'if not',[30] but the drafter had not done enough to make clear what that really meant: to answer the question 'if not *what?*'

The point is that 'otherwise' stands on its own, and its meaning has to be inferred from the language to which it draws a contrast. Though 'if not' can also stand on its own, a drafter who recognises the need to be explicit in framing a negative condition will find that beginning the sentence with 'if' will naturally lead to a clearer result ('if X does not happen' delineates clearly in what circumstances the consequence follows).

Do not use 'provided that': sometimes equivalent to 'if', but sometimes not

9.15 Used in ordinary speech, 'provided that' often means nothing more than 'if':

> Provided that we can find a baby sitter, we'll go to the theatre on Friday evening.

Drafters, however, sometimes use 'provided that' as a more general all-purpose linkage. Often, if they want to add some language to an existing clause, they may insert the extra language and introduce it, clumsily, by 'provided that'. But they do not mean 'provided that' to introduce an 'if'-clause, just an extra piece of drafting.

This means that 'provided that' is inherently ambiguous. For example, a sale and purchase agreement might provide

> The Buyer shall keep Seller Group Tax Information confidential provided that the Seller shall deliver to the Buyer by 31 December draft tax computations relating to the Target for the year to 30 September.

The ambiguity can be seen by asking: what happens if 31 December goes past without the Seller delivering anything to the Buyer?

If 'provided that' is used in a conditional sense and just means 'if', the meaning of the drafting is that no obligations arise. The Seller did not have an obligation to deliver the computations before 31 December. It was entitled

[29] [2023] EWCA Civ 61.
[30] ibid at [27] (Sales LJ), [44] (Andrews LJ) and [68] (Nugee LJ).

to do as it did and not deliver them. But neither does the Buyer have an obligation to keep the Seller Tax Information confidential. The condition that would have caused it to have such an obligation was not satisfied.

By contrast, if 'provided that' was not intended to signify a condition but functioned merely as a more general all-purpose linkage, there are two separate obligations. The Seller was under an obligation to deliver the computations by 31 December, which it has breached by not having done so. The Buyer has in principle a remedy for that breach. For its part, the Buyer must keep the Seller Group Tax Information confidential, regardless of the Seller's own breach, and a failure by the Buyer to do so would be a breach on its part, triggering a remedy for the Seller.

The drafter has therefore left the position wholly unclear by using 'provided that'. What is needed instead of 'provided that' is 'if' or 'and', depending on whether a conditional or non-conditional meaning is intended:

> The Buyer shall keep Seller Group Tax Information confidential if the Seller delivers to the Buyer by 31 December draft computations relating to the Target for the year to 30 September

or

> The Buyer shall keep Seller Group Tax Information confidential, and the Seller shall deliver to the Buyer by 31 December draft computations relating to the Target for the year to 30 September.

A sceptical reader may think from the above example that the problem surely never arises in practice: that the context always makes it clear whether 'provided that' is used as a pseudo-'if' or is a more general linkage. And indeed, in many cases the context *does* make the position clear, as for example in *Steria Ltd v Sigma Wireless Communications Ltd*[31] where the judge was unimpressed by arguments that 'provided' language, in context, could signify anything other than a condition. But in *Burford UK Properties Ltd v Forte Hotels Ltd*[32] the fog of confusion descended.

A hotel lease contained a rent review clause which turned on the meaning of an expression 'Net Bedroom Revenue'. After defining what that meant, the clause used the phrase 'PROVIDED ALWAYS that'[33] before two supplementary paragraphs, one of which was that

> The Tenant shall at all times use its best endeavours to obtain the maximum revenue from the use of bedrooms as sleeping accommodation…

31 [2007] EWHC 3454 (TCC).
32 [2003] EWCA Civ 1800.
33 Equivalent, of course, to 'provided that': the extra word 'always' is a pointless piece of intensification. This type of language is often, as here, awarded capital letters in drafting, which may make it easier to see on the page, but which does nothing to help indicate what meaning it is intended to carry.

Was the phrase 'PROVIDED ALWAYS that' used in an 'if' sense, so that if the Tenant did not use its best endeavours as stated, the 'Net Bedroom Revenue' definition as set out was disapplied, leaving the rent review to be determined on other, more general principles? Or was 'PROVIDED ALWAYS that' simply a semantically empty piece of language introducing a free-standing obligation on the Tenant, and giving the landlord a right in damages if it was not observed? The judges in the Court of Appeal were divided on the answer, which is hardly a testament to the drafter's skill.[34]

Drafters are recommended to shun 'provided that'. To use it reflects no credit on their sensitivity to the use of language or their awareness of the risks of ambiguity.

Conclusion: 'if' language is preferable, and should be used consistently

9.16 'If' language also gives the drafter an opportunity to cross-check whether, in combination, all the 'if'-clauses exhaust the range of possible circumstances that might foreseeably arise, so as to make the drafting comprehensive. If the answer is no, the agreement itself is flawed.[35] There is a further benefit. The drafter's clients, for their part, are more likely to recognise that a given provision is truly conditional: that the obligation it provides for will not be triggered unless the 'if'-clause is satisfied.

The recommendation for the drafter is therefore to use 'if' to frame conditional language, and to do so consistently. That consistency is important. In a case where an insurance contract sometimes used the negative form of 'if' ('not...unless') in one clause but labelled adjoining provisions as a 'condition precedent', the inconsistency opened the door to an argument that the two formulations must mean something different.[36]

At a level of detail, however, the question arises as to how the drafter can deploy 'if' language as clearly as possible. This is the next issue to consider.

Be sensitive to how to order the 'if'-clause and the consequence

9.17 English grammar allows the 'if'-clause and consequence of a conditional sentence to appear in either order. 'I'll take an umbrella if it's

[34] For another case where 'provided that' caused uncertainty, see *Dunward Properties Ltd v Isaac* [2022] EWHC 3276 (Ch) from [44] (Adam Johnson J) ('provided that' used to qualify rights reserved by landlord under lease).

[35] Or, in Lord Steyn's expression in *Total Gas Marketing Ltd v Arco British Ltd* [1998] UKHL 22, 'structurally incomplete': see **9.13** above.

[36] *George Hunt Cranes Ltd v Scottish Boiler and General Insurance Co Ltd* [2001] EWCA Civ 1964. Though the argument based on inconsistency of language ultimately failed, it would not have been possible to advance it if consistent language had been used.

raining when I set out' (consequence first) is just as grammatical as the 'if'-clause first version 'If it's raining when I set out, I'll take an umbrella.'

Though this means that there is no grammatical reason dictating the order, is there any stylistic reason for a drafter to choose one version over another?

Unless there is a good reason not to, the drafter is recommended to put the 'if'-clause first. A reader who encounters 'if'-type language up front will grasp more readily that the drafting is truly conditional.[37]

This advice has a long pedigree. In the 1840s George Coode, a Parliamentary draftsman, published a monograph *On Legislative Expression*, which recommended adopting the same order for the drafting of statute law. His recommendations retain their force today.

To illustrate this, compare the following two clauses. The first uses Coode's recommended order (*if*-clause before consequence): the second does not but reverses the order:

> First (Coode-compliant) version:
>
> If, on any date falling before 1 January 2025, the Company's market capitalisation falls below £15 million, then the Contractor may serve a Termination Notice and require the Company to provide security for any amount of Contract Charges unpaid at that date.
>
> Second version (not complying with Coode):
>
> The Contractor may serve a Termination Notice and require the Company to provide security for any amount of Contract Charges then unpaid if, on any date falling before 1 January 2025, the Company's market capitalisation falls below £15 million.

These two versions have the same meaning, but most readers will find the former version easier to grasp at first reading.

But though 'put the 'if'-clause first' is a sound general rule, a drafter should be alert to whether the usual order might deserve to be reversed. One example arises if the drafter has to record a long list of disparate conditions. The normal Coode order would place these first, but a reader may find it difficult to retain them all whilst waiting for the consequence. The reader's problems are compounded if the consequence is itself short, as in the following example.

> Coode's recommended order:
>
> If:
>
> (a) the Company or the Contractor becomes insolvent;

[37] And an incidental benefit is that it makes clear that 'if' is being used to signify a grammatical condition rather than in the sense of 'whether'. A sentence where 'if' is being used in a 'whether' sense does not generally allow the clause containing 'if' to come first: we say 'The inquiry will establish if the correct procedures were followed' rather than (other than in a stilted, old-fashioned style) 'If the correct procedures were followed, the inquiry will establish.'

> (b) it becomes illegal, under the laws applicable in any territory in which the Company carries on business, for the Contractor to carry out the Services in that territory;
>
> (c) the Company ceases to carry on its business in substantially all the territories listed in Schedule I;
>
> (d) a third party makes an unconditional offer to acquire the entire issued share capital of the Contractor; or
>
> (e) there is a Change of Control of either the company or the Contractor;
>
> this Contract shall immediately come to an end.

Most readers would prefer the reverse order, which puts the consequence before the long list of conditions:

> This Contract shall immediately come to an end in any of the following circumstances:
>
> (a) the Company or the Contractor becomes insolvent;
>
> (b) it becomes illegal, under the laws applicable in any territory in which the Company carries on business, for the Contractor to carry out the Services in that territory;
>
> (c) the Company ceases to carry on its business in substantially all the territories listed in Schedule I;
>
> (d) a third party makes an unconditional offer to acquire the entire issued share capital of the Contractor; or
>
> (e) there is a Change of Control of either the company or the Contractor.

Use 'if...then' for clauses in which the 'if'-clause comes first

9.18 'Then' is a marker that helps to signal to a reader that the sentence is pivoting from 'if'-clause to consequence. It is optional: 'If there are apples for sale, then I'm going to get some' could equally be 'If there are apples for sale, I'm going to get some.' And 'then' is not even grammatical if the consequence comes first: 'Then I'm going to get some, if there are apples for sale' is not good English.

In a contract, drafters are recommended, if they put the 'if'-clause first, to use 'then': anything that helps to make the grammar of a contractual sentence clear at the first reading is desirable.

Reserve 'if' for 'if'-clauses

9.19 A drafter who uses 'if' for any purpose other than a true 'if-clause' risks confusing the reader.

For example, in *Re Golden Key Ltd*[38] a drafter used 'if' to introduce an obligation that followed inexorably from the fulfilment of an 'if'-clause that had been assumed in the previous sentence. The court plainly felt that 'when' would have been better than 'if' in the later sentence, because the first sentence had already assumed that its 'if'-clause would be satisfied. It was confusing to suggest an additional element of contingency that did not truly exist.

'If' is also ambiguous if it might bear its other meaning of 'whether'.[39] In grammatical terms, 'if' meaning 'whether' does not signal a grammatical condition, but an interrogative clause. In

> The weather forecast will let us find out if rain is expected today

the words 'if rain is expected today' do not mark a grammatical condition or prerequisite. The weather forecast informing us does not depend on rain being expected: the sense is that the forecast will tell us *whether* rain is expected. Indeed, 'whether' could readily appear instead of 'if', with no change of meaning.

In that example, the context is clear enough: nobody would read the sentence as signifying a true condition. But the context is not always so helpful. Consider

> X Ltd shall notify the Stock Exchange if it believes that profits in the next quarter are likely to be lower than the current quarter's profits.

This is ambiguous: 'if' might signify a true grammatical condition, or might be equivalent to 'whether'. On the reading that 'if' *does* signify a grammatical condition', X Ltd does not have to notify the Stock Exchange in any quarter unless it expects profits to decline. But if 'if' means 'whether', X Ltd needs to say something to the Stock Exchange every quarter.

If the drafter intended a 'whether' meaning and had used 'whether' rather than 'if', no ambiguity would have arisen:

> X Ltd shall notify the Stock Exchange whether it believes that profits in the next quarter are likely to be lower than the current quarter's profits.

It follows that a drafter should prefer 'whether' to 'if' when that is the sense intended, reserving 'if' for grammatical conditions.

Cumulative and alternative conditions: consider whether to use 'and' or 'or'

9.20 If an 'if'-clause contains multiple grammatical conditions, they could be cumulative or alternative.

[38] [2009] EWCA Civ 636.

[39] See **9.12** above.

If the multiple conditions are *cumulative*, all of them must be satisfied before the consequence is triggered. In effect there is a single 'if'-clause comprising (say) three limbs. In ordinary speech someone might say

> If I bring my passport, supply a copy of a recent utility bill and make an appointment, I'll be able to open a bank account this afternoon.

The single 'if' and the 'and' that precedes 'make an appointment' indicate this type of cumulative condition. The speaker has to satisfy all three conditions to cause the consequence to follow.

The contract drafter can borrow this technique:

> If
>
> (a) the applicable tax regime allows the Company to claim tax relief in respect of its expenditure on the Leeds Facility;
>
> (b) the Company has as a result surplus tax relief that may be surrendered to a Consortium Member; and
>
> (c) a Consortium member requests the Company to surrender an amount of the surplus to the Consortium member to set against its own profits
>
> then the Company shall surrender the amount in accordance with the request.

With this drafting, it is clear that the Company's obligation to surrender amounts depends on *all* of (a), (b) and (c) being satisfied.

A drafter may instead have to draft for multiple grammatical conditions that are *alternative*. In ordinary language, a set of alternative conditions might be expressed like this:

> If there's an unusually high tide, a strong south-westerly wind or heavy rainfall in the hills, that area by the estuary tends to be flooded.

Here we understand that if any one of these conditions applies, the area will flood: flooding does not depend on them all happening at once (though the flooding will doubtless be worse if they do).

The difference in the language is of course that the word 'or' rather than 'and' before the final condition connotes that the conditions are alternative rather than cumulative.[40]

Again, in contract drafting, the use of 'or' naturally leads to multiple conditions being regarded as alternative rather than cumulative:

> If
>
> (a) the Asset Coverage Ratio falls below 2.5:1;
>
> (b) the Interest Coverage Ratio falls below 3:1; or

[40] For drafting implications of the words 'and' and 'or' more generally, see Chapter 8 above.

(c) the Borrower ceases to carry on business as a vehicle manufacturer

the Loan shall become immediately repayable.

The Borrower here could not plausibly argue that all three of the conditions have to be satisfied before the loan becomes repayable. The loan is plainly repayable if *any* of the three conditions is met.

There may still be a place for 'and' with alternative conditions, however. The example drafting immediately above would mean the same if the drafter had preferred:

If any of the following conditions is satisfied, the Loan shall become immediately repayable.

Those conditions are:

(a) the Asset Coverage Ratio falls below 2.5:1;

(b) the Interest Coverage Ratio falls below 3:1; and

(c) the Borrower ceases to carry on business as a vehicle manufacturer.

The sense that the three conditions are alternative rather than cumulative is forced by *any*.

'And' can also help the drafter if a consequence follows if (say) two out of three specified conditions are met. The following drafting is unambiguous:

If any two of the following conditions are satisfied, the Loan shall become immediately repayable.

Those conditions are:

(a) the Asset Coverage Ratio falls below 2.5:1;

(b) the Interest Coverage Ratio falls below 3:1; and

(c) the Borrower ceases to carry on business as a vehicle manufacturer.

It would be much harder to achieve that meaning using 'or'.

The discussion above suggests that a drafter can make it clear whether multiple conditions are cumulative or alternative simply through using 'and' and 'or' correctly (admittedly placing a lot of weight on those short conjunctions).

However, with alternative conditions, there is room for a grammatical argument that to use 'or' can lead to an unexpected result. In the example

If

(a) the Asset Coverage Ratio falls below 2.5:1;

(b) the Interest Coverage Ratio falls below 3:1; or

(c) the Borrower ceases to carry on business as a vehicle manufacturer

the Loan shall become immediately repayable

assume that the Borrower fails both the Asset Coverage Ratio and Interest Coverage Ratio tests. It is arguable, at a purely grammatical level, that the Loan has *not* become repayable. The argument runs that the usual meaning of 'or' connotes that only *one* of the alternatives applies (as in 'you can choose to receive payment in cash, by cheque or bank transfer', where the implication is that you can choose one only). In other words, the grammar is a matter of exclusive disjunction.[41] This is so obviously uncommercial a result in this context that the argument is unconvincing. But a drafter should strive to avoid relying on commercial context or the common sense of judges: decided cases show that judges can differ about what commercial logic dictates.[42]

A drafter who wants to achieve a sharper contrast can consider making the position clear by some more emphatic drafting using 'all' or 'any'.

For example, a set of *cumulative* conditions can be signalled by

> If all of the conditions in (a), (b) and (c) below are satisfied, the Company shall surrender the amount in accordance with the request.
>
> Those conditions are that
>
> (a) the applicable tax regime allows the Company to claim tax relief in respect of its expenditure on the Leeds Facility;
>
> (b) the Company has as a result surplus tax relief that may be surrendered to a Consortium Member; and
>
> (c) a Consortium member requests the Company to surrender an amount of the surplus to the Consortium member to set against its own profits.

And to signal that the conditions are *alternative*:

> If any one or more of the following conditions is satisfied:
>
> (a) the Asset Coverage Ratio falls below 2.5:1;
>
> (b) the Interest Coverage Ratio falls below 3:1; and[43]
>
> (c) the Borrower ceases to carry on business as a vehicle manufacturer
>
> the Loan shall become immediately repayable.

[41] See **8.8** above.

[42] 'It is, I am afraid, not unusual that an interpretation which does not strike one person as sufficiently irrational to justify a conclusion that there has been a linguistic mistake will seem commercially absurd to another' (*Chartbrook Ltd v Persimmon Homes Ltd* [2009] UKHL 38 at [15] (Lord Hoffmann). By 'one person' and 'another' Lord Hoffmann is referring to judges: he makes the point in the context of discussing a division of views in the Court of Appeal in the same case.

[43] Note that 'and' is in this version preferred to 'or': the conditions now function simply as a list and 'any one or more' demonstrates that the conditions are alternative. Indeed, 'or' would be inappropriate since it would not sit easily with the conclusion that if (say) two of the conditions were satisfied, the loan should be repayable just as much as if only one were, because of the same implication as discussed in the text: that 'or' tends to connote exclusivity.

Do not omit both 'and' and 'or' in a list of conditions

9.21 If no linking coordination is used between 'if'-clauses, it is unclear whether the conditions are cumulative or alternative. For example, when a drafter provided in a lease covenant for the tenant

> not to assign the whole of the Premises without first
>
> (a) obtaining the consent of the Landlord (such consent not to be unreasonably withheld);
>
> (b) procuring that such sureties as the Landlord reasonably requires covenant [in specified terms]

the drafter omitted, despite having dutifully separated subparagraphs (i) and (ii) of the *previous* covenant by 'or', to make clear whether (i) and (ii) were cumulative or alternative conditions. The room for potential dispute is clear.[44]

Do not repeat 'if' in cumulative conditions...

9.22 While the use of 'and' to separate a list of 'if'-clauses therefore strongly suggests that they are cumulative, in ordinary speech a different sense is introduced if the word 'if' is itself repeated:

> I tend to sleep badly if I'm worried about a work problem, if I read emails just before going to bed and if I eat too much cheese after dinner.

Here, though a case can be made for a cumulative reading, a listener hearing this sentence is likely, despite the three conditions being connected with a final 'and', to infer that if *any* of the three conditions is satisfied, the speaker sleeps badly. At the very least, the repetition of 'if' has thrown the meaning into doubt.

A drafter should always prefer to create unambiguous drafting version. So if aiming at cumulative conditions, the drafter is recommended to use a single 'if' (as well as to separate the last two conditions by 'and').

...or, though it is less dangerous, in alternative conditions either

9.23 The problem that the repetition of 'if' causes for cumulative conditions does not arise with alternative conditions.

> If (a) the Asset Coverage Ratio falls below 2.5:1;

[44] Though, when this drafting came to court, this clumsiness was not in fact the focus of dispute: the drafting is from *K/S Victoria Street v House of Fraser (Stores Management) Ltd* [2011] EWCA Civ 904.

if (b) the Interest Coverage Ratio falls below 3:1; or

if (c) the Borrower ceases to carry on business as a vehicle manufacturer,

the Loan shall become immediately repayable.

This means the same as the earlier example appearing in **9.20** above without the repeated 'ifs'. Nonetheless the drafter is recommended not to use 'if' more than once. A drafter who gets into the habit of repeating the word 'if' in framing conditions risks doing so in the dangerous context of a set of cumulative conditions, and not just in the safe one of a set of alternative conditions.

OTHER ASPECTS OF CONDITIONAL DRAFTING

'If P, then Q' drafting provokes the question: what if P is not the case?

9.24 It remains to consider a common feature of drafting conditionally. A grammatically conditional piece of drafting in its simplest form can be represented by

If P, then Q.

But this raises a 'What if?' question: what happens if P does not happen: what if 'not P'?

The normal negative implication: if not P, then not Q either

9.25 In ordinary conversation, a speaker who says 'If P, then Q' may often be taken to imply that Q will not happen if P does not.

For example, suppose that a speaker says to a friend:

If it's raining when I set out, I'll take my umbrella

the friend might be at least mildly surprised if, even though the sun was shining when the speaker set out, the speaker still took the umbrella. But the speaker has not told an untruth. What the speaker has said does not in grammatical terms *entail* or *demand* that if it isn't raining, the umbrella will be left at home. The speaker might decide to take it to the umbrella-mender, perhaps, or have just seen a forecast warning that it might rain later on. The speaker not taking the umbrella if the sun is shining is in other words an *implication* of what is said, but no more than that.

So 'If not P, then not Q either' is sometimes an implication of saying 'If P, then Q.' But how strong an implication is it? Sometimes, the very nature of the condition may make it clear. If a speaker says to a couple of nervous teenagers

If the police come, you'll have to answer their reasonable questions

it would not occur to the teenagers to ask whether they had to answer the police's questions, reasonable or otherwise, if the police did *not* come: plainly not. But if a speaker says

If we go to the Rose and Crown, we'll be able to see the football on live TV

the negative implication (that if the speaker and his friend do not go to the Rose and Crown, they will not be able to see the football) is much weaker. There might be any number of other venues they could go to that would be showing it.

So in ordinary speech, the strength of the 'If not P, then not Q' implication of 'If P, then Q' is heavily context-dependent.

Draft explicitly to make clear whether any negative implication applies

9.26 Contracts exist to impose obligations. So in a contract, if the 'Q' in 'If P, then Q' is likely to be equivalent to something like 'A shall do X'; 'If P, then Q' is therefore equivalent to

If P, then A shall do X.

But what happens if 'not P' – if P does not happen? The one thing that it seems possible to derive about the 'not P' circumstances from 'If P, then A shall do X' is that if 'not P', A is not obliged to do X. If A were obliged to do X whether P happened or not, the drafter would surely not have made the drafting conditional at all.

In a contract that states 'If P, then A shall do X' the very strong implication, then, is that A's obligation to do X depends on the 'if'-clause 'if P': if A was obliged to do X in circumstances where the 'not P' circumstance applied as well, the 'if P' part of the drafting of 'If P, then A shall do X' would be superfluous.

But what else can one say about what the contract requires in 'not P' circumstances? If the contract does not provide anything about what is to happen, the question arises whether anything is *implied.* Lord Hoffmann reflects on this question in *Attorney General for Belize v Belize Telecom Ltd*:[45]

> The question of implication arises when the instrument does not expressly provide for what is to happen when some event occurs. The most usual inference in such a case is that nothing is to happen. If the parties had intended something to happen, the instrument would have said so. Otherwise, the express provisions of the instrument are to continue

[45] [2009] UKPC 10 at [17].

> undisturbed. If the event has caused loss to one or other of the parties, the loss lies where it falls.

But though this is doubtless authoritative in cases where the circumstance is simply not addressed, it does not deal with the position addressed here: where the contract *does* deal with the position where a specified event happens, but is silent as to what happens if the event does *not* occur.

One question with 'If P, then A shall do X' is whether, if circumstance P does not happen (or has not happened yet), A is impliedly required not to do X: in other words is contractually forbidden from doing X. Whilst this will not always be the implication, it could be the case:

> If the N Shareholder ceases to hold a majority of shares in the Company, A shall resign as director of the Company

may at least plausibly be argued to imply that so long as the N Shareholder holds a majority of the shares, A shall continue to serve as director and will *not* resign.[46]

One notable case where the implication is at its strongest that if P does not happen, A is required not to do X is if, by doing X or a version of X, A would be prevented from *subsequent* performance if P later happens. So for example, if A agrees to sell a valuable painting to Y for £1 million if Y can raise the finance by 31 December, a judge may well regard it as an implied term of the agreement, enforceable by injunctive proceedings, that A will not sell the painting to another collector for a higher price beforehand.[47] Options to acquire specific property are the most obvious examples of contracts carrying this type of implied term.

But implied terms are problematic for a drafter. They are created by judges, not the parties to the contract. A drafter's objective should always be to be explicit: what is written down can be thought about and discussed in advance of the contract being signed. Implied terms, by their very nature, will not have been discussed by the parties, who will not have turned their minds to their consequences. And as we have seen, they are heavily context-dependent.

The drafter should resolve the matter by being explicit:

> If (but only if) the N Shareholder ceases to hold a majority of shares in the Company, A shall resign as director of the Company.
>
> If the N Shareholder ceases to hold a majority of shares in the Company, A shall, if she has not previously resigned, resign as director of the Company.

46 See the arguments raised on similar language in *Bonham-Carter v Situ Ventures Ltd* [2012] EWHC 230.

47 Although here of course it is not a question of A being prohibited from selling the painting to Y: A is prohibited from selling it *at all*.

These examples illustrate that drafting to cover the 'not P' circumstance can be achieved economically – the drafter cannot excuse a failure to draft comprehensively by arguing that it would be too long-winded to do so.

Drafting that missed the chance to be clear about the position 'if not P' featured in *NIHL Limited (Virgin Islands) v Infinite Ltd (Jersey)*.[48] Paragraph 1 of a Tomlin Order[49] obliged the parties to use 'reasonable endeavours to reach a full and final settlement' of their dispute. Paragraph 2 provided that if 'such settlement is not reached', the claimants could enter final judgment. The 'if'-clause in paragraph 2 did not expressly refer to the 'reasonable endeavours' contemplated by paragraph 1. The court held that the 'if'-clause in paragraph 2 could not be read as if it included, as part of the condition, that the parties had indeed used reasonable endeavours to reach full and final settlement. The 'if'-clause in paragraph 2 was limited to the question whether a settlement had been reached. What was missing was something that built on paragraph 1 ('if the parties do not use reasonable endeavours to settle their dispute, then [consequence]').

The negative implication where the consequence of P is permissive: 'If P, A may do X'

9.27 The drafter needs to grapple with a slightly different set of issues if the consequence in a grammatically conditional piece of contract drafting is permissive rather than obligatory, so that the drafting of the basic provision takes the form not of 'If P, A shall do X' but 'If P, A *may* do X.'

Here there is a strong implication that A's permission to do X depends on P happening, so that unless P does happen, A must not do X: is in other words forbidden from doing X. But the drafter may not always intend such an implication to arise:

> If, on any Calculation Date, the Borrower's Cash Cover Ratio falls below 2:1, it may sell Specified Securities in the open market to raise cash in an amount that the Lenders' Agent, acting reasonably, considers necessary to restore the ratio.

There may be no intention here to signify that whilst the Borrower still has a healthy Cash Cover Ratio above 2:1, it is prevented from selling Specified Securities. Indeed, it would be commercially surprising if it were so prevented. But again, to eliminate any ambiguity, it would be better to make that explicit, perhaps by inserting 'without prejudice to its right to do so at any other time' after 'may' to make the desired meaning clear.

48 [2020] EWHC 3136.

49 A consent order which records the parties' agreement as to the terms on which an action is stayed, and which falls to be interpreted in the same way as a contract not sanctioned by the court.

The tense of conditions: do not use 'if...shall'

9.28 Critics of 'shall'[50] as a modal verb in contracts sometimes point to one particular ambiguity that 'shall' can give rise to in grammatical conditions. They point out that language such as

> If the Consultant shall commit a criminal offence, the Company may immediately terminate the consultancy contract

is unclear. What if, at the date the consultancy contract is entered into, the Consultant has *already* committed an offence? Does the futurity aspect of 'shall' signify that only an offence committed *after* the contract is signed will give the Company the right to terminate?

This ambiguity certainly points away from using 'shall' in framing the 'if'-clause of a condition. But only a clumsy drafter would do so. The grammar of a contract is rooted in the grammar of ordinary English, and in ordinary English, even if the consequence is in the future, the correct tense for the 'if'-clause itself is the present tense. A speaker would say

> if it rains (present tense) this afternoon, I'll take (future tense) my umbrella

not

> if it shall rain (future tense)...

This tense convention should guide the contract drafter:

> If the Consultant commits a criminal offence, the Company may immediately terminate the consultancy contract.

This is less stilted than 'If the Consultant shall commit', and is preferable for that reason alone.[51] But it is still not clear what the answer is to the question: what if the offence has already been committed? It is better to be explicit about the period within which the offence must lie if it is to lead to the termination right:

> If, after the execution of this Agreement, the Consultant commits a criminal offence, the Company may immediately terminate the consultancy contract

or

[50] See **6.3** above and also, for example, Butt and Castle, *Modern Legal Drafting* (2nd edn, Cambridge University Press, 2006) from [131].

[51] If the drafter wants to trigger a condition in advance of an event occurring, it is possible to do so by a careful choice of verbs: see *James Kemball Ltd v 'K' Line (Europe) Ltd* [2022] EWHC 2239 (Comm) at [22] (Mark Pelling KC) ('commits a breach' (present event) to be contrasted with 'threatens to cease' (future event)).

> If, whether before or after the execution of this Agreement, the Consultant commits a criminal offence, the Company may immediately terminate the consultancy contract.

If the perfect tense is natural in the 'if'-clause, there is no harm using it:

> If at any time the Company has, in its two most recent sets of annual accounts, incurred a trading loss, it shall appoint the Agreed Consultants to report on the Company's business prospects for the three following years.

This is better than, as you sometimes see, a strained future perfect tense which does not correspond to orthodox English grammar:

> If at any time the Company shall, in its two most recent sets of annual accounts, have incurred a trading loss, it shall appoint the Agreed Consultants to report on the Company's business prospects for the three following years.

'Shall… have' here seems designed to emphasise that the test is applicable not merely at the point of execution of the contract but also during the life of the contract.[52] But it is again much better to stick to conventional grammar and be explicit about the time constraints:

> If the Company has, in its two most recent sets of annual accounts (whether or not covering a period falling in whole or part after the date of this Agreement), incurred a trading loss, it shall appoint the Agreed Consultants to report on the Company's business prospects for the three following years

or

> If the Company has, in its two most recent sets of annual accounts that each cover a period falling wholly after the date of this Agreement, incurred a trading loss, it shall appoint the Agreed Consultants to report on the Company's business prospects for the three following years.

The recommendation above forces the drafter to pay attention to, and draft appropriately for, the period when the fulfilment of a grammatical condition counts so as to give rise to the consequence provided for in the contract. This issue arises not only at the beginning of the contract but also at the end. Is there a backstop date by which, if the grammatical condition has not been fulfilled, the consequence does not follow? Or is the position still more complicated? There could perhaps be various successive contractual 'windows' within which the fulfilment of the grammatical condition causes

52 For an example of this odd distortion of tenses in a disputed contract, see *US Bank Trustees Ltd v Titan Europe 2007-1 (NHP) Ltd* [2014] EWHC 1189 (Ch) ('No termination of the Servicer's… appointment…shall take effect unless…the Servicer…shall have notified each of the Rating Agencies…of the identity of the successor Servicer').

the contractual consequence to follow, but outside (or between) which it does not.

Distinguish between trigger conditions and state-of-affairs conditions

9.29 The drafter must also consider whether or not fulfilment of a grammatical condition is for contractual purposes irrevocable – so that once it has happened, the contractual consequence of it happening lasts for the whole of the rest of the contract term. One might label this type of grammatical condition an 'event condition' or 'trigger condition'. The alternative is that when the grammatical condition is fulfilled, the contractual consequence exists for a period that is coextensive with the condition remaining fulfilled: if the condition ceases to be fulfilled, the contractual status quo is resumed. One could call this a 'state-of-affairs condition'.

A classic example of a trigger condition is

> If an A Director dies, the A Shareholder shall appoint a successor.

The A director cannot come back to life. By contrast

> If, but only for as long as, SONIA exceeds 3%, the interest rate on the Shareholder Loans shall be 8% per annum rather than 6%

is a state-of-affairs condition. Even without the decisive language 'but only for as long as', it would be commercially reasonable to think that the higher rate on the Shareholder Loans should last only for the period when SONIA exceeds the 3% threshold. That would suggest a state-of-affairs condition: if the condition is fulfilled but then, later, SONIA goes back down under 3%, the lower interest rate on the Shareholder Loans resumes. And 'If, but only for as long as' serves to put the matter beyond doubt.

In the A Director example, both the 'if'-clause trigger and the contractual consequence (death and appointment of a successor) are one-off events. And in the SONIA example, both are states of affairs.

But a trigger condition can exist with a state-of-affairs consequence, as in

> If the Company is placed into liquidation, the Shareholders shall each continue to maintain a representative office in Finland, employing as many staff as at the date of this Agreement.

And a state-of-affairs condition can give rise to a trigger consequence, though more usually this takes the form of the state of affairs giving a contracting party an ongoing right to trigger that consequence, as in

> If and for as long as the Company's net asset value is below £15 million, the Bank may call for the Loan to be repaid on one month's notice.

A drafter should be careful to distinguish between these various possibilities. Failure to do so risks ambiguity. In *Napier Park European Credit Opportunities Fund Ltd v Harbourmaster Pro-rata CLO 2 BV*[53] the destination of proceeds from a loan securitisation portfolio depended on whether

> the ratings of the Class A1 Notes have not been downgraded below their Initial Ratings.

When the test fell to be applied, the Class A1 Notes *had* previously been downgraded, but had also then subsequently been upgraded and their 'Initial Ratings' reinstated. But the drafter had not made it clear whether the 'have not been downgraded' condition was a trigger condition or a state-of-affairs condition. If it was a trigger condition, it had been satisfied when the original downgrade occurred, and that was that: the subsequent upward re-rating was irrelevant. But if it was a state-of-affairs condition, the state of affairs (that the Notes had a lower rating) no longer subsisted when the test fell to be applied, with the opposite result.

It is noteworthy that the tense the drafter used was not enough to make it clear which of the two alternatives – trigger condition or state-of-affairs condition – was intended. In the High Court,[54] the Chancellor suggested[55] that the perfect tense was more consistent with a trigger condition: the downgrade was 'perfect' in the grammatical sense (it had been completed). But the Court of Appeal disagreed. The perfect tense 'have been downgraded' was, in the Court of Appeal's view, capable of a state-of-affairs reading which, in the overall context of the arrangements, made more sense.

It is clear from this that careful drafting is needed to make clear what might otherwise have been opaque.

For example, the verb used in the contractual condition may be important. Compare the following two clauses with superficially similar 'if'-clauses:

> If the Competition and Markets Authority launches an investigation into the Company's affairs, then [consequence].
>
> If the Company's affairs are under investigation by the Competition and Markets Authority, then [consequence].

The former can only sensibly be regarded as a trigger: the CMA cannot *unlaunch* an investigation. Examples of other verbs that are naturally taken as occurring once at a particular point in time are 'become', 'enter', and 'leave'. Particular one-off actions are connoted by 'sell', 'transfer', and 'dispose'.

Lombard North Central PLC v European Skyjets Ltd (in liquidation)[56] illustrates a drafter succeeding in making a condition a trigger condition. A lender could

[53] [2014] EWCA Civ 984.
[54] [2014] EWHC 1083 (Ch).
[55] ibid at [42].
[56] [2022] EWHC 728 (QB) at [79] (Foxton J).

accelerate the loan it had made 'at any time after the occurrence of an Event of Default'. 'Default' included any default in the payment of principal or interest, as to which time was of the essence. It was held that this was clear enough to allow the lender to accelerate once a default had occurred: there was no need for it to be continuing.

By contrast verbs like 'be', 'remain', and 'continue' are all redolent of a continuing state of affairs.[57] So the latter example ('If the Company's affairs *are* under investigation') throws attention on the investigation as a continuing state of affairs, and will naturally be taken at least to imply that once the investigation has been formally concluded, the contractual consequence, if it is itself a state of affairs, will lapse, and the contractual regime that applied before the investigation began will resume.

To spell out that a state-of-affairs condition is intended, the drafter in *Napier Park*[58] could have used express language ('the notes have been, and remain, downgraded') or language, such as was used elsewhere in the documents, of something 'which is continuing'.[59]

A drafter may therefore find that detailed vocabulary will help make clear the status of grammatical conditions as triggers or state-of-affairs conditions. But other techniques may also be needed, like the 'If, but only for as long as' of the SONIA example above.[60] And if the drafter wants to achieve a 'trigger condition' instead, clear wording could make it clear that any inference that a grammatical condition had a state-of-affairs meaning was incorrect:

> If, at any time when the Shareholder Loans are outstanding, SONIA comes to exceed 4%, the interest rate on the Shareholder Loans shall then become 8% per annum rather than 6%, and shall remain at 8% until the Shareholder Loans are repaid.

57 In *Napier Park* [2014] EWCA Civ 984 at [27], Lewison LJ proposed 'they have been married for twenty years' as an example of a case where a state of affairs is clearly meant: the statement is taken as necessarily meaning that they are still married today. But the verb form 'have been married' is in itself capable of a trigger interpretation, as where a speaker responds: 'No, they have been married already' to someone who asks, 'Are they still waiting to tie the knot?'

58 ibid.

59 See ibid at [42] and also **13.23** below. The meaning of 'continuing' was explored, in the context of standard form ISDA documentation, in *Grant v FR Acquisitions (Europe) Ltd* [2022] EWHC 2532 (Ch).

60 The phrase 'for as long as' is slightly preferable to 'so long as' which is, when used on its own, technically ambiguous between a temporal connotation and a simple dependency one, giving a sense of not much more than 'if' and appearing naturally in the context of what are truly trigger conditions: 'I'll be able to lock the house when I leave, so long as I find my keys.'

Chapter 10

Negatives

Drafters overuse negative expressions in drafting. Negative drafting is a recipe for confusion, particularly when more than one negative expression appears. Double negatives have one meaning in informal discourse, but another in formal writing (including contracts). Drafters should understand the grammarian's concept of the 'scope' of the negative and the ambiguity it can cause. Negatives can cause particular problems when used with 'and' and 'or'.

NEGATIVE DRAFTING OFTEN CAUSES PROBLEMS

Do not fall into the habit of overusing negative expressions

10.1 A mistake in framing a negative has the potential to be particularly embarrassing, since the negative form of a statement carries the meaning that is the exact opposite of its positive equivalent. So a drafting error is not an error of nuance, but a glaring mistake.

Additionally, a reader finds it difficult to grasp negative concepts, particularly when they appear more than one at a time. The consequence is that a sympathetic drafter needs to avoid drafting in a negative form.

Lawyers' reputation for obscurity may in part be attributable to a tendency to express ideas in negative forms of expression.

Some drafters may perhaps be influenced knowing that it is restrictive covenants that run with the land they relate to. And restrictive covenants are more naturally couched as negatives. A contractual promise not to do X unless circumstance Y applies is more obviously described as a restrictive covenant than a promise to do X only if circumstance Y applies. But leaving aside any vagaries of land law, the result of the two forms of promise is the same. Nonetheless drafters reach instinctively for the formula 'not....unless' when 'only if' would be clearer.

To phrase an obligation in a negative form can itself have unintended consequences. Under English law, exclusion clauses (clauses that exclude or limit a party's liability for breach of contract) are often restrictively construed. But a clause that simply delineates the scope of a party's liability is not an exclusion clause in that sense.[1] The distinction is a fine one.[2] But it is obvious that negative language ('X shall not be liable in respect of doing Y unless...') is more redolent of an exclusion clause than is positive language that circumscribes a party's obligation ('X shall do Y only if...').

Drafting in the negative obscures obvious errors

10.2 Because negative drafting is harder for a reader to grasp than a positive statement, negative drafting often allows crass errors to creep in. For example, an insurance clause that provided

> The Insurance by Section A (Buildings) and B1 (Contents) will not be validated by [any act or omission beyond the insured's control][3]

clearly meant to provide that the insurance remained valid despite such an act or omission, or in the drafter's negative phrasing 'will not be *invalidated*'. But nobody noticed that what the parties signed meant the exact opposite of what they intended.

And negative drafting can obscure other shortcomings that have nothing to do with the negative phrasing in itself. A reinsurance contract provided that

> No settlement and/or compromise...shall be made and no liability admitted without the prior approval of Reinsurers.[4]

1 *JP Morgan Bank v Springwell Navigation Corporation* [2008] EWHC 1186 (Comm) at [602] (Gloster J).

2 That the distinction exists is evident from the Consumer Rights Act 2015, s 31(3), which in the context of contracts affected by that Act recognises the distinction: 'The reference in subsection (1) to excluding or restricting a liability also includes preventing an obligation or duty arising or limiting its extent.'

3 *Seashell of Lisson Grove Ltd v Aviva Insurance Ltd* [2011] EWHC 1761.

4 *Beazley Underwriting Ltd v Al Ahleia Insurance Co* [2013] EWHC 677.

The negative phrasing seems to have prevented the parties noticing that it was unclear whether the modifying wording 'without the prior approval of Reinsurers' applied to settlements and compromises as well as to admissions of liability (a classic unclear modifier case of the type discussed from **7.2** above).

RECOMMENDATIONS ON NEGATIVE DRAFTING

Reduce or eliminate negative expressions

10.3 To recognise the attraction, trembling on the edge of addiction, that lawyers feel for negative forms of expression, take the common phrase applied to the granting of consent or approval:[5]

> not to be unreasonably withheld.

In these five words are embedded three negatives: 'not', 'unreasonably' (the opposite of the positive adverb 'reasonably') and 'withheld' (the opposite of the positive verb 'granted').[6] Drafters use this language without noticing that it would be possible to convey the meaning positively

> which [name of party required to give approval/consent] shall grant if it is reasonable to do so

which, even though slightly longer, carries the same meaning without multiple changes of direction, and is consequently more immediately accessible to a reader.

A more elaborate example, drawn from a decided case:[7]

> The covenant contained in clause 2.1 shall not apply to any liability to the extent it would not have arisen but for ...any...thing done after Completion (other than one the...doing of which was taken into account in computing any provision...for Tax in the Accounts...).

There are three effective negatives, represented by 'shall not apply', 'no provision' and 'prevented from being adequate'.

There is nothing technically wrong with this drafting, or at least it was not this drafting that caused the dispute in the case in question. It is not however

5 'Consent' and 'approval' are in fact distinct: *British Gas Trading Ltd v Eastern Electricity PLC* [1997] CLY 4950 (right to withhold 'approval' a narrower right than a right to withhold 'consent'): see **11.17** below.

6 This illustrates that some language carries a negative meaning even though it is positive in form: in other words, it does not contain the clear negative signal of words like 'not', 'neither', 'nor' and 'none'. In particular, some verbs embody within their meaning a negative sense, such as the example here, 'withhold'. Other examples that drafters often use are 'prevent', 'refrain', 'prohibit', 'preclude', and 'desist'.

7 *Ludgate Administration No. 1 Ltd v Northern & Shell Media Ltd* [2002] EWHC 1023 (Comm).

surprising[8] that a dispute arose out of documentation drafted with this degree of complexity.

If negatives are piled up like this, it is formidably difficult even for a trained lawyer to perform the mental gymnastics demanded by the repeated reversals of direction that are required of a reader. And for anyone else, the task is more difficult still. It must be doubtful whether the clients for whom this drafting was prepared can have understood it clearly enough to establish whether it coincided with what they intended.

The drafter should try to eliminate as many negatives as possible to allow a reader to understand more readily. Such a process might result in

> The covenant in clause 2.1 shall apply only to the extent that the liability exceeds any provision for it in the Accounts. In determining the adequacy of a provision, the effect of any increase in rates of Tax announced after the Accounts Date shall be ignored.

This reduces the negatives to one (the negative sense of the verb 'ignored'). Most readers will find this easier to follow as a result.

Do not use double negatives

10.4 It is sometimes argued that the grammar of negative expression reflects mathematical conventions, in that the negative of a negative statement is tantamount to a positive. Prescriptive grammarians (those who are more concerned as much to 'correct' speakers than to understand them) use this argument to assert that the informal speech patterns of

> I never done nothing to hurt them

(though obviously intended by the speaker as a defence) is in reality a self-accusation, the two negatives of 'never' and 'nothing' cancelling each other out, and carrying the meaning that the speaker *did* do something to hurt them. But this is, it is submitted, a futile attempt at points-scoring. The speaker is plainly intending the utterance to be understood in a negative sense, and there is a tradition going back to Chaucer and Shakespeare of double negatives being used to emphasise, rather than undermine, the negative meaning of a sentence.

The type of emphatic double negative just discussed is, however, a characteristic of informal speech, and does not feature in more formal contexts. Contracts are formal documents, and in such a setting each negative is regarded as having its own significance. Accordingly, in drafting that provides that a joint venture shareholder X

[8] With the author's apology for the negative.

> shall not take any action in its capacity as shareholder that will not promote the interests of the Company

the two negatives respectively represented by 'not' will each be taken to have a separate significance, not to reinforce one another in the emphatic way that informal speech sometimes allows.

If, when a contract drafter serves up two (or more) negatives, they will be respected as negations, the recommendation in this paragraph to avoid double negatives may come across as unnecessary.

However, it can be difficult to establish exactly what a double negative means. The example above

> [X] shall not take any action in its capacity of shareholder that will not promote the interests of the Company

contains a double negative, obvious from the repeated 'not'. But the drafting does not impose a positive obligation on X to promote the interests of the Company. Indeed, it imposes no positive obligation *at all*. Rather, it is a prohibition: X is forbidden from doing anything as a shareholder that is counter to the interests of the Company.

It is easy for this to be missed on a superficial reading. It is easier for a reader to grasp the meaning of a sentence phrased positively. If the intention is to impose a positive obligation, it is best expressed as such

> X shall act as shareholder to promote the interests of the Company.

And if the intention is to preserve the same meaning as the drafting that features the double negative, that too can be expressed positively:

> X shall only take any action in its capacity as shareholder of the Company if the action promotes the interests of the Company.

Most readers will find that sentence easier to follow than the version containing the double negative. And all other things being equal, a drafter should always prefer language that a reader will understand.

Be conscious of the grammatical concept of the 'scope' of the negative

10.5 Clear drafting involving negative language requires that it is clear how far the negation extends. In grammatical terms the issue is the 'scope' of the negative,[9] a close cousin to the more general issue of how far modifying language extends.[10]

9 See Huddleston and Pullum, *The Cambridge Grammar of the English Language* (Cambridge University Press, 2016) at [790-9].

10 See from **7.2** above.

Take language from a non-contractual context such as

> All the aircraft in the squadron are not airworthy.

This is ambiguous between two possible meanings. One meaning is that *none* of the aircraft – not a single aircraft in the squadron – is airworthy. Here the scope of the negative (the words it affects within the grammar of the sentence) is narrow: it is confined to 'airworthy'. But the sentence is also capable of meaning that while some of the aircraft may be airworthy, it is not the case that all of them are. Here the negative represented by 'not' is said by grammarians to have wide scope over the whole of the rest of the sentence including 'all'.[11]

An example of this issue causing a dispute in practice is *McGeown v Direct Travel Insurance*.[12] A travel insurance policy promised to pay the insured £50,000 for a permanent physical disability on terms that

> If you are in paid work, we will provide the same cover for any permanent disability which prevents you from doing all your usual activities.

Mrs McGeown, who had taken out the policy, suffered an accident. Although afterwards she was able to do *some* of the activities she had previously enjoyed, there were some of them that she could not manage. Though the language of the insurance policy was not explicitly framed using negative language, 'prevent' is a verb that carried a negative meaning[13] ('which prevents you from doing' is equivalent to 'which means that you cannot do').

So the dispute was about the scope of the negative. Was the sense of the drafting (as Mrs McGeown argued) that she was covered even though she could still do some of what she used to be able to do? Or was it the other way round, so that (as the insurers maintained) she was covered only if she could show that *all* her usual activities were ones she could *not* now do?[14]

As so often, solving the problem is easier than identifying it in the first place. Some additional language would have made it clear what the scope of the negative is:

> Not a single aircraft in the squadron is airworthy.
>
> Not all the aircraft in the squadron are airworthy, though some may be.
>
> If you are in paid work, we will provide the same cover for any permanent disability which has the effect that none of your usual activities remains possible.

11 The scope of the negative is, it may be noted, why the language 'may not' is not recommended in drafting: see **6.6** above.

12 [2003] EWCA Civ 1606.

13 See n 6 above.

14 The insurers' arguments prevailed, but only because of clues from the remainder of the policy: the drafting of the clause itself was genuinely ambiguous.

> If you are in paid work, we will provide the same cover for any permanent disability which has the effect that, even if you remain able to do some of your usual activities, you are longer able to do all of them.

Drafters are recommended to be alert to the possibility that their drafting, if in a negative form, may not make it clear how far the scope of the negative extends.

Take care with negative clauses involving 'and' and 'or'

10.6 As discussed in Chapter 8, the words 'and' and 'or' can be used in ways that do not make it easy to interpret what is meant. But when 'and' and 'or' are used in a negative formulation, the hazards multiply.

The normal disjunctive meaning of 'or' ('her mother was in her forties or fifties'[15]) switches when both elements of the coordination are within the scope of the negative. A sentence in the form

> He won't eat meat or dairy

is normally equivalent in meaning to two negatives separated by 'and':

> He won't eat meat and he won't eat dairy either.

But it is possible for

> He won't eat meat or dairy

to have a different meaning, equivalent to

> He either won't eat meat or he won't eat dairy, I can't remember which.

So there is an ambiguity.

With 'and', a similar issue arises. The normal effect of 'and' in positive speech is conjunctive:

> The chairman is fluent in Dutch and English

means he can speak both languages. Often a negative in connection with 'and' is equivalent to a combination of two negative statements:

> I couldn't find my passport and tickets anywhere

is equivalent to

> I couldn't find my passport and I couldn't find my tickets.

It thus has the same meaning as the same sentence using 'or' instead of 'and':

> I couldn't find my passport or tickets anywhere

[15] Clearly disjunctive because she cannot be both.

with perhaps a flavour, if the 'and' version is preferred, that the speaker thought they had been left in the same place.

But things are not always that simple. A sentence in the form

> He can't be chairman and chief executive

is not taken as equivalent to

> He can't be chairman and he can't be chief executive either.

Instead, the speaker is taken as meaning that what is forbidden is that he has both posts at the same time.

There is therefore scope for ambiguity when a sentence in the negative features either 'and' or 'or', which can cause contractual drafting to go awry. An ambiguity of this type duly surfaced in *Gan Insurance Ltd v Tai Ping Insurance Co Ltd*.[16] A reinsurance contract included, in apparently common language:[17]

> It is a condition precedent to any liability under this Policy that....no settlement and/or compromise shall be made and liability admitted without the prior approval of Reinsurers.

The question arose: what happened if one limb of the coordination was satisfied (a settlement and/or compromise had been made) but the other was not (no liability had been admitted)? The courts made slightly heavy weather of this, perhaps hindered by phrasing the question in terms of whether there had been a *breach* of the provision when the contract did not impose an obligation on the reinsured not to compromise, but simply exonerated the reinsurers if they did so. In the High Court, the decision was that the reinsurers remained on the hook, but the Court of Appeal reversed that decision. In effect what the Court of Appeal said was (surely correctly) that the provision was equivalent to a cumulative negative condition: the reinsurers' liability depended on: (a) no settlement and/or compromise having been reached; and (b) no liability having been admitted either. Though (b) was satisfied, (a) was not, and so the condition precedent was not satisfied.[18] It would have been clearer, in fact, if the drafter had preferred to use 'or':

> It is a condition precedent to any liability under this Policy that....no settlement or compromise shall be made or liability admitted without the prior approval of Reinsurers

would have led, rather more clearly, to the same result.

The moral is that a drafter should therefore consider particularly carefully when choosing between 'and' and 'or' in a negative clause.

16 [2001] EWCA Civ 1047.

17 A version of which duly resurfaced in *Beazley Underwriting Ltd v Al Ahleia Insurance Co* [2013] EWHC 677: see **10.2** above.

18 [2001] EWCA Civ 1047 at [15] (Mance LJ).

Chapter 11

The right words

The wide vocabulary of the English language presents the drafter with many choices. The drafter should strive for clarity, which is not guaranteed by using precedents or drafting in the second person. Word order matters. Modern, straightforward language is better than old-fashioned legalese or Latin. A single word can have various meanings, one of which is favoured in a legal or business context: the drafter needs to be clear which meaning is intended. Particular care is needed with expression of time. The drafter should not choose a word with too wide or too narrow a meaning; should be sensitive to nuances of meaning; and should use words consistently within the contract. The drafter should not hesitate to use the obvious word, and should be consistent in the level of detail; every word counts. No special rules apply for parties who are not adept in English. Spell-check is no panacea.

THE ENGLISH LANGUAGE: SIMULTANEOUSLY OPPORTUNITY AND THREAT

11.1 The English language is notoriously a mongrel. English speakers use words that have entered the language over centuries from many other languages. The English used by lawyers has developed alongside the language used by everyone else, and from time to time has taken a different path. In medieval and early modern England, for example, Latin and Norman French were used in the law far more than they were used outside it.

The richness of English means that the drafter is often faced with a choice between different words, each of which carries a slightly different nuance. In one sense this gives the drafter a valuable opportunity. The right word can capture the drafter's intended meaning precisely. But for the unskilful drafter, the choice is a threat. A drafter who is insensitive to subtleties of meaning may, by choosing the wrong word, cause the contract to miss the mark, giving rise to confusion and the possibility of an expensive dispute.

This book is not intended to rival a judicial dictionary. Judicial dictionaries are valuable resources that illustrate how often judges strive to discern the meaning of a contract by examining the possible shades of meaning inherent in a particular word. Hours of court time, coming at a frightening cost for one party or another, can be spent on the meaning of a word that the drafter paid scarcely any thought to when including it in the contract.

But that is the wrong way round. If the drafter had made the effort to choose the right word in the first place, the meaning should have been clear, and the dispute avoided. Lawyers are often derided for being pedantic: for over-concentrating on the minutiae of language. But this trait is in this context a strength. If lawyers use enough care about the language they use, they are more likely, when drafting a contract, to frame provisions that precisely record the parties' consensus. And that is what they are paid to do.

This chapter is intended to help the drafter select the right words. Many of the recommendations here are quite obvious, and the reader may feel that each on its own is not such that to ignore it risks the silk purse of effective drafting crumpling into a sow's ear of incoherence. That may be so, but a reading of the case law suggests that cumulatively, good choices can make a significant difference.

FOUR GENERAL PRINCIPLES

Spell out what you mean

11.2 One overarching theme of this work is that drafters should aim to be explicit about what they want to convey. Contracts are not the place for a writer to rely on the reader inferring what is intended: the risk is that different readers may draw different inferences.

This principle applies at the detailed level to the choice of words and expressions as much as it applies more generally. The drafter should be wary of assuming that even a simple and familiar word will always be clear enough to carry its obvious meaning in any particular contractual context.

Take for example a simple word such as 'pay'.

In *Charter Reinsurance v Fagan*[1] the House of Lords considered the phrase 'actually paid' in a reinsurance contract, persuading themselves[2] that in that context 'actually paid' did not connote a transfer of money. It connoted merely a *liability* to pay.

1 [1997] AC 313.

2 Despite a forceful dissenting judgment from Staughton LJ in the Court of Appeal [1996] 1 Lloyd's Rep 261 who objected 'There must come a time when efforts to bend meaning (or, as I would say, reverse it) have to stop.'

Drafters considering the result of that case must feel dispirited. What more could the drafter have done to achieve the opposite effect? But there is one lesson to be learned. In considering precedents, the courts noted that in an earlier case[3] a drafter had used a more expansive phrase 'shall have become liable to pay and shall in fact have paid'. There the opposite conclusion was reached. It was clear that the phrase 'shall in fact have paid' must mean something more than simply 'shall have become *liable* to pay'. By expanding the language so as to illustrate that 'shall in fact have paid' meant something going beyond mere liability to pay, the drafter had made it clear that 'pay' had its more familiar meaning of an actual transfer of funds.

An echo of this issue can be discerned in the drafting considered by the Supreme Court in *Sara and Hossein Asset Holdings Ltd v Blacks Outdoor Retail Ltd*,[4] this time in the context of the conclusiveness of a landlord's certificate in a lease in the absence of 'manifest or mathematical error or fraud'. Again, the drafting did not explicitly distinguish between an obligation to pay an amount over in cash (to protect the payee's cash position) and an underlying liability to pay. That the same issue can arise in such different contexts, both times needing the highest court in the land to resolve it, suggests that drafters should be particularly on their guard to make sure that they distinguish clearly between a liability to make a payment in cash and the delivery of cash in satisfaction of that liability.

These cases carry an important lesson for drafters, not just when they are dealing with this particular issue but in the task of drafting more generally. If what they write is explicit enough, they can reduce the risk of black being held in context to mean white (as some, including Staughton LJ, would argue happened in *Charter Reinsurance*). The drafter is not helpless in the face of an inventive judge. The drafter who writes 'black but not white' may perhaps be accused of overdoing things. But by being what may seem at first glance unnecessarily explicit, the drafter may have forestalled a dispute.

Do not assume that language is clear just because it is contained in a precedent

11.3 The respect for precedent embedded in the common law breeds conservatism among the lawyers who practise it. Drafters are often tempted to believe that language that has been used in an earlier contract is in some way safer than language they choose themselves. If someone suggests new language, the drafter resists change by arguing that the language, having been used in earlier contracts, has either not been litigated (so that it must

3 *Firma C-Trade S.A. v Newcastle Protection and Indemnity Association (The Fanti)* [1991] 2 AC 1.
4 [2023] UKSC 2.

be dispute-proof)[5] or that it has been litigated and so its meaning is clear. On either basis it would be foolhardy to change it.

This stance deserves to be treated sceptically. Many drafters cannot, with any particular form of words, explain which of two directly contradictory propositions applies to any particular piece of language. In any case, the premiss is flawed. That language has not been litigated yet does not mean that it cannot be disputed in the future: a lawyer should not be playing Russian roulette. And it is dangerous to assume that because a particular form of language has been interpreted in one way in the context of a particular contract, its meaning is fixed. Judges emphasise that their interpretation of what particular words mean in a particular contract is heavily dependent on the context of that particular contract: in another contract, they might not mean the same thing at all.[6]

Do not assume that second person drafting is automatically clear

11.4 Most contractual drafting is in grammatical terms written in the *third person*. The contract is not addressed by one party to another. Instead, both parties are referred to neutrally and separately.

Sometimes, however, drafters formulate their contracts in terms of one party addressing another. The contract then takes the form of a mixture of first person (the party from whom the contract is drafted as emanating usually referred to as 'we') and second person (the party addressed, recast as 'you').[7] The technique is most common in consumer contracts, where the usual technique is for the drafting to come from the corporate supplier of services as 'we' and the consumer addressed as 'you'. This drafting style is attributable to a wish, commendable in itself, to make the contract more accessible and comprehensible to readers who might be thought likely to be intimidated by the formality of more orthodox third person drafting.

Whatever its tonal advantages, drafting in the first and second person is no guarantee of clarity. For example, in *Investors Compensation Scheme*[8] the drafting

5 The absence of positive evidence of X being taken as proof that X could not exist: a fallacy similar to that which prompted people to argue that a black swan could not exist.

6 See, for example, *Hawley v Luminar Leisure Ltd* [2006] EWCA Civ 18 at [103] (Hallett LJ) (dispute over whether an injury suffered in a late night fracas was 'accidental' or 'fortuitous' for the purposes of an insurance policy).

7 Although in the document considered one landmark case on the interpretation of contracts, *Investors Compensation Scheme v West Bromwich Building Society (no. 1)* [1998] 1 WLR 896, the Investors Compensation Scheme preferred a halfway house, referring to itself in the third person as 'ICS' but addressing the investor as 'you'.

8 ibid: Lord Hoffmann's judgment remains a landmark exposition of the courts' approach to how to interpret documents.

of a declaration by an investor was addressed to the investor by the Investors Compensation Scheme. That did not save it from incoherence:

> I.C.S agrees that the following...claims shall enure to you absolutely: Any claim (whether sounding in rescission for undue influence or otherwise) that you have or may have against the West Bromwich Building Society.

The bracketed words did not, on analysis, appear to make any sense, and the House of Lords held that 'something must have gone wrong with the drafting'.[9]

A slightly different danger of second person drafting emerges from *Laemthong International Lines Company v Fahem.*[10] A letter of indemnity written in the second person was expressed to indemnify *you, your servants and agents*. The consequence of the use of the second person is that it raises the question of who is the 'you'[11] being referred to. In the case, the question arose: did it refer to the charterer of the vessel, or to its owners as well? Third person drafting is more naturally specific, which is an advantage.

The right words...in the right order

11.5 If contract drafters use a coherent word order in their drafting, the contract is easier to understand than if the word order is illogical or haphazard. Within a clause, particularly a conditional clause, this can point towards using a particular word order: see generally Chapter 9 above. But quite apart from affecting how easily a reader can understand the drafting, word order can substantively affect meaning. In *BJ Aviation v Pool Aviation Ltd,*[12] a lease of a private airport provided for what might happen at the end of the lease term:

> If...the Operator shall serve written notice upon the Owner requesting renewal of the Agreement...then subject to the re-negotiation of the rent payable...the Owner shall grant to the Operator a fresh [lease].

The renewal arrangement was held unenforceable as an agreement to agree. But the Court of Appeal suggested that the result might have been different if the stipulation as to rent had come at the end of the clause ('the Owner shall grant to the Operator a fresh lease at a rent to be renegotiated'). The word order in the clause, in other words, was crucial to its meaning.

9 To be fair, the Investors Compensation Scheme also produced an explanatory note for investors, also addressed to investors in the second person as 'you', which Lord Hoffmann described as a 'model of clarity'. It is depressing to reflect that when the drafter switched into trying to draft a contract, clarity fled.

10 [2005] EWCA Civ 519.

11 English is unusual in not having separate pronouns for the singular and plural forms in the second person: both *are 'you'*. The old singular forms 'thou' and 'thee' are extinct, and although distinctively plural forms exist in some dialects ('youse' and 'you all'), they are probably too informal for the drafter of even the raciest second person contract.

12 [2002] EWCA Civ 163.

THE TYPE OF LANGUAGE TO CHOOSE

Prefer modern language to the outdated, and the straightforward word to the obscure one...

11.6 Lawyers' language is often with good reason criticised as old-fashioned. This is true of contracts as of lawyers' writing more generally. Nobody uses the term 'legalese' as a compliment. Old-fashioned expressions that nobody other than a lawyer would use confer a cobwebby feel on drafting. It would be impossible to give an exhaustive list of expressions of this type, but these two examples from decided cases will serve as an illustration:

> In the event of the sales distribution by [EMI] or its Associates (whether directly or by licence) of the[EMI] Recordings by the Artists hereunder by Online Distribution...such sales shall be deemed sales of Records for all purposes SAVE THAT the royalty in respect thereof shall...be a [xx]% share of EMI's receipts.[13]

'Hereunder' would be better as 'under this Agreement'; 'save that' is a legalese version of the everyday expression 'except that'; replacing 'such sales' by 'those sales' would be an improvement; if 'in respect thereof' had been 'for those sales', the reader would have felt less put off..

The second example:

> If the Tenants shall be desirous of determining the said term hereby granted at any time after the expiration of the third thirteenth and twenty third years of the said term and of such desire shall give to the Landlords not less than six calendar months' notice in writing ...then on the expiration of such notice as aforesaid the said term shall cease and determine.[14]

Here, 'shall be desirous of determining' could be rendered more straightforwardly as 'wish to determine'; 'the said term hereby granted' is better as 'the term granted by this lease'; 'such notice as aforesaid' could simply be 'the notice'; and 'cease and determine' could just be 'come to an end'.

The drafters of contracts like these seem at best indifferent to whether their clients (ranging here between accountants and rock musicians) are likely to understand it. And if the clients do not understand the contract before it is signed, how can they point out if they do not consider that the language embodies their consensus?[15] How many times must parties have decided that a draft contract is too obscurely worded for them to be able to understand;

[13] *Pink Floyd Music Ltd v EMI Records Ltd* [2010] EWCA Civ 1429.
[14] *KPMG LLP v Network Rail Infrastructure Ltd* [2007] EWCA Civ 363.
[15] For a counterintuitive observation to the contrary in the context of one particular building contract, see *West v Ian Finlay & Associates* [2014] EWCA Civ 316 at [57] (Vos LJ).

relied accordingly on their lawyers to draft it so as to reflect their wishes; and ended up by regretting their decision when they find out too late that they have not done so?

Lawyers are often tempted by obscure language rather than the straightforward. Why is 'commence' preferred to 'start' or 'begin'? Why, when A sells an asset to B, is A the 'Vendor' rather than the 'Seller', and B the 'Purchaser' rather than the 'Buyer'? Why are documents effecting a lease of property referred to as 'these presents' when nobody plans to wrap them up?

...but remember that simple language can disguise uncertainty

11.7 Just because a word is a familiar one, it does not follow that it is unambiguous. This can matter a lot, particularly where the word is pivotal to the operation of the contract.

Cases are legion.

In *Ardagh Group v Pillar Property Group,*[16] a tax scheme depended on when a capital loss had been used

> by virtue of... effective off set

against a capital gain. But what 'effective off set' meant was unclear in the context of an overall settlement of a range of disputes with the tax authorities.

In another case, 'operations' must have appeared a straightforward term when used to describe the activities of a garage proprietor. But when it came to committal proceedings for alleged breach of an undertaking given by the proprietor, the exact meaning of the term (did it include work in the workshop preparatory to actual business operations?) demanded careful analysis.[17]

In a case[18] where householders agreed to pay builders

> any monies due for work authorised by me/us which is not paid by my/our insurer

it became crucial to determine whether 'work authorised by me/us' related only to additional works authorised by the householder, or also to the basic work covered by the insurance policy (the insurance company's intermediary having gone into administration without paying the builders). A simple phrase over which the contracting parties' eyes may have skimmed turned out to be controversial.

In a case where an offer was expressed to be 'open for 21 days', the question arose whether that meant that it could not be withdrawn within the 21-day

16 [2013] EWCA Civ 900.
17 *Lait v Williams* [2006] EWHC 633 (TCC).
18 *AJ Building and Plastering v Turner* [2013] EWHC 484.

period, or that it could not be accepted after that period had elapsed.[19] The drafter would have been better to be explicit about what being 'open' meant.

When in another case a prohibition on assignment was expressed to any assignment or transfer 'by any Party to a third Party', the simplicity of the language may have tempted the drafter into thinking it was dispute-proof. But what later happened was that an insurer acquired some contractual rights by subrogation, a process that under the applicable law (Japanese law) clearly involved a transfer. Did such a transfer fall foul of the prohibition on assignment, or could the insurer validly enforce the subrogated rights on the grounds that, having taken effect by operation of law, the transfer was not 'by' the insured? The meaning of this single word 'by' gave rise to a dispute on which the High Court and Court of Appeal took different views.[20]

In all of these cases, what the drafter needed was to have added to or expanded the (superficially straightforward) expressions used so as to be explicit about what they meant. The drafter needs to be constantly alert to whether even the simplest of words conceals the potential for dispute.

The main technique is one that drafters can learn from judges who interpret disputed expressions in court. Judges construe contracts iteratively, testing their initial assumption about what contractual language means by considering whether the consequences of that assumption seem to fit the purposes of the contract, or whether a rival interpretation would do so better.[21]

That is how drafters should think. Looking at any particular expression in the contract, is it clear enough what it means in the contract as a whole; and if not, what additional or alternative language would be clearer? Not least among the successful drafter's qualities is the humility to acknowledge that one's first attempt is not necessarily the best. Asking as many 'What if?' questions as possible (see Chapter 13 below) is another way of flushing out potential problems.

Avoid Latin expressions that are not in everyday use

11.8 Though Latin has a long history in English legal language, it should be used as sparingly as possible by the drafter of a modern contract. English speakers who are not lawyers never knew much Latin, and today few have

[19] *C v D* [2011] EWCA Civ 646.

[20] *Dassault Aviation SA v Mitsui Sumitomo Insurance Ltd* [2022] EWHC 3287 (Comm) and [2024] EWCA (Civ) 5; the Court of Appeal's view was that the transfer, being by operation of law, was not 'by' the insured, and that the transfer was thus not caught by the prohibition: Sir Geoffrey Vos MR at [29].

[21] See, for one of many cases, *Wood v Capita Insurance Services Ltd* [2017] UKSC 24 at [12] (Lord Hodge): 'This unitary exercise involves an iterative process by which each suggested interpretation is checked against the provisions of the contract and its commercial consequences are investigated…'

learnt Latin at all.[22] It is off-putting to the parties who need to understand what the contract means without a lawyer having to explain it to them.

Not every Latin expression should however be off-limits for the drafter. One or two Latin expressions, chiefly abbreviations, are so common in ordinary usage, and consequently so well understood by everyone, that they can safely be used by the drafter. An example is 'per cent'. This is now so clearly part of English that most users of English use it without noticing or remembering its Latin origin. So if a more authentically English-derived equivalent were used such as 'out of every hundred', it would strike most readers as contrived and indeed unnecessary. The Latin version is both shorter and instantly understood.

A drafter who uses 'per capita' may be understood by most readers, but perhaps not by everyone: a drafter might be better to use 'each' or 'a head'. But though most legal readers would remember what another lawyer meant when describing a 'per stirpes' distribution of an estate,[23] nobody else would. be likely to. To achieve the objective of comprehensibility, a drafter should prefer an English equivalent.

Many abbreviations have Latin origins. Again the drafter's task is to see whether an English equivalent is available, and to use the English equivalent if there is any risk that a reader will not understand the Latin.

Some are so easily understood by readers that the case for recasting them in English is weak. Though readers may not know the actual Latin derivations,[24] 'a.m.' and 'p.m.' are so familiar that it is unnecessary to substitute 'in the morning' or 'in the afternoon'.

'Etc' meaning 'and the rest' is similar, but its imprecision should sound a warning note. It is always better to be as explicit as possible in contracts: 'etc' in a contract suggests the drafter running out of steam. It inevitably raises the question: is some unenumerated item within the 'etc' concept or not? That is a species of the problem known to lawyers by another Latin term, 'eiusdem generis'. It is discussed in Chapter 5 above.

In contrast, the abbreviation 'viz' (short for the Latin 'videlicet') is less well understood, so the English equivalent 'that is to say' or 'in other words' is to be preferred.[25]

22 Before an attempt in 2021 to boost the learning of Latin, it was taught in under 3% of state schools.

23 Literally 'through the roots', signifying a distribution equally among separate branches of a family rather than equally among family members.

24 Which are 'ante meridiem' and 'post meridiem' respectively.

25 In *Ambatielos v Anton Jurgens Margarine Works* [1923] AC 175, the two abbreviations 'viz' and 'etc' were used together, causing difficulties ('viz' suggesting that what followed it was comprehensive, but 'etc' suggesting the contrary). The lesson from the dispute that resulted from the appearance of the two in combination is that abbreviations, just because they are so succinct, tend to be underestimated in terms of their contribution to the meaning of drafting in which they are included.

Shun 'redundant doubles'

11.9 Lawyers' prolixity causes them to draft in redundant doubles – unnecessary repetition that serves no real purpose. For example, the drafter of a standard form release document that came before the House of Lords in 2001[26] framed the release by providing

> The applicant agrees to accept the terms set out in the documents attached in full and final settlement of all or any claims…

The double 'full and final settlement' added nothing to 'final settlement'; nor did 'all or any claims' signify anything that 'any claim' would have not.

This drafting illustrates a common feature of redundant double: the doubled phrases come across as almost incantatory. The lawyer gives the impression of having reached unthinkingly for the double phrase without considering whether both components are needed, and succeeds only in making the drafting more remote from ordinary use of language, and harder for a reader to follow. A drafter who thinks that the pile-up of words ensures that the language is *comprehensive* is deluded: in *BCCI v Ali*,[27] for example, it was held that the language, despite the double expressions, did not extend to cover particular claims arising from the stigma of having worked for a corrupt and dishonest employer.

'All or any' resurfaced in *Peregrine Aviation Bravo Ltd v Laudamotion Gmbh.*[28] A provision referring to an aircraft lessee threatening to suspend 'all or any' of its debts or other payment obligations was held not to be engaged by the lessee writing to its lessor in relation to obligations under only some particular leases. The reader is forced to conclude that the word 'any', which would normally be accepted as referring to a single payment obligation, was robbed of some of its literal force by being included in the stock lawyer's redundant double 'all or any'.

Among the more common examples of this type of redundant double formulation are 'each and every', 'full force and effect', 'understood and agreed' and 'last will and testament', but these are only examples. It would take too much space (and would depress the reader) to attempt a comprehensive list.[29]

A double expression may represent a fault worse than mere prolixity. The two components, even in combination, may miss the drafter's target. For example, in *BOC Group v Centeon LLC*[30] a sale and purchase agreement[31] contained

26 *Bank of Credit and Commerce International SA v Ali* [2001] UKHL 8.
27 ibid.
28 [2023] EWHC 48 (Comm) at [152] (Henshaw J) (who was heavily influenced by the context in which the provision appeared: an event of default with drastic contractual consequences).
29 Though the indefatigable Bryan A Garner identifies over 120 in *The Redbook: A Manual On Legal Style* (2nd edn, Thomson West, 2006) at [192]–[194].
30 [1999] 1 All ER (Comm) 970.
31 Described by Evans LJ as a 'massive document'.

a clause that required payment of a later instalment of the purchase price should be 'absolute and unconditional'. But the drafter had not thought to exclude set-off, and the omission of that type of language was held to amount to an 'eloquent silence'. The language the drafter had used was therefore not enough to preclude set-off.

This case illustrates a particular danger of a formulaic double expression. It *appears* comprehensive, but flatters to deceive. The two components may do no more than cover the same ground (what did 'absolute' add to 'unconditional'?) The drafter needed to think about whether the contractual language did what it needed to.[32]

HITTING THE TARGET

Do not simply use the wrong word...

11.10 The drafter risks undermining the contract if the wrong word is chosen. Tin-eared drafting does a drafter no favours. So for example, a drafter who stipulates what is to happen 'on expiry of this Agreement'[33] can scarcely complain if the question is raised as to whether the obligations provided for have any contractual force: if the agreement has expired, it self-evidently cannot have any more contractual force.[34]

...or a word that is vague

11.11 Many words and expressions are by their nature imprecise. They admit a range of possibilities as to what they mean. Indeed, it is arguable that most words are of this type:

> There are few, if any, words in the English language which, viewed in splendid isolation, are capable of only one meaning.[35]

This point was echoed in the intellectual property dispute *Oxonica Energy Ltd v Neuftec Limited*.[36] The judge pointed out that in the case of patents the concept of an 'application' for a patent might mean the legal state of affairs that subsists when someone has applied for a patent, or the contents of the

[32] Ironically, in this case, the drafter, or those acting for the recipient of the payment, would have done better to use the familiar expression that payments be made 'without withholding, deduction or set-off'.

[33] *Dwr Cymru Cyfyngedig (Welsh Water) v Corus UK Ltd* [2007] EWCA Civ 285.

[34] Prudent drafters are careful to make sure in this type of circumstance that following the agreement substantially coming to an end, some provisions remain in force, including for example confidentiality provisions, and dispute resolution provisions that control any issues arising between the parties after the contract has otherwise terminated.

[35] *European Film Bonds A/S v Lotus Holdings LLC* [2021] EWCA Civ 807 at [46] (Stuart-Smith LJ).

[36] [2008] EWHC 2127 (Pat) at [33]–[34] (Peter Prescott QC).

document in which that is done. The former can come to an end when the process is completed: the document does not come to an end at any point in time.

Again, in *Daewoo Heavy Industries v Klipriver Shipping*,[37] clause 6 began:

> Neither the carrier nor the ship shall in any event be or become liable for any loss [exceeding a specified monetary limit].

The simple phrase 'in any event' here carried the meaning of 'in any circumstance'. But the phrase can of course be read simply as suggesting, without much if any content, a link between the clause in which it appears and what has gone before.[38]

Language with a legal or business meaning may bear that meaning in a contract

11.12 Words may have a particular legal meaning and if they do, a court may ascribe that meaning to the word when used in a contract. The very nature of a contract is that it is intended to be a legally binding document: it is meant to have legal consequences. When a contract contains a word with legal baggage, the word is therefore likely to be interpreted accordingly.

For example, when a particular success fee payable to an investment manager depended on the 'sale' of investments, the Privy Council held that 'sale' meant 'sale' in its ordinary legal meaning. In the words of Lord Sumption:

> 'Sale' has a well understood meaning. It means a transfer of property to another party for a money consideration. So the investment manager, which had not managed to find a buyer for any of the investments within the time allotted, was not entitled to the fee.[39]

Similarly, the word 'representation' used in a contract with investors was held to carry its legal meaning of a statement of fact made by one person to another, on the truth of which the representee was intended to rely.[40]

But this is no more than a presumption: it may be rebutted.[41] The context may show that the technical meaning of the word was not intended, and that

37 [2003] EWCA Civ 451.

38 Another common phrase that, like 'provided that', is inherently ambiguous (see **9.15** above).

39 *Krys v KBC Partners LP* [2015] UKPC 46.

40 *The Financial Services Authority v Asset LI Inc* [2013] EWHC 178 (Ch), citing *Cassa di Risparmio della Repubblica di San Marino SpA v Barclays Bank Plc* [2011] EWHC 484 (Comm). See also *Marlborough Knightsbridge Management Ltd v Fivaz* [2021] EWCA Civ 989 at [11] ('It is common ground...that the expression 'landlord's fixtures' ...is one which has a very long usage in this area of the law...It is therefore idle to suppose that it should be interpreted as if it were free from any technical meaning.')

41 *LG Schuler v Wickman Machine Tool Sales Ltd* [1972] 1 WLR 840 (Lord Simon).

the word was being used in some more general sense.[42] Nor is it the case that just because a word is often used by lawyers, the way that lawyers use it will determine its contractual meaning. A word in general use, even if it has a legal flavour, may bear the meaning in which non-lawyers would understand it.[43]

Similarly, words that have a particular meaning in the context of a particular business in which the parties are engaged may well be found to bear that meaning when they are used in a contract. A drafter should always consider whether a particular expression has a particular technical meaning in the context of the business milieu in which the contract is entered into. For example, with a lease that permitted an airport to provide facilities for 'business aviation', it became important to establish exactly what that expression meant in the context of the lease.[44] The drafter did not however appear to have consulted documents relevant to the field to see whether the expression was used in them in a way that squared with the contractual purpose.[45]

If, in that case, a clear business meaning of the term could have been established, it would have influenced the court in deciding what it meant in the lease. But because no such business meaning could in the end be discerned, its meaning had to be derived from the words themselves. And it was unclear whether the expression meant, for example, any case where the travellers, or most of them, had a business reason for travelling; or a narrower meaning excluding passenger flights, where the owner or charterer of the plane just wanted to use the flight for the purposes of their own business. In linguistic terms, the significance of the adjective 'business' in the context of the term 'business aviation' was unclear: the drafter had not done enough to make it so.

Be specific as to which meaning is intended

11.13 It follows that in choosing contractual language, the drafter must be alive to the range of meanings any proposed contractual language could conceivably bear, and whether any of those meanings is its usual legal or business meaning. The drafter should also think about whether any such legal or business meaning differs from the popular meaning of the language.

42 The conclusion drawn by the courts in the *Schuler* case itself (ibid) (description of a clause as a 'condition' not signifying that any breach of it, however trivial, justified termination): see **9.5** above.

43 For example, a lawyer's understanding that the term 'compensation' would not include exemplary damages but only compensatory damages 'would not command universal acceptance' (*Lancashire County Council v Municipal Mutual Insurance Ltd* [1996] EWCA (Civ) 1345 (Simon Brown LJ)).

44 *Biggin Hill Airport Ltd v Bromley London Borough Council* [2001] EWCA Civ 1089.

45 For example, the drafter might perhaps have thought of asking whether the way the term was used in a document issued by the Board of Trade in 1983 entitled 'Facilities for dealing with Business aviation in the south east of England' might have thrown some light on how the expression fell to be understood.

The drafter's job is to be clear. Accordingly, where language is used that may have more than one meaning, the drafter should spell out, whether by defining the term or through other explicit language, which of the meanings is intended.

The drafter should also bear in mind that language with a narrower potential range of meanings is likely to achieve more precision. For example, in the *European Film Bonds* case referred to at **11.11** above,[46] the drafter had chosen to draft a stipulated contractual trigger by referring to the 'return' of an item to an original sender. But that was, as the court said, capable of meaning the process of returning it to the original sender, or its delivery back to that person. The drafter could have thought of words like 'despatch' and 'deliver' – each a narrower term than 'return' – to make it clear which alternative was meant.

If language is too vague, more radical problems arise.

In an extreme case, the enforceability of the contract itself may be threatened. *G Scammell and Nephew Ltd v HC and JG Ouston*,[47] discussed in **3.11** above, was a case that turned on whether language was so woolly that the whole contract was vitiated.

Even if the contract is not put at existential risk, vague language can cause uncertainty. In *Yuanda UK Co v WW Gear Construction Ltd*,[48] the drafter referred airily, in a part of the contract dealing with adjudication of disputes, to 'a multi-party dispute situation'. As the extremely general word 'situation' suggests, this was susceptible of a wide range of interpretations. The enforceability of the contract *as a whole* was not in doubt: the vagueness infected only the adjudication provisions. But the looseness of the concept failed to make it clear what disputes, and between whom, might be within that concept. The judge managed to give the expression a sensible meaning by making what he described as 'fairly modest amendments'[49] to the drafting. But the drafting was too vague for its meaning to be clear without resort to the court.

It may be that to use a vague expression is the only way that the parties can reach a consensus. But the drafter owes it to the parties to explain to them that whilst the term may allow the parties to sign the contract, the uncertainty inherent in the language may store up trouble further down the road. An obvious example is a test of reasonableness. Effectively, if a contractual test is made subject to a test of reasonableness, as where consent is 'not to be

46 [2021] EWCA Civ 807.
47 [1941] AC 251 (order of vehicle given 'on the understanding that the balance of the purchase price can be had on hire purchase terms over a period of two years' without any guidance on what terms might be acceptable).
48 [2010] EWHC 720.
49 ibid at [77].

unreasonably withheld'[50] or a party is required to take 'reasonable steps' or 'reasonable efforts' to accomplish a desired state of affairs,[51] the parties are leaving it to the future to debate whether in future uncertain circumstances the reasonableness criterion is satisfied. A court will be happy to adjudicate this question. Drafting that applies this test may therefore reduce the risk of the contract being subject to such a degree of uncertainty that it is void for uncertainty; but the room for debate about what is and is not 'reasonable' leaves plenty of scope for future dispute.[52]

The more specific the drafting, the less likely it is to be unenforceable, and the less room for doubt about what it means. The risk of the contract being disputed is reduced if the scope of reasonableness is defined to some degree, making it clear whether it is reasonable or not for a party to take some specified consideration into account, or how far it is reasonable (if at all) for the party to consider its own commercial interests outside the four corners of the contract.[53]

Use an illustration to indicate what meaning is intended

11.14 A useful technique for the drafter who wants to delineate the meaning of an expression is to provide an *illustration* of it. This is a move in the direction of defining the expression, but does not go so far.

For example, the drafter of the contract discussed in *The Football Association Premier League Ltd v PP Live Sports International Ltd*[54] used the concept of the 'format' of the Premier League competition undergoing a 'fundamental change'. Without trying to define exactly the scope of that concept – on its face somewhat elusive – a 'fundamental change' was stated to 'include' a change that resulted in 'the total number of Clubs being reduced to less than eighteen', or 'the Competition ceasing to be the premier league competition played between professional football clubs in England and Wales'. The illustrations fell short of a conventional exhaustive definition in two ways: it was clearly non-exhaustive ('includes' rather than 'means'),[55] and related not to the change itself but to the *result* of the change. But the illustrations helped make it clear that changes to the scheduling of games in reaction to

[50] As in *Porton Capital Technology Funds v 3M UK Holdings Ltd* [2011] EWHC 2895, where consent to discontinuance of a business was required 'which shall not be unreasonably withheld'. The drafter was attracted by adverbs other than 'unreasonably': products were required to be 'actively marketed' and regulatory approval to be 'diligently sought'. A 23-day court hearing predictably (to use a further adverb) ensued. For adverbs generally, see **7.23** above.

[51] See from **3.14** above.

[52] As for example in *Landlord Protect Ltd v St Anselm Development Co Ltd* [2008] EWHC 1582 (Ch) (landlord's consent to lease assignment not to be unreasonably withheld; question whether landlord's requirements in relation to personal guarantee 'reasonable').

[53] See **3.16** above.

[54] [2022] EWHC 38 (Comm).

[55] See **4.8** above.

the Covid-19 pandemic, and playing games in empty stadiums for the same reason, were not a 'fundamental change' in 'format'.[56]

Use particular care with expressions of time

11.15 A drafter should always consider, when referring to a date or time, making it clear in which time zone the time is to be determined.[57] Otherwise there is room for debate about what a specified time means.[58] A reference to '12 a.m.' or '12 p.m.' is ambiguous: there is no consensus as to which means 12 noon and which 12 midnight, which are the better terms. But a reference to 12 midnight 'on' a particular day is itself ambiguous: is it the midnight that marks the beginning or the end of the day that is signified? So many drafters stipulate 11.59 p.m. as the relevant time, achieving certainty[59] if perhaps at the expense of elegance.

Drafters expressing deadlines need to consider how to make them clear. A regrettable reason to sharpen their concern is that those responsible for taking action by a particular contractual deadline seem to be drawn to the brinkmanship inherent in serving (say) notice of a warranty claim at the very last possible date, so that if anything can go wrong, it is sure to. Cases often reach the courts in which one party is arguing that the deadline has accordingly just been missed.[60]

One obvious point is that drafting is clear if it states the deadline in terms, by stating (say) that a notice of claim, to be valid, must be served by 11.59 p.m. London time on 30 November 2026. That is better than providing that the notice must be served 'within three years from the date of this Agreement'. The

56 [2022] EWHC 38 at [77] (Fraser J).

57 References to the time in a particular country can be ambiguous if the country spans more than one time zone: it is safer to refer to a particular city instead ('New York time' rather than 'US time' for example) or to specify the time zone by name ('Eastern Standard Time' for example). In referring to time in the UK, it is better not to succumb to the temptation to refer to 'Greenwich Mean Time' or 'GMT', as this is not the time to which the nation works during the summer months, when British Summer Time operates (by virtue of the Summer Time Order SI 2002/262). Either of 'UK time' (safe enough, since the UK does not span time zones) or 'London time' is better.

58 See, for example, *Euronav NV v Repsol Trading SA* [2021] EWHC 2565 at [13] (charterparty in standard form containing 'no general provision regarding dates and times'; consequent uncertainty over day on which unloading completed and so over deadline for service of demurrage notice).

59 And avoiding the type of dispute that surfaced in *Elements (Europe) Ltd v FK Building Ltd* [2023] EWHC 726 (TCC) (payment application under a JCT standard form, which had been delivered by email at eight minutes past ten in the evening, argued (in the end unsuccessfully) to be delivered late because outside normal site opening hours).

60 See, for example, *Zayo Group International Ltd v Ainger* [2017] EWHC 2542 (Comm) at [66] Simon Bryan QC) (final day for service of notices: six motorcycle couriers involved in trying to serve notices in London on six separate parties, one of whom had alas moved to New Zealand).

latter formula raises the question whether the date on which the Agreement is executed counts towards the three-year period or does not.[61]

It will, however, not always be easy to provide a specific date in an agreement. The parties may have agreed on a particular period from the date of the agreement, but the date of the agreement is not fixed until the negotiations are complete. The drafter has too much to do to remember to update a specific reference to a date in the notice clause: it is easier to refer to the agreed period. In such a case the drafter should as a minimum try to make clear whether periods are inclusive of the dates on which the periods begin and end. Since agreed periods are often whole numbers of years, the word 'anniversary', plus a reference to a specific time on the anniversary, can be useful to fix the date by which a notice must be given.

Strike a balance between expressions that are too precise and ones that are not precise enough

11.16 A drafter can trip up by using a word or expression that turns out to be over-precise. For example, when a force majeure clause referred to the 'mechanical breakdown' of a conveyor belt, that was not language which could be stretched so as to be regarded as applying to the complete destruction of the belt by fire.[62]

In another case, an employer's insurance policy was expressed to exclude protection against liability in respect of 'pneumoconiosis'. But the definition of that term referred to fibrosis of the lungs due to asbestos dust, and did not extend to the different disease of mesothelioma. Had the policy referred to a wider category – for example, asbestos-related diseases – the exclusion might have helped the insurer. But the language used was too specific, so the exclusion failed.

But the drafter can also cause problems by falling into the reverse trap: using an expression that is not precise enough. Standard forms, in particular, often use language that is deliberately general so that the forms can be used in a range of circumstances. So in a clause that allowed a purchaser not to complete the purchase of two companies if a 'Material Adverse Effect' had occurred, the question turned on identifying the 'industries' in which the target companies operated.[63] But the parties could not agree on what 'industries' meant: the general language raised the question, but did not answer it. The

61 The general rule is that it does not: see the discussion of the authorities in *Matthew v Sedman* [2021] UKSC 19, another case where the notice turned out (in the light of the court's decision) to have been served too late, but would, even if the court had reached the contrary view, have been served only on the last possible day. A special rule applies to periods that start running at midnight (as in *Matthew v Sedman* itself).

62 *ED & F Man Sugar Ltd v Unicargo Transportgesellschaft mBH* [2012] EWHC 2879 (Comm).

63 *Travelport Ltd v Wex Inc* [2020] EWHC 2670 at [148]–[149] (Cockerill J).

judge observed: 'the wording is probably largely taken from a pro forma …the parties could have but did not specify what industries they meant. It may well be that one of the results of this case is that future drafters will do differently.'

THE VIRTUES OF ACCURACY AND CONSISTENCY

Be sensitive to nuance with words that are close in meaning but not synonymous

11.17 In a long term gas supply agreement, a clause restricted assignment without the prior written approval of the other party

> which approval shall not be unreasonably withheld.

A casual reader might have thought there was no real difference between this formulation and a stipulation that the assignment required 'consent' which should not be unreasonably withheld. But it was held in the Court of Appeal[64] that the difference was crucial. 'Consent' would have been more like 'permission', giving the person whose consent was required more leeway in deciding whether to grant it. 'Approval' was a narrower concept, and connoted a sort of vetting process that could consider only whether the proposed assignee was fit for purpose.

In another case,[65] a settlement agreement provided that a cash payment would not be necessary if extra work was 'awarded' to one of the parties. Although some extra work was *offered* to the relevant party, the opportunity to carry it out was not pursued: the court held that work would be 'awarded' only if taken up, not merely offered.

In another settlement agreement, a settlement of disputes arising out of a customer's cancelled orders was held not to apply to the customer's 'forecasts'.[66] And in the (admittedly non-contractual) context of deciding on the education of a child with special educational needs, the Administrative Chamber of the Upper Tier Tribunal concluded that there was a difference between a school being 'suitable' and being 'appropriate' for the child in question.[67]

The point for the drafter here is that near synonyms may have slightly different meanings, so that the choice of one rather than the other drives the contractual outcome.

64 *British Gas Trading Ltd v Eastern Electricity PLC* [1997] CLY 4950.
65 *Jacobs UK Ltd v Skidmore Owings and Merrill LLP* [2012] EWHC 3293 (TCC).
66 *Global Display Solutions Ltd v NCR Solutions Group Ltd* [2021] EWHC 1119 (Comm) at [322] (Jacobs J).
67 *LC v Hampshire CC* [2023] UKUT 281 (AAC) (the distinction being that 'suitability' was statutorily confined by reference to specific criteria, whereas 'appropriateness' was not).

Do not vary language other than to signal a change in meaning

11.18 A drafter invites trouble if using, within the same document or suite of documents, words or expressions that are similar, but on their face distinct. For example, if a contract sometimes refers to 'negligence' and sometimes to 'gross negligence',[68] the drafter will be taken to mean that the two concepts are distinct.[69] Why else would the contract have used different standards? The alternative possibility – that the drafter and the parties had not noticed the difference between the two and that the existence of two apparently different standards was accidental rather than deliberate – strikes a cynical reader as perhaps more likely. But when the contract comes before a court, a judge will generally approach the contract with the expectation that the parties meant what they said.[70]

The moral is: be consistent. It is dangerous to refer to the same thing by two different names, because the very difference in the names will suggest to the reader that two different things are being referred to.

In *Richards v Wood*[71] a declaration of trust was entered into following the purchase of a council house under a right-to-buy scheme. Clause 3 of the declaration of trust recorded the discount from market value inherent in the price at which the sale was effected, together with the amounts of the purchase price provided for by the tenants and another family member. In clause 4 the declaration of trust allocated the trust property in proportion to the 'initial respective contributions' set out in clause 3. But clause 3 had not referred to 'contributions' at all, and it was disputed whether the reference to 'contributions' referred just to the actual purchase price or extended to the discount. The inconsistency in the drafting caused an ambiguity[72] that would not have arisen if the drafter had borne in mind more closely how the previous clause had itself been framed.

Again, in *NKD Maritime Ltd v Bart Maritime (No. 2) Ltd*,[73] the drafter of an agreement for the sale of a vessel sometimes referred to 'delivery' of the vessel and at other times to 'transfer of title' to it. The court accepted that the use of different terms must be deliberate and so must refer to different things. And in *Green v Petfre (Gibraltar) Ltd*,[74] a betting company's standard form gaming

68 Itself a concept with a doubtful pedigree in English law: *Armitage v Nurse* [1997] EWCA Civ 1279.

69 *Winnetka Trading Corporation v Julius Baer International Ltd* [2011] EWHC 2030 (Ch).

70 'The habit of the draftsman is to eschew synonyms. He uses the same words throughout the document to express the same thing or concept and consequently if he uses different words the presumption is that he means a different thing or concept' (*Prestcold Central Ltd v Minister of Labour* [1969] 1 WLR 89 (Lord Diplock).

71 [2014] EWCA Civ 327.

72 An ambiguity that caused a dispute that cost so much that it exhausted the trust entitlement of one of the contending beneficiaries: ibid at [38] (Lewison LJ).

73 [2022] EWHC 1615 (Comm) from [51].

74 [2021] EWHC 842 (QB) at [131] (Foster J).

contract with a customer was criticised for failing to distinguish between 'rules', terms' and 'conditions'.

Drafters should strive to avoid accidental minor inconsistencies in language. An inconsistency allows one side to a contract to argue that the minor linguistic difference must be deliberate and intended to signify an intention to distinguish between two different cases and treat them differently.

This happened in a case that reached the Supreme Court in 2015, *Tael One Partners Ltd v Morgan Stanley & Co International PLC.*[75] The LMA standard terms at one point referred to

> fees accrued up to…the Settlement Date.

Another clause used slightly different language:

> fees…to the extent that they accrue in respect of the period before the Settlement Date.

These two versions are so similar that a casual reader might assume that they must surely mean the same thing. But at first instance the High Court judge saw the difference as potentially crucial to the interpretation of the contract.[76]

Do not shun the obvious word

11.19 The drafter should not be mealy-mouthed but should allow the drafting to speak plainly. The dangers of not being plain can be seen in *PEC Ltd v Thai Mapam Trading Co Ltd.*[77] Buyers under a GAFTA[78] standard form alleged that they had made a valid claim to extend the delivery period. But the alleged claim was not expressed as a 'claim' at all, and indeed contained some additional language that made it look still less like a document intended as a 'claim'. The drafter would have been better to express outright the intention to make a 'claim'.

Be consistent in the level of detail

11.20 The drafter should avoid variations in how explicitly issues of similar importance are dealt with. If the drafter varies in detail, sometimes mentioning a particular matter and sometimes not, an inference can be drawn that the variation is deliberate, so that the cases where the specific item is not mentioned are intended not to cover it. For example, in *Shell UK Ltd v*

75 [2015] UKSC 12.
76 [2012] EWHC 1858 (Comm) at [33] (Popplewell J). See also **6.3** above (unhelpful to be inconsistent between 'shall', 'will' and similar formulations).
77 [2011] EWHC 3306 (Comm).
78 The Grain and Feed Trade Association.

Total UK Ltd[79] the court considered a complex set of interlocking indemnity provisions, some of which dealt expressly with negligence and some of which did not. The court stated:[80]

> We suggest that where parties have drawn up a series of detailed agreements and the draftsmen have expressly dealt with negligence, … where it has not been expressly referred to that would be likely to be a deliberate decision by the draftsman to exclude negligence.

And in *Brookfield Construction (UK) Ltd v Foster and Partners Ltd*,[81] a contract stipulated that obligations under some provisions were to be time-limited. The consequence was that where another provision was not expressly time-limited, it was to be inferred that the parties intended the obligation to carry on.[82]

Every word counts

11.21 Drafters aiming for comprehensive coverage can sometimes include language as a lawyer's reflex, without considering whether it is needed or appropriate. When the language is scrutinised in context, however, it can turn out to be much more important than the drafter can ever have ever expected.

For example, in *RSPCA v Sharp*,[83] the words 'if any' appeared in a will after a reference to inheritance tax. That pointed strongly towards one of the two rival contentions as to what the will meant (because on the other interpretation, inheritance tax would always be due, so 'if any' would not make sense). The drafter may well have added 'if any' without any suspicion that the meaning of the whole document depended on that innocent-seeming phrase. But so it proved.

MISCELLANEOUS

Do not assume that non-Anglophone readers' contracts will be specially interpreted

11.22 English law and the English courts are considered comparatively reliable and predictable, so they are widely used in international business. This means that contracts drafted in the English language, and destined to

79 [2010] EWCA Civ 180.
80 ibid at [15].
81 [2009] EWHC 307 (TCC).
82 'I accept the submissions of Mr Stewart QC on behalf of BC that where the parties wanted to place time limits on WST's performance of specific obligations, they did just that' (ibid at [29] (Coulson J)).
83 [2010] EWCA Civ 1474 at [40] (Lord Neuberger MR).

be adjudicated by English judges, are often entered into by parties (or at least one party) for whom English is not their first language. In such cases it is realistic to wonder whether the parties fully understand the legal effect of the contracts they are entering into. Examples are *Rainy Sky SA v Kookmin Bank*,[84] *WS Tankship BV v Kwangju Bank Ltd*[85] and *SNCB Holding v UBS AG*.[86]

Judges are resistant to arguments that if the parties are not native English speakers, their contracts should be interpreted under some special rules. To concede that point would be to expose a judge to a process 'fraught with difficulty'.[87] Nonetheless, if the parties themselves are not familiar with English, let alone the sometimes rarefied English encountered in contracts, the drafter has a correspondingly greater responsibility to draft simply enough to make the contract comprehensible. When this is borne in mind, the recommendations contained in many of the earlier sections of this chapter are reinforced.[88]

Do not rely on spell-checking

11.23 When documents are reproduced electronically, a drafter may often be tempted to rely on spell checking software to highlight typographical problems. But though doubtless useful, this type of device cannot identify a case where a word or series of words are simply omitted,[89] or a word is not merely misspelled but is replaced by another word that exists, but is simply the wrong word for the context.[90]

84 [2011] UKSC 50 (performance bond issued by Korean bank).
85 [2011] EWHC 3103 (Comm) (guarantee issued by Korean bank).
86 [2012] EWHC 2044 (Comm) (Belgian railway company entering into complex financing arrangement).
87 *Hin-Pro International Logistics Ltd v Compania Sud Americana de Vapores SA* [2015] EWCA Civ 401 at [58] (Christopher Clarke LJ).
88 For example, those in **11.6** (prefer modern language).
89 As in *KPMG LLP v Network Rail Infrastructure Ltd* [2007] EWCA Civ 363; *Homburg Houtimport BV v Agrosin Private Ltd (the Starsin)* [2003] UKHL 12.
90 As in *Royal Bank of Scotland Plc v Highland Financial Partners Ltd* [2010] EWCA Civ 809 (the correct word 'notice' somehow appearing as 'which').

Chapter 12

What prevails?

If a contract contains two provisions that appear to contradict each another or are otherwise inconsistent with each other, the question arises: which one prevails? The parties, having regard to their own interests, may disagree about the answer, leading to unpredictability and dispute. Some types of contractual circumstances make disputes more likely. Drafters need to answer 'What prevails?' questions through making the hierarchy clear at various levels: as between documents, parts of documents, and individual provisions. Some expressions like 'subject to', 'without prejudice to' and 'notwithstanding' can regulate how provisions interrelate, but drafters need to use them accurately, as well as understanding that the law may step in to prevent a relationship being characterised inappropriately.

THE PROBLEM IN OVERVIEW

PARTICULAR CASES WHERE 'WHAT PREVAILS?' ISSUES ARE MORE COMMON

12.10 When overlapping documents are designed for different purposes

12.11 When the drafter adopts a 'torrential' drafting style

12.12 When the drafter does not appear to identify an overlap

GENERAL TECHNIQUES FOR FIXING 'WHAT PREVAILS?' ISSUES

12.13 Confine the problem by consolidating the arrangements into a single document

12.14 Provide an explicit hierarchy between documents, or parts of documents

12.15 Beware wording that solves one dispute only to invoke another

LANGUAGE THAT CAN BE USED TO MAKE IT CLEAR 'WHAT PREVAILS'

12.16 To make clear what prevails, drafters customarily use the phrase 'Subject to'

12.17 'Subject to' does not does not automatically obliterate the subordinate provision entirely, but it may do so

12.18 'Subject to' requires care, however, if the dominant provision supplements the subordinate one rather than otherwise modifying it

12.19 'Without prejudice to' is safer to add an obligation

12.20 'Notwithstanding': a feasible alternative to 'subject to' in the dominant provision, but less recommended

12.21 'Notwithstanding anything else in this Agreement' and similar language can be used to make a provision 'superdominant'

12.22 More limited degrees of superdominance are possible

12.23 'Supersubordinate' drafting is less likely to be useful than drafting for 'superdominance'

12.24 'Subject only to'

12.25 'Otherwise' not suitable to express subordination

12.26 'Except as provided in' is sometimes (but only sometimes) an alternative to 'subject to'

'WHAT PREVAILS?' LANGUAGE: RECOMMENDATIONS AND LIMITATIONS

12.27 Answer 'what prevails?' issues with as much precision as possible

12.28 Remember that rules of law classifying legal relationships can impose a limit on the parties' ability to determine what prevails

12.29 But do not assume that to ascribe a label to a contract is always ineffective

THE PROBLEM IN OVERVIEW

Some examples are, or should be, obvious

12.1 The most glaring type of inconsistency occurs when a drafter serves up *directly contradictory* provisions.

In the most extreme cases, hapless drafters contradict themselves within a single provision, sometimes even within a single sentence. In *Neilson v Poole*[1] a parcel of land known as 'Brooklands South' was identified

> as the same [is] for the purposes of identification only more particularly delineated on the plan drawn hereon coloured blue.

So what was the status of the plan? The words 'for the purposes of identification only' suggested that the plan was there merely to identify where Brooklands South was located. But 'more particularly delineated' suggested the exact reverse: that, if there were any doubt about the boundaries of Brooklands South, the plan would resolve those doubts. The sentence contradicted itself.[2]

Most readers who are professional drafters will react to cases like this by refusing to believe that they could themselves make such an obvious error. And indeed, one would hope that this is usually the case. But it did not stop the drafter of the contract under consideration in *Kangol Ltd v Hay & Robertson Plc*[3] from putting the following into a licence agreement:

> In the event that[4] the licensee fails to pay Kangol the minimum royalty level specified in Clause 2.2 of this agreement, Kangol may terminate this agreement forthwith unless the licensee pays Kangol such sums as are required to meet such minimum royalty level at the time such payments are due.

The first part of the sentence gives the licensee a right to terminate with immediate effect, but the second, beginning with '*unless*', seems to take it

1 (1969) 20 P & CR 909.

2 Megarry J, when a dispute about the boundaries of Brooklands South duly reached the courts, said with some justification 'The collocation of [the phrases] may be said to be unfortunate; and in that I think I speak temperately' (ibid).

3 [2004] EWCA Civ 63.

4 The appearance of the phrase 'in the event that' rather than 'if' is itself a reliable sign of less than ideal drafting: see **9.12** above.

away. So can the licensee terminate or not? The judge in the High Court said no; the Court of Appeal said yes. The drafter had failed to see the inherent logical contradiction embedded in a single sentence.

Almost as bad as an inconsistency within a single sentence is a pair of successive sentences that contradict each other. In *Peabody Trust v Reeve*[5] the standard terms (on which the trust had somehow let ten thousand properties without anyone noticing) contained this drafting:

> 5 (a) With the exception of any changes in Rent this Agreement may only be altered by the agreement in writing of both the Tenant and the Trust.
>
> (b) The terms of this Agreement may be varied by the Trust by a notice of variation served on the Tenant...

The judge observed[6] that the trust's counsel, in arguing unsuccessfully that the trust had the right to effect a unilateral variation, 'candidly accepts in his written argument that the wording of the two sub-clauses of clause 5 appear to be "directly contradictory"'.

Where overlapping issues are not dealt with in adjacent clauses, the risks of the drafter missing a contradiction are increased

12.2 The further apart that provisions appear in a contract, the more likely it is that contradictions between them will be missed.

In some cases, the provisions are close together, so the drafter's failure is almost as stark as in the extreme examples in **12.1** above. For example, the (apparently non-professional) drafter of a golf club catering contract in *Thorney Park Golf Limited v Myers Catering Ltd*[7] provided for a fixed term of three years in clause 4 of the contract, going on (after clause 5 dealt with the caterer's responsibilities) to provide a right to terminate on four months' notice. On its face this allowed the notice to be given at any time, regardless of the fixed, three-year period provided for in clause 4: a classic 'What prevails?' problem.

Only slightly further apart were the offending provisions in *Paros PLC v Worldlink Group PLC*.[8] Paragraph 4 of a letter agreement provided that

> Paragraph 1... is not intended to be legally binding

5 [2008] EWHC 1432 (Ch).
6 ibid at [7] (Gabriel Moss QC).
7 [2015] EWCA Civ 19: the Court of Appeal had little difficulty in concluding that the notice could not be given so as to terminate the contract within the three-year fixed period.
8 [2012] EWHC 394 (Comm).

but also that

> all other paragraphs...are legally binding.

Among those 'other paragraphs' was paragraph 6, which said that the obligation imposed by the paragraph

> is not intended to be legally binding.

So there was a direct contradiction between paragraph 4 and paragraph 6.

Such an error obviously opens the way to a dispute: if it becomes important to decide whether or not paragraph 6 is binding, the agreement affords no clue to the answer.[9] But also, even if (as in *Paros* itself[10]) the contradiction did not itself become contentious, the evident incoherence of the drafting is likely to call into question whether *other* parts of the drafting, which *are* in dispute, are credible evidence of the contractual intention.

A greater gap between two provisions makes it harder for the drafter to recognise that they contradict each other.

For example, in *Woodford Land Ltd v Persimmon Homes Ltd*,[11] the question arose whether Persimmon, which was buying some development land in Doncaster from Woodford, was allowed to deduct the cost of providing social housing from the purchase price. In the body of the agreement, clause 17 suggested that the answer was no. The drafting provided that

> The parties will bear any provision for affordable or social housing on the Site in the Agreed Shares

and it was clear that, in the circumstances that applied, Persimmon's 'Agreed Share' was 100%. So clause 17 suggested that Persimmon should bear the whole cost, and so could not deduct it from the purchase price.

But in clause 1, it had been specifically provided that what were called 'Development Costs' *should* be deducted from the purchase price; and Schedule 7 provided that costs of 'complying with a Section 106 Agreement', which on any view was part of the cost of providing social housing, were included in 'Development Costs'. That would mean that Woodford, not Persimmon, ended up bearing the cost.

The two provisions were thus flatly contradictory. The only plausible drafting explanation is that the drafter had not identified the contradiction (and thus neglected to draft anything to make it clear which of the two provisions

9 The specific provision in paragraph 6 might possibly prevail under the principle that specific provisions prevail over more general ones. But this is no more than guesswork.

10 [2012] EWHC 394 (Comm).

11 [2011] EWHC 984.

prevailed). The matter had to be resolved by a judge, itself a clear indication that the drafting had failed.[12]

Direct contradictions are just the tip of the iceberg: less obvious inconsistencies matter too

12.3 'What prevails?' questions do not arise only where two provisions can be seen to be directly contradictory. Less obvious cases of inconsistency can be just as controversial.

In *Mamidoil-Jetoil Greek Petroleum Co v Okta Crude Oil Refinery*,[13] for example, the drafter of an agreement appointing Jetoil to handle oil was at one level clear enough about the term of the agreement, clause 7 providing:

> This agreement is valid for 10 years starting from the date of the Signature.

But Jetoil's fee for providing its services was specified only for *two* years. So when the refinery wanted to escape the agreement before the ten years had elapsed, they argued[14] that if a term as fundamental as Jetoil's fee was set out for only two years only, the clear implication was that the agreement should end at the end of those two years if the parties could not agree about the fee to be paid after that time.

The drafting point here is that the two provisions did not on their face contradict each other. One clause stipulated a ten-year term. The other stipulated a fee payable for two years. But the co-existence of the two provisions led to a dispute because they could be argued to be *impliedly* inconsistent. And any inconsistency between two provisions, whether express or implied, raises the question of which of the two is to prevail over the other.

Contradictions and inconsistencies shade into wider questions as to how different provisions interact

12.4 The type of drafting problem under discussion here – one where a contradiction or inconsistency between two provisions provokes the question 'What prevails?' – is arguably a subset of a wider drafting issue: one whether the contract is fully internally coherent.

[12] The conflict was resolved in favour of the interpretation that superficially favoured Woodford: clause 17 dealt in terms with the cost of social/affordable housing, and so inferentially was what the parties must have thought was the dominant provision. This was, however, a Pyrrhic victory for Woodford, who paradoxically had conceded the point for the purposes of an earlier expert's determination that was binding on them. They therefore really wanted to lose the 'What prevails?' argument so that they could mount a rectification claim. All in all, not a happy result.

[13] [2001] EWCA Civ 406.

[14] In the end, unsuccessfully.

A lack of coherence can sometimes be seen even in drafting that superficially appears not to embody any contradictory or inconsistent provisions at all. An example is *RSPCA v Sharp*,[15] a case concerning a will. Clause 3 of the will gave specified beneficiaries

> the amount which at my death equals the maximum I can give them… without Inheritance Tax being payable in respect of this gift.

Clause 4 bequeathed a house to another set of beneficiaries and directed that the inheritance tax on that bequest should be borne out of residue. Clauses 5 and 6 bequeathed the residue to the RSPCA.

At first glance, therefore, none of the clauses seemed to conflict with any other. Nor was there any obvious inconsistency between the provisions. Nonetheless a dispute arose: the drafting problem was that the drafter of the will had not made it clear how the clauses *interacted*.

The executors took the view that the effect of clause 3 was to confer a bequest of £300,000, the amount of the then nil rate band for inheritance tax. In other words, they took the view that clause 3 should be applied without taking account of any IHT that might arise because of the bequest in clause 4. But the RSPCA argued that this could not be right. IHT, when it applies, is regarded as payable in respect of the *whole estate*: it is not allocated to any specific bequests. Accordingly, the only way that no IHT could arise in respect of the clause 3 bequest ('without Inheritance Tax being payable in respect of this gift') would be to restrict it to the amount which, taken *together with* the house bequeathed under clause 4, made up the £300,000 nil rate band.[16]

This was not a case of contradiction or implied inconsistency. Clarity would not have resulted if the drafter had simply addressed the question of whether clause 3 prevailed over clause 4, or the other way round. If clause 3 had been expressed as 'subject to clause 4',[17] for example, it would not really have resolved the issue. Clause 4 dealt on its terms only with the bequest of the house and the IHT on that bequest, saying nothing about the clause 3 bequest. And if clause 4 had been made 'subject to clause 3', the only effect would seem to be a rather different one: if there had not been enough cash to satisfy the clause 3 bequest, it might have cast doubt on whether the bequest of the house under clause 4 should be compromised in some way.

What the drafter needed to have done (if the testator's intention was indeed to pass a gross amount equal to the nil rate band under clause 3) was more sophisticated than that. The will would have needed to state that for the purposes of calculating the amount of the bequest to be made under clause 3, the executors should consider what the position would have been if the clause 4 gift had not been made.

15 [2010] EWCA 1474.
16 The Court of Appeal, after weighing the arguments carefully, found in favour of the RSPCA.
17 The usual method of resolving 'What prevails?' questions: see **12.16** below.

This case illustrates how delicate the drafter's task is to craft a fully coherent document. A contract must be viewed holistically, not as a set of completely independent provisions. Nonetheless, by far the most common category of case where the drafter fails to achieve coherence is where two provisions embody a contradiction or inconsistency that invites the 'What prevails?' question; which is why the rest of this chapter is devoted to it. The wider term 'inconsistency' is generally preferred to 'contradiction': a contradiction is no more than a very obvious inconsistency.

If the drafter does not make clear what prevails, unpredictability results

12.5 If the drafter does not make it clear which of two conflicting provisions prevails, the parties may take opposing views. Since the contract provides no answer to the conundrum, the question can only ultimately be resolved by a judge or any different dispute resolution mechanism provided for in the contract.

A judge will be faced with the task of interpreting the contract as a whole to work out which provision is to be preferred over the other. So the 'What prevails?' question may turn on, for example:

- which of the competing provisions' supremacy fits better with what the rest of the contract, taken together with the admissible background, suggests is the contractual purpose (for example, because it would be irrational for the other provision to prevail);[18]
- which provision seems likely to be the one which the parties can be assumed to have considered was specifically applicable, either because it appeared in some bespoke language rather than in general terms contained in a borrowed standard form,[19] or because simply more obviously narrowly targeted;[20] or
- which provision is given greater prominence in the contract.[21]

These factors may not all point the same way. And another consideration blurs the picture still further. Faced with a set of provisions that at first glance seem to contain an internal conflict, a judge will strain to conclude that the drafter thought the provisions were in fact reconcilable. Judges often express

[18] As for instance in *DnaNudge Ltd v Ventura Capital GP Ltd* [2023] EWCA Civ 1142 (provision in articles of association requiring class consent held to prevail over provision for 'automatic' conversion of shares, which would otherwise have inexplicably allowed a class of preferred shareholders' rights to have been taken away by the other shareholders).

[19] As for instance in *Pagnan SpA v Tradax Ocean Transportation SA* [1987] 3 All ER 565.

[20] A principle sometimes referred to by lawyers, presumably to the bafflement of most of their clients who are saddled with the legal costs of sorting out the dispute, by the Latin phrase 'generalia non specialibus derogant'.

[21] See **1.23** above.

a generous if sometimes inaccurate presumption that the drafter has tried to enshrine a fully thought-through and coherent consensus in a document which is itself internally harmonious.[22]

If a judge takes this line, a court may try to pre-empt a 'What prevails?' question by asking itself a different, and logically prior, question: is there a reading of the contract that does not involve a conflict *at all?* A court will approach this prior question in a

> cool and objective spirit, without presupposing that one answer is more likely than another.[23]

The outcome of any dispute of this type is accordingly unpredictable, depending as it does on the instinct of the judge and even on the quality of the presentation of the parties' respective arguments. Even if one party succeeds in persuading a judge that its view of the meaning of the contract is to be preferred, it will have been forced to spend valuable time doing so. It may not recover all its costs; its business relationship with the counterparty is likely to have been poisoned. For the other party, the result is of course still worse: its view of the contract has not prevailed, and it is likely to have to bear the lion's share of the legal costs of the journey to what must seem a desolate destination.

The task of the drafter is to forestall all this. Where provisions potentially conflict, or where they can only reconciled with some distortion to their surface meaning, the drafter should intervene to make it clear how they interact. As **12.4** above suggests, this is a far-reaching question. But the main objective of the drafter should be to make clear the answer, in any particular case, to any 'What prevails?' question that the drafting throws up.

If the contract acknowledges that provisions may be superficially inconsistent and makes it clear which provision is to prevail if that occurs, a judge is freed from straining to come up with a reading of the contract that reconciles all the provisions.

This means that drafting so as to answer 'What prevails?' questions has a benefit going beyond merely corroborating the credibility of the drafting. It allows the process of applying a contract to be more straightforward and economical, by providing for the contract to operate both coherently and predictably.

Only diligent checking will flush out inconsistencies

12.6 To identify inconsistencies, a drafter has no alternative to undertaking a careful and thorough read-through of the whole of the contract before it

[22] For an example of this type of approach, see *Adactive Media Inc v Ingrouille* [2021] EWCA Civ 313 (David Richards LJ) (contrary to High Court's conclusion, no conflict between governing law clause and arbitration clause in consultancy agreement).

[23] *Pagnan SpA v Tradax Ocean Transportation SA* [1987] 3 All ER 565 (Bingham LJ).

is signed. The drafter needs to identify provisions that overlap; to determine whether, in overlapping, they conflict so as to invite the question 'What prevails?'; and, if that question arises, to answer it. The techniques for doing so are discussed below.

Professional drafters reading this advice may retort that it is unrealistic to expect that a read-through like this can in practice happen, bearing in mind many clients' determination to negotiate their contract right up until the last minute, requiring the drafter to devote all available time to reflecting the outcome of those negotiations. But if the drafting turns out to contain conflicting provisions without resolving which of them is to prevail, clients are likely to blame the drafter, who will plead in vain that there was not enough time[24] for the drafting to be checked before the contract was signed. Drafters might consider asking a colleague hitherto uninvolved in the contract to read it through solely with a view to picking up unresolved internal conflict.

PARTICULAR CASES WHERE 'WHAT PREVAILS?' ISSUES ARE MORE COMMON

When a document is not just one drafter's work

12.7 The longer and more complex an agreement, the easier for an inconsistency to elude the attention of even an alert drafter. And the modern tendency is for contracts to become ever longer and ever more complex. It is routine for ready-made clauses to be inserted into an agreement through a 'cut and paste' process. Even if the drafter has checked that the clause to be inserted appears to be appropriate in itself, that does not guarantee that the new provision does not clash with something else in the contract.[25] As Chadwick LJ observed in *Taylor v Rive Droite Music Ltd*:[26]

> the process of adaptation from other documents lends itself more readily to sloppy and careless draftsmanship than the process of drafting as a coherent whole…

[24] For a drafter to spend time identifying and fixing inconsistencies may strike the contracting parties as representing an unnecessary expense. A drafter might respond by pointing out that, compared with the cost of resolving an inconsistency that finds its way into the final contract, the extra expense is a mere drop in the ocean. In *Taylor v Rive Droite Music Ltd* [2005] EWCA Civ 1300, for example, inconsistencies in a publishing contract meant that it was unclear whether its term was two or three years. Admittedly, this was not the only issue in dispute. But it gave rise to a 19-day hearing in the High Court, which was not in itself enough to stop the bleeding: the dispute went up to the Court of Appeal.

[25] *Macquarie Internationale Investments Ltd v Glencore UK Limited* [2010] EWCA Civ 697: 'now that documents are routinely drafted by electronic means, with provisions in previous contracts being used and adapted for new contracts, the likelihood of superfluity of expression and duplication of protective provisions is all the greater' (Lord Neuberger MR). The same, he might have added, goes for the likelihood of internal inconsistency.

[26] [2005] EWCA Civ 1300 at [42].

Inconsistencies often arise when the different sections of an agreement are bolted together to form a single document. In many law firms, different groups of specialist lawyers may be responsible for the different sections: each group's attention will tend to be focussed on the particular section for which it has responsibility. But somebody has to make sure that the different sections all work together properly. This becomes harder still if more than one document is involved, particularly if the parties have entered into different agreements at different times. Such contracts may often overlap, and the risk of their dealing inconsistently with particular circumstances is increased.

It is instructive to look at the risk areas in which difficulties most often tend to arise.

When more than one document tries to achieve the same contractual effect

12.8 In a multi-document contract, more than one document may play the same role in the contractual framework.

For example, in *HIH Casualty & General Insurance Ltd v New Hampshire Insurance Company*,[27] insurance arrangements were entered into on the basis of an initial insurance slip and some subsequent policy wording. It was not made clear whether the slip prevailed over the policy wording, or the policy wording over the slip. This inevitably provoked extensive argument in court when it turned out that the parties' respective interests led them to take opposing sides on the question.

When bespoke provisions supplement a standard form

12.9 It is common for internal conflicts to arise when parties enter into a contract based on a standard form, but agree on some particular provisions directed to their own circumstances. It is in the nature of such an arrangement that the parties will want their bespoke provisions to prevail over anything in the standard form that conflicts with them. Judges infer this, even if the contract does not say so explicitly.[28] But it is always better to be clear about the issue in the contract than to rely on a court drawing the correct inference. A practical issue arises for the drafter if a standard form is overlain by some specially-drafted provisions contained in a separate bilateral document. The drafter has to bear in mind what is said in the standard form, and to achieve the desired contractual result through the combination of two different

[27] [2001] EWCA Civ 735.
[28] *Homburg Houtimport BV v Agrosin Private Ltd (The Starsin)* [2002] 1 AC 715 at [11] (Lord Bingham).

documents. But it is harder to achieve consistency and coherence when the drafter has to wrestle between two documents that interact and overlap.[29]

Sometimes the drafter will want to incorporate not the whole of a standard form, but only specified parts of it. The drafter needs to be explicit about what part is being incorporated. If that is unclear, the drafter risks an argument that something else has been incorporated that the drafter meant to leave out.[30] The more specific the language of incorporation, the better, and it can do no harm to add '(but not any other provisions of [name of document])' or similar language to put the matter beyond doubt.

All that this technique achieves, however, is to make clear whether or not any particular provisions have been adopted. It does not resolve any conflict which then arises between the incorporated provisions and the rest of the document. To do that, a drafter needs to identify and address the conflicts using the techniques described later in the chapter.

When overlapping documents are designed for different purposes

12.10 This type of problem sometimes arises (see **12.15** below) in securities offerings, when a complex series of contractual relationships is created by a set of documents (which may have a hierarchy among themselves), which themselves form the basis of an offering circular under the terms of which investors are invited to subscribe for securities.

Other cases that tend to carry a particular risk of overlap, and thus of potential inconsistency, arise in consumer contracts. The actual contractual drafting is often (with good reason) regarded[31] as too inaccessible for the consumer to understand, so a more straightforward explanation is prepared. Vigilance is needed to ensure the two coincide. If they do not, doubt is cast on whether the contractual drafting accurately reflects the parties' intentions.[32] In cases where contracts have been carefully put together to achieve (say) a particular tax effect, the house of cards can easily collapse if simpler documentation, prepared with a consumer in mind, does not pay careful enough attention to

[29] For example, the various contracts and appendices in *Bovis Land Lease Ltd v Cofely Engineering Services* [2009] EWHC 1120 (TCC); and the standard form and 'recap email' in *BP Oil International Ltd v Target Shipping Ltd* [2013] EWCA Civ 196.

[30] As for example may have happened in *Cottonex Anstalt v Patriot Spinning Mills Ltd* [2014] EWHC 236 (Comm) (incorporation of arbitration bylaws of the International Cotton Association argued to extend to rules relating to closing out of contracts).

[31] Though this in itself does not reflect well on the drafter.

[32] Very often, the explanation prepared for the consumer is a refreshingly easy read when compared with the contract itself. For example, the document prepared for individual investors in *Investor Compensation Scheme Ltd v West Bromwich Building Society No. 1* [1998] 1 WLR 896 was a model of clarity, whereas the actual contractual drafting in respect of the critical point was obvious gibberish: see **11.4** above.

the intricacies of the contract.[33] And the urge to make a product attractive to a consumer can lead to the consumer-facing document stressing the attractions of the product to the point where rights reserved to the supplier in underlying documents are effectively extinguished.[34]

In the context of employment contracts and analogous arrangements, a side letter may be put in place alongside some more general document. In such a case, inconsistencies between the side letter and the more general document may well cause difficulties.[35]

When the drafter adopts a 'torrential' drafting style

12.11 Some drafters appear to throw as many clauses as come to hand at a perceived problem, in the hope that enough of them stick for any problems to be avoided: a drafting method described by Lord Hoffmann as 'torrential'.[36] The problem is that the clauses may not work together.

Take for instance the contract scrutinised in *Brown v Drake International Ltd*.[37] Drake supplied workers to work at Southampton Docks, which were operated by Southampton Container Terminals Ltd.

Under the Drake/SCT contract, Drake agreed in clause 22 to indemnify SCT against liability for personal injury 'however caused' arising 'in connection with the execution of the contract'. In clause 23, Drake also agreed to indemnify SCT against damages payable by SCF in respect of injury to Drake employees. But the clause 23 indemnity contained an exception in respect of injury 'resulting from any act or default of SCT'.

So both clauses contained an indemnity in favour of SCT, but one had a carve-out for things that were SCT's fault. When a Drake employee suffered a fatal accident for which SCT was partly responsible, could SCT claim an indemnity against Drake? SCT argued yes, on the basis that clause 22 provided for an indemnity against losses 'however caused'. Drake, though, argued no, pointing to the clause 23 indemnity, which specifically carved out any SCT indemnity right when the losses arose as a result of SCT's own fault.

The drafter did not, it seems, identify that the two clauses were in conflict. The conflict was not one of direct contradiction. Both provisions pointed towards an indemnity in favour of SCT. But one contained an exception that the other did not. Either clause *on its own* would have made it clear whether

33 As happened in *A1 Lofts Ltd v HMRC* [2009] EWHC 2694 (Ch); [2010] STC 214.

34 *Alexander v West Bromwich Mortgage Co* Ltd [2015] EWHC 135 (Comm).

35 As with the side letter and a limited partnership agreement in *Liontrust Investment Partners Ltd v Flanagan* [2017] EWCA Civ 985 (limited partnership terminable on six months' notice, but side letter providing for notice not to apply in first 24 months of Mr Flanagan's participation in Liontrust).

36 *Norwich Union Life Insurance Society v British Railways Board* [1987] 2 EGLR 137 at [138].

37 [2004] EWCA Civ 1629.

SCT was entitled to an indemnity: it was the fact that they *both* appeared, and dealt inconsistently with the issue, that caused the dispute. More drafting did not mean *clearer*: 'more meant *worse*'.[38]

When the drafter does not appear to identify an overlap

12.12 Even competent drafters can leave the reader baffled when they provide clearly for a particular consequence to follow from a stated event, but fail to make it clear what amounts to the occurrence of that event. The sense this type of drafting gives is that the drafter has drafted each clause in isolation, without ever looking at them alongside one another.

This issue caused a dispute over a sum in excess of $17 million in *BMA Special Opportunity Hub Fund Ltd v African Minerals Finance Ltd.*[39] A borrower under a loan facility decided to refinance the whole amount borrowed under the facility. This uncontroversially triggered an obligation under clause 8.3 of the loan agreement to prepay to the original lenders the amount that had been borrowed. But was the prepayment also a 'voluntary prepayment' as described, a little further down, in clause 8.5? If yes, a prepayment fee of $17 million was payable; if no, no prepayment fee was due.

Despite the significant legal fees spent by the parties when the facility was drafted and negotiated, the answer to this was unclear, and arguable either way. The borrower had decided to refinance: its decision to do that was clearly a voluntary one. But when it refinanced, the obligation to prepay became compulsory: the borrower had no choice but to prepay. So was it a 'voluntary prepayment' or not? [40]

GENERAL TECHNIQUES FOR FIXING 'WHAT PREVAILS?' ISSUES

Confine the problem by consolidating the arrangements into a single document

12.13 A common drafting technique is to reduce the risk of inconsistency as between different documents by consolidating all the contractual arrangements into a single final contract that is explicitly stated to deal comprehensively with the parties' relationship and supersedes any earlier arrangement.[41] This

[38] To adapt Kingsley Amis, writing in *Encounter* (1960) about a proposed expansion of higher education.

[39] [2013] EWCA Civ 416.

[40] The judge and the Court of Appeal found that the prepayment fee was not due, but not without more legal fees having to be embarked to arrive at the answer.

[41] See from **1.15** above.

customarily takes the form of an 'entire agreement' clause that makes it clear that the parties intend only the provisions of the final contract to apply to regulate their future relationship: earlier agreements are wholly replaced.

The technique is not of course a panacea. Even if all the contractual arrangements are brought together into a single document, the drafter still has to check that the document itself is internally coherent and does not embody conflicts between the provisions it contains.

Provide an explicit hierarchy between documents, or parts of documents

12.14 An explicit hierarchy answers the 'What prevails?' question directly: as between A and B, either A prevails over B, or B prevails over A. If the hierarchy between or within specific provisions is made clear, the drafting has no internal conflict. A judge does not need to indulge in a Procrustean effort to reconcile provisions that do not fit neatly together: the hierarchy language means that they do indeed operate together smoothly.

A contractual hierarchy can function at many levels. In complex arrangements involving a series of contractual documents, a hierarchy might apply as between separate documents,[42] or between separate parts of documents, as a whole. Or a hierarchy may operate at a more detailed level, making clear the relationship between individual clauses, or smaller units still. At whatever level, the intended effect is the same: the question 'What prevails?' has an answer.

Some model language to provide a clear hierarchy of this type was supplied by the drafter in the contract under consideration in *Bovis Lend Lease Ltd v Cofely Engineering Services*:[43]

> If any conflict appears between the DOM/2 conditions and the Appendix then the Appendix shall prevail. If any conflict appears between the terms of Subcontract DOM/2 and the numbered documents the terms of Subcontract DOM/2 shall prevail. If any conflict appears between the provisions of the Main Contract and the terms of the Subcontract documents the terms of the Subcontract documents shall prevail.

The judge in that case could therefore be unequivocal:[44]

42 See, for example, *Yieldpoint Stable Value Fund LP v Kimura Commodity Trade Finance Fund Ltd* [2023] EWHC 1212 (Comm) (framework agreement expressed to be subject to the terms of particular transactions entered into pursuant to it).

43 [2009] EWHC 1120 (TCC) at [25] (Coulson J): the passage quoted from the contract appears at [25]. This was the high water mark of the clarity of the drafting: elsewhere the drafter was less successful, the judge observing at [22]: 'Each side has to accept that, even taking their case at its highest, there are infelicities of drafting, cross-referencing and the like, which cannot be easily resolved'.

44 ibid at [25].

> It is clear therefore that the Subcontract itself provides that the Appendix is the most important document.

Given that the case went to court, however, it is evident that the drafter did not go far enough by simply providing a hierarchy at this broad-brush level. What the language sought to do was to place various documents and parts of documents in a hierarchy of significance if any conflict arose between them.

But this language is by its nature cruder and less satisfactory than more balanced and targeted drafting that can follow if the drafter has taken the trouble to identify particular potential conflicts between particular provisions, or even within a single provision, and cater for them each case by case. Only that type of detailed drafting is enough to resolve difficulties.

In *Brown v Drake*[45], the problem was an unacknowledged conflict between clauses 22 and 23 of a contract. Clause 22 contained an unqualified indemnity. Clause 23 repeated the indemnity, but provided for a carve-out for things that were the fault of the contractor SCT. The drafter needed to have made clear which of them prevailed. Either clause 22 should have been expressed not to apply in circumstances falling within the clause 23 exception, or clause 23 should have been expressed to yield to, or be without prejudice to, clause 22, so that the clause 22 indemnity fell to be read as paramount. But as it stood, the drafting left open a question that should have been answered.

Similarly, in *BMA Special Opportunity Hub Fund*,[46] the conflict was within a single provision, clause 8. The drafter would not have to done much extra drafting to have avoided a dispute. Some simple language in clause 8.5 like 'Unless clause 8.3 applies' or 'Whether or not clause 8.3 also applies' would have made it clear whether or not a prepayment of the loan in the clause 8.3 circumstances was meant to be the type of 'voluntary prepayment' that triggered the clause 8.5 prepayment fee. Not for the first time in this work, the remedy is simple if the disease is only identified.

Beware wording that solves one dispute only to invoke another

12.15 Another case where simply providing a hierarchy between documents proved inadequate is *Septo Trading Inc v Tintrade Ltd*,[47] in which a drafter struggled to coordinate bespoke provisions and a general standard form: as **12.9** above suggests, often a recipe for confusion.

In a contract for the sale of oil, some bespoke provisions were contained in a 'recap email'. But the arrangement also embodied some standard form BP terms.

45 [2004] EWCA Civ 1629: see **12.11** above.
46 [2013] EWCA Civ 416: see **12.12** above.
47 [2021] EWCA Civ 718.

The drafter did gesture towards imposing a hierarchy as between the recap email and the BP terms: the BP terms were to apply 'where not in conflict with' the recap email.

On its face, this looks a promising route to resolving any conflict. But it did not prevent a dispute. The problem was that the recap email and the BP terms did not deal with expert determinations in the same way. The recap email said that the determination could apply to the quality of the oil, whereas the BP terms suggested that the determination was relevant only for invoicing purposes. The drafting that purported to deal with the 'What prevails?' question simply led on to another: did the BP terms indeed conflict with the recap email, or could effect be given to them both?

The case warns the drafter that 'document X prevails over document Y if they conflict' is language that goes in the right direction, but may not go far enough.[48] The drafter needs to go further and consider 'What prevails?' questions at a detailed level.

Nor, in a case involving bespoke provisions interacting with some general drafting, should the drafter deal with only *some* of the instances in which the intention is (say) to make the bespoke provisions prevail over the general ones. If the drafter does that, the inference can be that in a case where the drafter has *not* provided expressly for the bespoke conditions to prevail, they do not do so (because where the drafter wishes to make the bespoke conditions prevail, the contract expressly so provides).[49]

Another expression that promises more than it delivers in this context, among others,[50] is 'Except where the context otherwise requires'. A drafter who provides

> Except where the context otherwise requires, A shall prevail over B

purports to deal with a 'What prevails?' question issue, but in reality just ducks it.

On its face, this drafting introduces a rule which is only partially applicable: the context, the reader is told, may disapply or override the normal rule that 'A shall prevail over B'. But the reader is given no clue as to where, if at all, the context may 'otherwise require', and all that is achieved is that an uncertainty is placed in the mind of the reader. The suspicion is that the drafter has lacked the determination to go through the contract and decide where – if anywhere – the rule 'A shall prevail over B' should be disapplied. Instead, the drafter has merely included the phrase in an unconvincing effort to make the contract

48 See also *Kuoni Travel v Boyle* [2013] EWHC 877 (drafting provided that 'in the case of any conflict' between a sale and purchase agreement and a tax covenant, the tax covenant should prevail: dispute over whether a conflict existed when the sale and purchase agreement applied a thirty-day time limit for notifying claims, but the tax covenant did not).

49 *Alchemy Estates v Astor* [2008] EWHC 2675 (Ch).

50 See **4.1** above (n 1).

appear more coherent than it truly is. The scope for arguing about whether the context *does* 'otherwise requires' is obvious. The drafter should have taken the trouble to decide when the context did 'otherwise require', and provided specifically that the rule was overridden in those (but only those) instances.

A clear answer to a 'What prevails?' question can cause a problem at a different level.

For example, take the case where investors subscribe for an issue of securities in a financing arrangement.[51] The issue will be undertaken on the basis of an offering circular that purports to describe the effect of a complex set of underlying documents. To guard against the risk of inconsistency as between the offering circular and the underlying documents, a drafter will often provide that the underlying documents prevail over the description given in the circular. An example of this can be seen in *US Bank Trustees Ltd v Titan Europe 2007-1 (NHP) Limited*.[52] The provision in the offering circular that established the documentary hierarchy was admirably clear:[53]

> The obligations of the parties to the transactions contemplated herein are set forth in and will be governed by certain documents described herein, and all of the statements and information contained herein are qualified in their entirety by reference to such documents.

The difficulty with this is that there should, of course, be no discrepancy or conflict between the terms of the offering circular and the underlying documents. The circular is meant to describe the underlying legal relationships faithfully. If the offering circular conflicts (as it did in this case) with what the underlying documents say, the drafting makes it clear that the investors' rights are governed by the latter. But the resolution of the 'What prevails?' question has solved one problem, only to cause another: the investors may have a claim in respect of the inaccuracies in offering circular.[54]

LANGUAGE THAT CAN BE USED TO MAKE IT CLEAR 'WHAT PREVAILS'

To make clear what prevails, drafters customarily use the phrase 'Subject to'

12.16 In the discussion that follows, it is assumed that the drafter has identified that two provisions are in conflict in some way: clause A and clause B. The dominant provision (the one that the drafter intends to prevail) is clause B and the subordinate provision (the one that is intended to yield to clause

[51] Of the type referred to in **12.10** above.

[52] [2014] EWHC 1189 (Ch): the drafting is quoted at [36].

[53] If stylistically unattractive: note the triple appearance of 'herein' in a single sentence.

[54] [2014] EWHC 1189 at [84].

B) is clause A. That is not meant to imply that the subordinate provision will always appear before the dominant one.[55] The order could easily be reversed.

The most common method of indicating that clause B is to prevail is to insert 'subject to clause B' in clause A. The reader then readily understands that clause B prevails over clause A to the extent they are inconsistent with each other.

'Subject to' does not does not automatically obliterate the subordinate provision entirely, but it may do so

12.17 When a drafter uses language which expresses the hierarchy of provisions, the effect is not necessarily to supplant the subordinate provision entirely and render it of no effect. In other words, if clause A is made 'subject to' clause B, clause A is not consigned to the wastepaper basket if clause B applies. Clause A yields to clause B only to the extent that clause B is inconsistent with it.[56] So a contract might provide:

(a) Subject to (b), P shall deliver [a specified amount of a specified type of] timber to Q once a week.

(b) In circumstance J, P shall deliver the timber referred to in (a) to Q once a fortnight.

Here the dominant clause (b) does not, when it applies, supplant clause (a) entirely. Clause (a) is still relevant to identify what timber it is that P must deliver on the timetable prescribed by (b).

That principle is seen in action in *RWE Npower Renewables Ltd v JN Bentley Ltd*,[57] where the contract contained some language that made it clear what hierarchy applied among various contractual provisions.[58] When the arrangements were considered in court, the judges made it clear that although a subordinate

[55] Indeed, when judges find it impossible to decide otherwise which of two competing provisions prevail, they sometimes refer to a principle that what comes first deserves to prevail. This was pronounced confidently to be a 'principle of law' by Lord Wrenbury in the Privy Council in *Forbes v Git* [1922] 1 AC 256, but it is submitted that it is not one that does the law any more credit than would be done by the judge tossing a coin.

[56] The author has heard experienced drafting professionals describing 'subject to' as language that directs the reader to apply clause A 'through the lens of' clause B. This is a useful metaphor: a lens is not an eyepatch, and the image acknowledges that where clause B is engaged, clause A may still have an effect, modified or qualified in some way by the operation of clause B. But as the paragraph in the main text goes on to suggest, the modification or qualification required by the dominant provision may go so far as to disapply the subordinate provision completely.

[57] [2014] EWCA Civ 150.

[58] The language used in the contract was not conventional 'subject to' language, but instead provided for various contractual provisions, some of which appeared in other documents, 'to be read and construed as part of this Agreement in the following order of preference'. However, the author considers that the same result would have applied if the provisions had all appeared in the same agreement and the drafter had imposed the hierarchy using the 'subject to' concept.

provision yielded to a dominant one, the subordinate provision remained relevant to the extent that it did not conflict with the dominant one.[59]

'Subject to' is however perfectly capable of having the more radical effect of disapplying the subordinate provision *completely*. There is nothing wrong, in other words, with drafting that takes the form

(a) Subject to (b), P shall do X.

(b) In circumstance J, P need not do X.

Here the effect of the dominant provision (b), where it applies, is to nullify the obligation in the subordinate provision (a) completely. There is no difficulty in reading 'subject to' as having that effect.

'Subject to' requires care, however, if the dominant provision supplements the subordinate one rather than otherwise modifying it

12.18 Assume that the usual position under a contract is that P has to do X. But in circumstance J, P has to do Y *as well as* X. In other words, the dominant provision *adds* an obligation to the one required by the subordinate one.

With care, 'subject to' can cater for this:

(a) Subject to (b), P shall do X.

(b) In circumstance J, P shall [also do Y] [do X and Y] [do Y as well as X].

However, this works to convey the required meaning only because of the repeated reference in (b) to the obligation to do X, either expressly ('do Y as well as X' or 'do X and Y') or impliedly ('also do Y'). Consider what would happen if the drafter did not repeat the reference to X but provided:

(a) Subject to (b), P shall do X.

(b) In circumstance J, P shall do Y.

This drafting would not carry the required meaning of 'P shall do both X and Y'. The reason it would not work is that 'subject to' implies that where (b) applies, it modifies (a) in some way. But the only way (b) could be read as modifying (a) would be by *cancelling* the obligation to do X. But this is not the meaning the drafter intends.

The conclusion is therefore that although 'subject to' language can be used so as to add an obligation, the drafter must take particular care to convey the right meaning.[60]

59 [2014] EWCA Civ 150 at [17] (Moore-Bick LJ).

60 'Subject to' is not the right language to use in a case where the clause in which it appears cannot conceivably be affected by the dominant clause. 'Subject to' would then be meaningless or, in the words of Waksman J in *Drax Energy Solutions Ltd v Wipro Ltd* [2023] EWHC 1342 (TCC) at [65], 'would not make any sense').

'Without prejudice to' is safer to add an obligation

12.19 The risks inherent in using 'subject to' when an obligation is added are eliminated if the drafter uses 'without prejudice to' instead. In the example, this language should appear in paragraph (b) rather than (a). There is then no need to refer in (b) to the doing of X at all:

(a) P shall do X.

(b) Without prejudice to (a), in circumstance J, P shall do Y.

A cautious drafter might add 'as well as X' to the end of (b), but this is unnecessary: 'without prejudice to' does the trick on its own.[61]

'Without prejudice to' is, however, ill-equipped for use in clauses that are in any way inconsistent with one another, Where a drafter does use 'without prejudice to' in such a case, it is likely to be read as signifying that being equivalent to 'subject to'. In other words, if A is expressed as 'without prejudice to' B, B will be the dominant provision and A, the subordinate provision, will yield to it.[62] But the skilful drafter will use 'without prejudice to' only with provisions that do not conflict, when it straightforwardly signifies that both clauses apply, without any question arising as to any hierarchy between them.

'Notwithstanding': a feasible alternative to 'subject to' in the dominant provision, but less recommended

12.20 Where 'subject to' is used, it appears in the subordinate provision. Some drafters prefer to signify the hierarchy of provisions by inserting language in the dominant provision instead. So Clause B might open with language such as 'Notwithstanding clause A…'[63]

The two formulations (clause A beginning 'Subject to clause B' and clause B beginning 'Notwithstanding clause A') are equally clear in meaning. But there is a reason for preferring the 'subject to' version.[64] If 'Notwithstanding clause A' is used in clause (b), clause A is on its face unqualified. Nothing in clause A gives any hint that it is intended to yield to clause B to the extent the

61 Some drafters prefer 'without affecting' to 'without prejudice to', but this is a purely stylistic preference: the two expressions mean the same.

62 *Scottish Widows Fund and Life Assurance Society v BGC International* [2012] EWCA Civ 607 at [20] (Arden LJ).

63 Some drafters think the quadrisyllabic (and slightly old-fashioned) 'notwithstanding' should be replaced in modern drafting by some shorter and more modern alternative like 'despite'. That is, again (n 61), a purely stylistic choice.

64 Drafters should confine their use of 'subject to' to achieving this type of subordination. If it is used to disguise a condition, it can cause problems, as in *BJ Aviation v Pool Aviation Ltd* [2002] EWCA Civ 163, when a purported lease extension right was held void because 'subject to renegotiation of the rent payable' meant no more than 'if the parties can agree on the rent payable', which was an unenforceable 'agreement to agree': see **9.14** above.

two conflict. Readers of clause A only realise that it does not fully mean what it appears to say when they get around to reading clause B as well.

By contrast, if 'subject to clause B' appears at the beginning of clause A, a reader of clause A is already on notice that there is a provision which overrides clause A and indeed is directed to where to find it. There is no warrant for the reader imagining that clause A is unqualified.

To this it might be retorted that in the examples under discussion, a reader will encounter clause B straight after clause A, and so the chances of confusion are low. But this is doubtful. A reader of a contract that has already been entered into will normally not read it sequentially, but will be hunting for the answer to a particular question that has arisen. Such a reader may very well go straight to clause A and spend time analysing it without ever getting to clause B. And in any event, the example may be unrealistic in suggesting that the two clauses in conflict succeed one another: the dominant clause may lie very far from the subordinate one, especially in a complex contract.

'Notwithstanding anything else in this Agreement' and similar language can be used to make a provision 'superdominant'

12.21 Despite[65] the recommendation in the previous paragraph, there is one case where a drafter may reasonably prefer to place 'What prevails?' language in the dominant provision rather than the subordinate provision. This is where the dominant provision is intended to be 'superdominant': in other words, it prevails not just over one other provision but over the whole of the rest of the agreement. In this type of case the superdominant provision can be introduced by

> Notwithstanding anything else in this Agreement...[66]

The attraction of this is that it removes the need to identify all those provisions which contain anything that might conflict with the superdominant provision and to make them explicitly 'subject to' it. This alternative not only would be tedious and time-consuming, but would also carry another risk. If the drafter were to overlook one of the provisions which was intended to be subordinate, it might well be inferred to prevail over the superdominant provision – exactly contrary to the drafter's intention. The argument would be that the drafter had, when any provision was intended to yield to the superdominant one, always made that clear by using 'subject to' language in that provision. The

65 Or perhaps even 'notwithstanding' the recommendation.

66 Or even, in a transaction regulated by a series of documents, something like 'Notwithstanding anything else in this Agreement or in any other Transaction Document...' But see also n 69 below.

omission of 'subject to' from that one provision must accordingly have been deliberate.[67]

'Notwithstanding anything else in this Agreement' is therefore attractively economical language.[68] But it leaves the problem identified in **12.20** above, namely that readers of any of the subordinate provisions, each on its surface unqualified, may not appreciate that it is overridden.[69] To guard against this, a considerate drafter should consider how to draw attention to the superdominant provision, perhaps by placing it in a prominent position in the contract or referring to its predominance in the recitals which act as an introduction framing the contract.[70]

'Notwithstanding anything else in this Agreement' is therefore drafting of considerable power, and needs accordingly to be deployed carefully. It would be impossible to apply rationally if it appeared twice in the same contract in provisions that could themselves conflict, since each would on its face sterilise the other. A similar result would flow if the provision in which the superdominant language was contained was stated elsewhere in the contract not to apply in certain circumstances.[71]

More limited degrees of superdominance are possible

12.22 The drafter is free to narrow the scope of sovereignty enjoyed by the superdominant provision by restricting the overriding effect to something less than the entire agreement:

> Notwithstanding anything else in this clause…
>
> Notwithstanding anything contained[72] in Part IV of this Agreement…

Again, however, the drafter should beware an 'expressio unius' argument[73] that might arise. What happens if a provision X with this limited version of

67 A process of reasoning that judges often bring to questions of contractual interpretation, which rejoices in the Latin name 'Expressio unius est exclusio alterius', broadly that in generally explicit drafting, omissions must impliedly be deliberate: see **5.9** above.

68 And is effective to achieve super-dominance: *Optimares SpA v Qatar Airways Group QCSC* [2022] EWHC 2461 (Comm) at [27]–[28] (Calver J).

69 A problem that is exacerbated if the drafting is as in n 66, when a reader might read through a whole document without realising that its effect is subverted by something contained in another document entirely. This is accordingly a technique that the drafter should think twice before employing.

70 See generally Chapter 2 above.

71 A case that the author has seen in practice. The problem is that the clause disapplying the superdominant provision is within the ambit of the 'anything else in this Agreement' which the superdominant provision insists it overrides. So the drafting is circular.

72 'Notwithstanding anything contained…' is better than 'Notwithstanding anything else…' if the superdominant provision does not itself fall in Part IV: 'anything else' suggests that the superdominant provision is itself contained within the area of the contract over which it is accorded supremacy.

73 See n 67 above.

'superdominance' is found to conflict with a provision Y that lies outside X's stated sphere of supremacy? The limited 'notwithstanding' language might be argued to signify that the drafter meant to imply that Y should itself prevail over X.

A less confident version of this type of superdominant language is 'Nothing in this Agreement is intended to...' It is often used in the context of trying to make sure that the arrangements do not accidentally assume a different legal character from that which the parties want. The general position (see **12.28** below) is that the parties cannot ascribe to their relationship a different character from that which it bears on an analysis of the rights and obligations it creates. But evidence that the parties intend their relationship to fall on one side of a dividing line can sometimes be relevant.[74] So 'Nothing in this Agreement is intended...' may be of some, though limited, use.

'Supersubordinate' drafting is less likely to be useful than drafting for 'superdominance'

12.23 The foregoing paragraphs discuss with language which widens the scope of 'notwithstanding' language to create a 'superdominant' provision. Is there any case for using the same technique with 'subject to' language that attempts the reverse? In other words, in a clause intended to be subordinate, might it make sense – rather than referring to a specific overriding provision – to draft the subordinate provision as ' subject to anything else in this Agreement'?

Whilst in theory such drafting is feasible, it seems unlikely to be useful in practice. It strikes a reader that the drafter is timorous (not really believing in the drafting that is being advanced), or lazy (the drafter cannot be bothered to think through which other provisions might be engaged), or both. In *Apache North Sea Ltd v Ineos FPS Ltd*[75] Foxton J fairly referred to the phrase 'subject to the terms of this Agreement' as a 'drafting reflex'. Drafters should not rely on reflexes.

Just occasionally, however, drafting of this type can appear justified. For example, in a lease under scrutiny in *Goldmile Properties v Lechouritis*,[76] a tenant's right to quiet enjoyment of the premises was expressed as follows:

74 *National Car Parks Ltd v The Trinity Development Co (Banbury) Ltd* [2001] EWCA Civ 1686 ('This Licence is not intended by either party hereto to confer upon the Licensee any right or interest in the nature of a tenancy' regarded as of some relevance to the legal categorisation of an arrangement in circumstances where the parties were sophisticated and of equal bargaining power).

75 [2020] EWHC 2081 (Comm) at [23].

76 [2003] EWCA Civ 49.

> That the Tenant... shall peaceably hold and enjoy the Demised Premises during the Term without any interruption (except as herein provided) by the Landlord.

'Except as herein provided' has the flavour of something inserted by the drafter without considering exactly how and why the right to quiet enjoyment might be qualified. But when it came to the landlord wanting to clean and repair the building as was required elsewhere in the lease, those very general words were held to allow the landlord to do so and to achieve the contractual purpose, despite the disruption to the tenant's restaurant business.

'Subject only to'

12.24 Drafters sometimes use the expression 'subject only to' rather than merely 'subject to'. This formulation goes beyond mere emphasis.

The difference can be seen as follows.

If clause A is stated to be 'subject to clause B', the meaning is restricted to signifying the relationship between the two clauses: the meaning is that B prevails over A to the extent they would otherwise conflict with each other. But if clause A is also in conflict with a different clause, clause C, the drafter has not resolved whether clause A or clause C should prevail. That remains unclear.[77]

If, however, clause A is expressed to be 'subject only to clause B', the position is different. It is still clear that as between clause A and clause B, clause B prevails. But the reader has also been given a steer as to how to resolve a conflict between clause A and clause C. 'Subject only to clause B' is linguistic shorthand for 'subject to clause B, but not subject to any other provision'. So the meaning is reasonably clear: if there is a conflict between clause A and clause C, clause C must yield to clause A. So the single word 'only' has an effect more far-reaching than may at first seem obvious.

Not all drafters exhibit the necessary discipline in using the phrase *'subject only to'*. For example, in *Attorney General for Belize v Belize Telecom Ltd*[78] the drafter of articles of association provided that certain directors should hold office 'subject only to' a particular provision relating to some specified disqualifying circumstances. But the drafter plainly did not mean that: other provisions relating to retirement by rotation plainly applied to those directors, so 'subject

[77] An astute advocate trying to persuade a court that clause A should prevail over clause C would doubtless argue that by omitting to say that clause A was 'subject to clause C' when the drafting *did* provide that clause A was 'subject to clause B', the drafter was clearly indicating that clause A should prevail over clause C: the drafter was plainly capable of making it clear when clause A should be overruled, but had not chosen to do so in the case of clause C. But that is by no means a conclusive argument.

[78] [2009] UKPC 10.

only to' did not have the force that it superficially carried. The lesson from this is a common one: if a drafter uses expressions carelessly, without thinking through whether they have their usual meaning, the credibility of the drafting is undermined.

'Otherwise' not suitable to express subordination

12.25 It is tempting for a drafter to reach for the word 'otherwise' where the drafting provides for an exceptional case and then follows it with a general rule:

> If the Tenant serves a termination notice before 31 December 2024, this lease shall come to an end on 31 March 2025. Otherwise, it shall come to an end on 31 March 2027.

This works neatly enough if the dividing line between the exceptional case and the rest is sharp enough, as in the example.

But the drafter should not assume that 'otherwise' is always clear enough.

It did not prevent a dispute arising in *Cobelfret Bulk Carriers N.V. v Swissmarine Services SA*.[79] A charterparty for a specific voyage was entered into between the owner and charterers on the basis of some specific terms contained in an email. The email went on to say that the charter was 'otherwise' in accordance with a proforma charterparty.

The term 'otherwise' was held not to point conclusively towards the terms of the email prevailing over the terms of the charterparty. The pro forma charterparty contained some terms covering some of the same issues as had been dealt with in the email. The reader was forced to try to reconcile the two documents.

The drafting lesson is that 'otherwise' is in truth not language of subordination at all. Where it is appropriate, as in the example language earlier in the paragraph, it simply enables the reader to take the right fork in the road depending on whether a condition is satisfied.[80] But the *Cobolfret* case[81] shows that it is ill-equipped to do any more sophisticated job of resolving the priority intended to be according to competing provisions.

'Except as provided in' is sometimes (but only sometimes) an alternative to 'subject to'

12.26 Drafters sometimes use 'except as provided in' instead of 'subject to' when they are wanting to signify the relationship between provisions. Take for example the simple example used in **12.17** above:

79 [2009] EWHC 2883 (Comm).
80 For more on the undesirability of 'otherwise', see **9.14** above.
81 [2009] EWHC 2883 (Comm).

(a) Subject to (b), P shall do X.

(b) In circumstance J, P need not do X.

This could equally well be drafted as:

(a) Except as provided in (b), P shall do X.

(b) In circumstance J, P need not do X.

But 'except as provided in' is generally appropriate only if what the clause does is to eliminate or override an obligation otherwise required by the subordinate clause. It does not work if the provision referred to supplements the basic obligation. As explained in **12.18** above, in such a case 'subject to' can, with care, be used:

(a) Subject to (b), P shall do X.

(b) In circumstance J, P shall [also do Y] [do X and Y] [do Y as well as X].

By contrast, drafting using 'except to' in these circumstances simply fails:

(a) Except as provided in (b), P shall do X.

(b) In circumstance J, P shall [do Y] [also do Y] [do X and Y] [do Y as well as X].

Whichever formulation is chosen for (b), the drafting does not work. The implication in (a) of 'except as provided in (b)' is that when (b) applies, P does not have to do X. But the contractual intention is the reverse: that it must.

'Except as provided in' is ill-suited to other cases where the more flexible 'subject to' should be preferred.

For example, 'Except as provided in' does not work well when the dominant clause makes the obligation when the specified circumstance applies similar, but more onerous. Take the case where P's basic obligation is to deliver timber to Q at least once a fortnight, but in circumstance J it has to increase the frequency of deliveries to at least once a week. If this is drafted for using 'except as provided in', the result is:

(a) Except as provided in (b), P shall deliver timber to Q at least once a fortnight.

(b) In circumstance J, P shall deliver timber to Q at least once a week.

But this reads uneasily. The issue is that the greater includes the lesser. When (b) applies, P's new obligation is not truly an exception to the obligation to deliver 'at least once a fortnight'. If P does deliver 'at least once a week', as (b) requires, it is necessarily also required to deliver 'at least' (in fact more than) 'once a fortnight'.

But no such difficulty applies if the drafter reaches for 'subject to':

(a) Subject to (b), P shall deliver timber to Q at least once a fortnight.

(b) In circumstance J, P shall deliver timber to Q at least once a week.

'Except as provided in' is also the wrong choice for a drafter when, for example, imposing a limit on liability.

(a) Except as provided in (b), A shall indemnify B for A's breach of contract.

(b) The maximum liability for A's breaches of contract is £5 million.

This does not work well, because (b) does not linguistically (or in what it means) operate as an exception to A's liability under (a). It represents a cap on the amount of liability, but that is an exception only in the strained sense that losses exceeding £5 million are excepted from the obligation in (a). It would be possible to draft (b) in such a way that 'Except as provided in' would work better in (a), by providing

(a) Except as provided in (b), A shall indemnify B for A's breach of contract.

(b) A shall not indemnify B for A's breaches of contract if and to the extent that A's losses arising from such breach of contract exceed £5 million.

But the natural drafting of (b) takes the form of a cap, and 'except as provided in' is not well-equipped to deal with it.

'Subject to', however, works readily to impose a cap:

(a) Subject to (b), A shall indemnify B for A's breach of contract.

(b) The maximum liability for A's breaches of contract is £5 million.

Unsurprisingly the same effect can be seen where the modification takes the form of a minimum threshold rather than a cap:

(a) Except as provided in (b), A is liable for losses suffered by B arising out of a breach of the warranties contained in Schedule 1.

(b) A is not liable under (a) unless and until the total damages suffered by B exceed £1 million.

Again, 'except as provided in' does not work. The language of (b) does not function as an exception to (a), but stipulates positively that (a) applies only once the threshold is reached. By contrast, 'subject to' would work perfectly well:

(a) Subject to (b), A is liable for losses suffered by B arising out of a breach of the warranties contained in Schedule 1.

(b) A is not liable under (a) unless and until the total damages suffered by B exceed £1 million.

The general point is that 'except as provided in' is only suitable for exceptions properly so-called, not for different cases where one provision modifies or overrides another.

'WHAT PREVAILS?' LANGUAGE: RECOMMENDATIONS AND LIMITATIONS

Answer 'what prevails?' issues with as much precision as possible

12.27 The drafting of a subordinate clause can proceed with varying degrees of specificity. In descending order, a drafter might consider:

> Subject to clause 12 (1)(a)...
>
> Subject to clause 12.1...
>
> Subject to clause 12...
>
> Subject to anything below...
>
> Subject to anything else in this Agreement...

The more specific the drafting, the more useful the language. The more general the language that is used to refer to the dominant provision, the greater the risk that the language will mistakenly be believed to refer to some other conflict which was either not identified or not intended to be resolved by it.[82] And as **12.23** above suggests, the most general form of 'subject to' language is unlikely to be useful at all.

A drafter is of course able to refer to the dominant provision as specifically as 'Subject to clause 12.1(a)' suggests only if clause 12 has been sub-divided into separately numbered and lettered sub-clauses and paragraphs.[83] If, however, that technique is not used, and the drafting of the dominant provision is an undifferentiated slab that continues for several lines, the drafter cannot focus on a particular paragraph (clause 12.1(a) in the example), but only to clause 12.1 or perhaps even clause 12 in its entirety. This would impose on the reader the unenviable task of reading all the way through clause 12.1 or clause 12 to identify which element of it the drafter intended to make the subordinate clause yield to.

If breaking the dominant provision down into shorter units matters for the dominant provision, it also helps to do the same with the subordinate provision. If the drafting is broken down in that way, as for example in:

[82] See, for example, *K/S Victoria Street v House of Fraser (Stores Management) Ltd* [2011] EWCA Civ 904, where the drafter provided in sub-clause (F) 'Notwithstanding the provisions in this clause', leading to a lively debate about whether sub-clause (F) overrode the whole of the rest of the clause, or just those sub-clauses to which it was plainly applicable.

[83] As **1.28** above recommends.

10. 3 (a) Subject to clause 12.1(a)...;

(b) ...; and

(c) ...

the reader can instantly identify that it is only clause 10.3(a), but not either 10.3(b) or 10.3(c), that is subordinated to the dominant sub-clause 12.1(a).

Within a single paragraph, there are further choices to be made. If the 'subject to' language appears at the beginning of the paragraph in which it appears, a reader will naturally assume that what is made subordinate is the entirety of (say) the obligation that the subordinate paragraph imposes. That is the right way of drafting if the dominant clause does indeed override the obligation to the extent of eliminating it. But if the dominant clause does not *override* the obligation but merely *modifies* it, it may be necessary to locate the subordinating language more carefully:

10.3 (a) The Borrower shall deliver the Required Information, together with any further information relating to the Borrower's financial position reasonably requested by the Lender, to the Lender and the Agent at least (subject to clause 12.1(b)) five Business Days before any Interest Payment Date

12.1 (b) In an Enforcement Period, clause 10.3(a) shall apply as if 'five' read 'ten'.

As this example also demonstrates, this approach has another virtue: the dominant clause can be more economically drafted because it is unnecessary to repeat the majority of the subordinate provision in an attempt to make it clear how the subordinate provision is affected.

The confident and careful drafter, therefore, is as specific as possible. And specific drafting breeds confidence that it has been deliberately framed: the overriding effect of the 'What prevails?' language will not extend beyond the circumstance the drafter has taken care to delineate. In a case where a right to rescind was expressed to apply

> save where the party purporting to serve such notice is in default of its obligations under this clause 6.2

it followed that the right to rescind was not overridden by breaches of obligations arising under other provisions.[84]

[84] *BDW Trading Ltd v JM Rowe (Investments) Ltd* [2011] EWCA Civ 548 at [37] (Patten LJ).

Remember that rules of law classifying legal relationships can impose a limit on the parties' ability to determine what prevails

12.28 Although parties generally have freedom to determine the answer to the question 'What prevails?' as between competing contractual provisions, that principle sometimes collides with rules of law that constrain that freedom.

One often-encountered case is seen when parties seek to ascribe to characterise their contract as amounting to a particular legal relationship, usually because that type of contract gives rise to preferable tax or regulatory treatment for one or both of the parties. But whilst the parties can as a general rule agree what they like as between themselves, they cannot award their contract a particular legal characterisation: that characterisation is a matter of law.

Accordingly, when (for example) a contract purports to style itself as a consultancy contract,[85] that does not close the door to a conclusion that it is, as a matter of law, a different type of contract. That would seem to remain the case even if the contract said that the clause attempting to characterise the contract prevailed over the other terms of the contract. The point is that the characterisation of the contract is not to be arrived at as a matter of contractual interpretation, but is a statutory question.[86]

A statement that the relationship between contracting parties is not intended to create a partnership will similarly not prevent the relationship amounting to a partnership if the effect of the contract is that the parties are carrying on a business in common with a view to profit.[87] By the same token, labelling an arrangement a partnership in an attempt to avoid the so-called partners being regarded as employees will fail if the true relationship is of an employment nature.[88]

Similarly, where for VAT reasons one party purports to provide a comprehensive service to a customer as principal, rather than as agent introducing other contractors who contract with the customer as principal, the categorisation of the supply for VAT purposes depends on analysing the contractual

85 As in *Autoclenz Ltd v Belcher* [2011] UKSC 41 where the contract provided: 'The Sub-contractor and Autoclenz agree and acknowledge that the Sub-contractor is not, and that it is the parties' intention that the Sub-contractor should not become, an employee of Autoclenz.'

86 In *Autoclenz*, the question was whether the contract was a worker's contract for the purposes of minimum wage regulations and working time regulations. The point that the question to be answered was a statutory one is 'critical to understanding' *Autoclenz*: see *Uber BV v Aslam* [2021] UKSC 5 at [68] (Lord Leggatt).

87 Again, a statutory question: 'carrying on business in common with a view to profit' is the definition of a partnership in the Partnership Act 1890, s 1(1). In reality a clause of the type described is often more aimed at preventing any implication that the parties have the rights to bind one another as agents. It is better, if this is the real concern, to state as much explicitly; but if in reality the arrangement is a partnership, the acts of a 'partner' may still bind the others unless the third party to whom the partner makes a commitment knows about the denial of rights of agency: see the Partnership Act 1890, s 5.

88 *Protectacoat Firthglow Ltd v Szilagyi* [2009] EWCA Civ 98.

relationships on the basis of which the supply is made, rather than being determined by how the parties describe it.[89]

In another well-known case, where parties to an arrangement for occupation of a flat agreed on exclusive possession, but labelled their contract a licence, the court concluded that it was, instead, a lease.[90]

The point in all these cases is that the characterisation clause is in reality not a provision on all fours with the underlying terms of the contract, so that it can be contractually agreed to prevail over them. The characterisation is a legal *consequence* of the effect of the underlying terms. A clause that purports to determine the quality of the relationship overreaches itself.

When, in cases like this, drafters misdescribe the legal relationships created by the contract they have drafted, they are accused of ascribing the wrong 'label' to it. The drafter has sought to determine the classification of the contract *despite* the true nature of the underlying rights and obligations being inconsistent with that classification.

But do not assume that to ascribe a label to a contract is always ineffective

12.29 'Mislabelling' is conceptually different from a case where the underlying contractual provisions *are* modified to the point that a particular undesired legal classification does not apply. For example, if a provision goes to the nature of the rights and obligations of the parties in such a way that the indicia of partnership are absent, that goes beyond mere 'labelling'. For example, if the 'partners' do not share income or contribute to costs in the same way, the relationship may not fall to be classified as a partnership, and even if the objective of including such a provision is that the parties do not want to create a partnership, there is no reason that objective should not be achieved.

Nor should a drafter conclude that it is always futile to state the parties' *intentions* on the classification of the contract they are trying to enter into. For example, where an agreement over land is involved, sophisticated parties can be assumed to know that the parties are aware of the difference between a lease which confers an interest in the land itself (and a right of exclusive possession) and a purely contractual licence, which does not. If therefore the parties refer to their agreement as a 'licence' and state, as happened in *National Car Parks Ltd v The Trinity Development Co (Banbury) Ltd*,[91] that

89 *A1 Lofts Ltd v HMRC* [2009] EWHC 2694 (Ch).
90 *Street v Mountford* [1985] AC 809.
91 [2001] EWCA Civ 1686.

> This Licence is not intended by either party hereto to confer upon the Licensee any right or interest in the nature of a tenancy and gives no proprietary interest to the Licensee in the Licensed Premises

the clause was not regarded by the court as an irrelevant or misleading piece of mere 'labelling'. The feature that led to a different conclusion from *Street v Mountford*[92] was that in *National Car Parks*,[93] the parties recognised that a licence did not confer exclusive possession, and by choosing to describe their arrangement as a licence, impliedly agreed that NCP should not enjoy it.

If one tries to analyse the two different types of case through a 'What prevails?' lens, they can be seen to be quite different. In a case like *National Car Parks*, there is in truth no conflict within the contract. The parties did not provide in one clause that there should be exclusive possession and then seek to characterise the contract as something inconsistent with that right.

By contrast, in the type of case exemplified by *Street v Mountford*,[94] the parties intend that possession should be exclusive but attempt to characterise the contract as something inconsistent with that right. The two provisions *do* conflict. And the reason the drafter does not attempt to resolve the 'What prevails?' question is that to resolve it in either direction causes an unwelcome consequence. If the contract provides that the underlying rights prevail over the characterisation clause, they make it clear that the characterisation clause is a mere label that can be ignored. But if the characterisation clause is stated to prevail over the provisions that confer the substantial rights and obligations in the contract, the contract is not the one that the parties want to enter into. There is an irreconcilable conflict that no amount of language aimed at resolving 'What prevails?' questions will help with.

92 [1985] AC 809.
93 [2001] EWCA Civ 1686.
94 [1985] AC 809.

Chapter 13

'What if?' questions

Drafters who fail to ask enough 'What if?' questions leave gaps in their drafting. The drafter needs to try to predict the future. Some future events are inevitable. Some future circumstances are readily foreseeable; others less so. The drafter owes it to the parties to create drafting that deals as comprehensively as possible with the circumstances that, were they to come to pass, would affect the parties' contractual relationship in a material way.

THE DRAFTER WHO DOES NOT ASK ENOUGH 'WHAT IF?' QUESTIONS IS FAILING

BAD FAILURES

13.2 Do not ignore the inevitable

13.3 Check whatever can be verified at the contract date

13.4 Do not overlook what a party is highly likely to want to do as soon as the contract is signed, or what it needs to do to implement its contractual rights

OTHER READILY FORESEEABLE CIRCUMSTANCES

13.5 What if a condition is not fulfilled?

13.6 What if the contract is not strictly conditional, but contemplates an event that turns out not to happen?

13.7 What if a party does not behave as expected?

13.8 What if the timetable slips?

13.9 What if the existing legal structure changes?

13.10 What if assets change hands?

13.11 What if one of the parties becomes insolvent?

13.12 What if a transaction's objectives are achieved, but not in the way expected?

13.13 What if something goes wrong between the parties?

THE DRAFTER WHO DOES NOT ASK ENOUGH 'WHAT IF?' QUESTIONS IS FAILING

13.1 The future is unknowable. No drafter can foresee all future circumstances that, if they were to come to pass, would affect the parties. Nor are all foreseeable circumstances equally likely. But a drafter cannot hide behind that as an excuse for failing to consider circumstances that *are* reasonably foreseeable, and, having considered them, then to draft for them.

If drafting does not cater for something that happens, the parties are likely to react to it by trying to agree on a way forward. But circumstances will have changed since the contract was entered into. One party may now want to walk away from the contract; the other, to stick to it. Or the parties' relationship may be so deeply intertwined that they both want the contract to continue, but differ markedly from one another on the terms on which that should happen.

Faced with this, the parties will be thrown back on any remedies they might have under common law, or be reduced to arguing that a term is implied in the contract that applies in the circumstances that have in fact arisen.

In *Casson v Ostley PJ Ltd*,[1] Sedley LJ makes some instructive observations on the nature of how a judge should deal with a drafting dispute:

> In the present case, as in most cases on the interpretation of contracts which reach this court, the words fall short of the facts. It may be axiomatic that we are to deduce the parties' intention from the words they have used, but the intention itself is in most such cases a fiction. Occasionally, it is true, something which has been agreed on has just been poorly expressed and can be elucidated; but far more often the parties have simply and understandably not even thought about the event which has now caused a problem… It might be no more than a recognition of human fallibility if we were to acknowledge that all contractual and legislative provision can usefully be subjected to a 'What if?' test, and that its response to the test may legitimately affect the meaning the courts accord it…

Sedley LJ is being generous in saying that drafters 'understandably' overlook possible future events. Professional drafters should hold themselves to a higher standard. An important item on any self-respecting drafter's checklist is to ask enough 'What if?' questions to mean that that all reasonably foreseeable circumstances are catered for and that the contract does therefore comprehensively set out what duties the parties would owe one another in any such circumstance.[2]

Another way of expressing this proposition is to say that drafters should challenge their own drafting by identifying what *assumptions* their drafting makes about the future and see what might happen to give the lie to those assumptions. The drafter needs a dose of self-awareness to do this, or at least to be able to analyse the drafting to see what assumptions it reflects.

The unknowability of the future makes this a counsel of perfection. And it is in the nature of things that the longer the period between the drafting of the contract and the date on which a contractual provision falls to be applied, the more sharply the circumstances may have changed and the more important, therefore, the thoroughness of the drafter in asking enough of the right 'What if?' questions when the contract was being drafted.

By looking at decided cases where drafters had not asked themselves the right 'What if?' questions, so that their drafting contained embarrassing holes, it is possible to identify the most common ones where drafting turns out to prove

1 [2001] EWCA Civ 1013 at [29] and [31]. The author is grateful to adopt the judge's language as the heading for this chapter.

2 For a contrary view, more generous to the drafter whose drafting has gaps, see Lord Leggatt's dissenting judgment in *Barton v Morris* [2023] UKSC 3 at [127]: 'life is too short to negotiate contract terms designed to cover every contingency that may occur. Even the most comprehensive and carefully drafted written contract cannot anticipate and provide expressly in advance for every possible contingency. And even where contingencies are foreseeable, commerce would be stultified if time and cost was routinely incurred in discussing and making provision for situations that are not thought likely to happen.'

defective. The remainder of this chapter deals with 'What if?' questions of this type, starting with the most embarrassing failures.

BAD FAILURES

Do not ignore the inevitable

13.2 'What if?' questions are to do with contingencies. The challenge for the drafter is to identify a circumstance which might possibly arise in the future. The drafter's culpability, if circumstances arise that are not contemplated by the drafting, is proportionate to how likely it was, when the drafting is carried out, that what *has* happened *would* happen. A drafter who does not cater for circumstances that are not reasonably foreseeable may perhaps be excused. But the drafter who fails to spot a stone cold certainty[3] has failed abjectly.

Such was the drafting in *Arnold v Britton*,[4] in which a service charge was levied on lessees of chalets in a holiday park under 99-year leases granted in the 1970s. The initial service charge was a comparatively modest £90 a year, but the service charge was to increase at 10% annually throughout the term of the lease. With no contingency other than the lapse of time, the service charge would rise inexorably at a 10% compound rate. The drafter had not attempted a mathematical calculation which would have led to the disturbing conclusion that the annual service charge would exceed a million pounds before the lease expired.

Astonishingly, and reflecting little credit on anyone involved, over 20 chalets were sold containing this provision.[5] In every case, either the lawyer acting for the purchasers did not identify the effect of the offending provision, or the buyer decided to go ahead anyway. This is, to say the least, surprising.

Check whatever can be verified at the contract date

13.3 Drafters may assume that a state of affairs exists at the date of contract, and focus their 'What if?' questions (and the drafting that flows from the answers) on what should happen under the contract if that state of affairs changes. But more immediate difficulties arise if the facts are not as the drafter has assumed them to be in the first place.

3 The drafter's failure is so extreme that it scarcely deserves to be called a failure to ask a 'What if?' question at all.

4 [2015] UKSC 36.

5 And with the exception of Lord Carnwath, all the judges refused to find that the leases could be interpreted in any other way: they did not accept that, to adapt Lord Hoffmann's formulation, 'anything ha[d] gone significantly wrong with' the drafting (Lord Neuberger ibid at [34]).

For example, in *BS & N Ltd (BVI) v Micado Shipping Ltd (Malta) (The Seaflower)*,[6] the charterer of a vessel was given the right to cancel the charterparty if the vessel 'lost' certain approvals on the part of oil majors. The absence of the approvals would have made sub-chartering the vessel impossible or uneconomic. The drafter assumed that the approvals were all in place at the start of the charterparty. But this was not so. The vessel had never received an approval from Exxon, one of the oil majors specified. So the charterparty's termination right did not look as if it applied:[7] the vessel could not 'lose' an acceptance it never had in the first place. The drafter's assumption about the state of affairs existing at the contract date had undermined the drafting.

A similar failure undermined the drafting of a pension trust deed in *The Pensions Regulator v A Admin Ltd*.[8] The deed referred to a method of computing benefits 'prescribed by Part 4 F[inance]A[ct] 2004'. But (as could easily have been established at the time) part 4 of the Finance Act 2004 did no such thing. The result was that the purported trust failed completely.

Part of a drafter's checklist should therefore be to verify that the factual assumptions on which the drafting is based are indeed true. This may not be easy. But it will help if the drafter maintains a list of those assumptions which can be checked off as the date for signature approaches. A lawyer drafting the contract will often not have any personal knowledge of the matters on the checklist, and so will have to rely on what the parties say. But the drafter owes it to the parties (if they are in the best place to verify it) to ask them explicitly to confirm what has been assumed in the drafting.[9]

Do not overlook what a party is highly likely to want to do as soon as the contract is signed, or what it needs to do to implement its contractual rights

13.4 In *RIG Holdings LP v Aeroflex Test Solutions Ltd*,[10] a company was sold by one group to another. The company being sold had a calendar year end for its accounts, but the sale took place on 31 July. A clause in the deed of tax indemnity accompanying the sale made perfect sense if the company being sold had retained its calendar year end. But the purchaser group's usual year end was 30 June, so it changed the year end of the company being sold to

6 [2001] CLC 421.

7 Though the Court of Appeal mercifully found that the charterer should be allowed to terminate.

8 [2014] EWHC 1378.

9 As an alternative to a checklist, a drafter might consider including a detailed set of *recitals* that include the assumptions of fact which have shaped the drafting of the contract (see **2.2** above). It is then the recitals, which appear in the contract document itself, that fall to be verified, rather than a separate extra-contractual list, on which it might be more difficult to focus the parties' attention.

10 [2009] EWHC 1440.

30 June, as it was allowed to do. That meant that the tax deed did not work as might have been expected. The drafter of the deed of indemnity had made an implicit assumption that the year end of the company being sold would stay as it was. But for the purchaser group to change it was not only a foreseeable event, but a likely one. The drafter had not challenged an assumption that could easily have been seen to be an unwarranted one.

Rig Holdings[11] illustrates how a drafter needs to look ahead to what a party might naturally be expected to want to do. But the drafter might fairly point out that there was nothing in the contract itself to nudge attention onto the target company's year end.

A drafter has less excuse for overlooking what is needed for the contract itself to make coherent sense. This happened in *Perhar v Freestone (Re the Sustainable Bathroom Company Ltd).*[12] The drafting of a debenture representing security for a financing facility simply failed to provide for the circumstances in which the security would become enforceable. Though the court was able to persuade itself to fill the gap with an implied term, the drafter had exposed the lender to unnecessary risk.

OTHER READILY FORESEEABLE CIRCUMSTANCES

What if a condition is not fulfilled?

13.5 The difficulties thrown up by the variety of meanings of the term 'condition' are explored more fully in Chapter 9. But a common 'What if?' question is often associated with conditions in the grammatical sense of contingencies. If an agreement, or some aspect of it, is subject to a condition in that sense, the drafter is often focussed on what happens once the condition is fulfilled. But it may not be, even if one or both of the parties have undertaken to try to make sure the condition is fulfilled.

This is what happened in *Total Gas Marketing Ltd v Arco British Ltd.*[13] A proposed long-term gas supply agreement was expressed to be conditional on Arco becoming party to an 'allocation agreement' by 1 March 1996. Arco agreed to use its reasonable endeavours to do so. But when March 1996 arrived, no allocation agreement had been agreed. So it was apparent that the drafting of the agreement was 'structurally incomplete… the consequences of [1 March 1996] passing without the Seller becoming a party to the allocation agreement are not spelt out'.[14] It was thus not clear whether that failure meant that Total

11 ibid.
12 [2023] EWHC 2065 (Ch).
13 [1998] UKHL 22.
14 ibid (Lord Steyn in the section of his speech headed: 'Clearing the decks: The terminology and structure of Clause 2.8').

was no longer bound by the contract, or its obligations merely suspended, a question that had to be left to the courts to decide. The drafter had simply assumed that the 'reasonable endeavours' obligation would lead to the condition becoming satisfied.

In a case where one party fails to act as expected to bring about the fulfilment of a condition, the innocent party might instinctively think that the same result should follow as if the condition *had* been fulfilled. The other party should surely not be able to rely on its own default to escape the consequences that would have followed fulfilment of the condition. But *King Crude Carriers SA v Ridgebury November LLC*[15] suggests that this is not so: English law does not recognise a principle of 'deemed fulfilment' of a condition.

What if the contract is not strictly conditional, but contemplates an event that turns out not to happen?

13.6 A similar danger lurks in a contract of this type. The drafting may assume that something will happen, reflecting the parties' common assumption that it will. They may even have agreed (in a non-binding way) that it *should* happen. But it may not.

In *Paros PLC v Worldlink Goup PLC*[16] it was assumed (and agreed, though in a part of the agreement that was not legally binding) that Worldlink, a PLC, would re-register as a private company. It did not do so.

Worldlink's failure to re-register had a consequence when it came to costs. The agreement on costs in paragraph 5 of the agreement dealt separately with what was to happen

> between signing this Agreement and the re-registering of Worldlink as a Private company

and

> after Worldlink is re-registered as a Private company.

The drafter had made an assumption: that Worldlink *would* re-register. The assumption was not express, only implied. Seemingly, the drafter either did not recognise that the drafting embodied an assumption, or did recognise the assumption but failed to challenge it by asking: what if Worldlink does not re-register as assumed? Whatever the answer, the result was a (doubtless unwelcome) dispute.

15 [2023] EWHC 3220: in the contract in question, the condition went to the obligation to pay a deposit, but was disguised by the contract simply assuming that the obligation would be fulfilled, rather than being clearly expressed as an 'if'-clause: compare **9.14** above.
16 [2012] EWHC 394 (Comm).

Again, in *Retirement Villages Developments Ltd v Punch Partnerships (PTL) Ltd*,[17] an option over land was framed so as to expire on an 'End Date', expected to arrive within 30 months. But the drafting also assumed that the local planning authority would at some point allocate the land for development. Unless and until they did so, no 'End Date' would occur and so the option – for which the optionholder had paid a premium of a mere £1 – would not come to an end. The planning authority did not allocate the land for development; no planning application was submitted; so the option remained in force indefinitely. The drafter did not seem to have asked: what if the planning authority does not allocate the land?

What if a party does not behave as expected?

13.7 Sometimes a contract does not expressly oblige the parties to behave in a particular way, but contains a provision that only makes sense if they do so. What if, when the provision falls to be implemented, the party does not behave in the way that the drafting assumes? This caused a difficulty in *Mapeley Acquisition Co (3) Ltd (in receivership) v City of Edinburgh Council.*[18] A lease of office premises obliged an outgoing tenant to pay remedy disrepairs or, if it did not, to pay to the landlord

> such reasonable sum as shall be certified by the Landlord's surveyors as being equal to the cost of carrying out such work.

But what if, for its own reasons, the landlord had no intention of carrying out that work? The lease did not expressly *require* it to do so, and arguably required the tenant to stump up for imaginary work that the landlord had no intention of carrying out. The Court of Session interpreted the provision as not requiring the payment to be made. But the drafter would have done better to consider the 'What if?' question and to make the payment depend on the work being carried out.

A similar difficulty arose in *Sheffield City Council v Scotfield Group Ltd.*[19] An agreement for the sale of a development site contemplated that, after planning permission had been granted, the developer/purchaser would provide evidence of a construction contract demonstrating to the seller (the Council) that the development could be carried out. But if the purchaser did not do that by a stipulated longstop date, the contract was simply extended indefinitely, leaving the Council in limbo. Doubtless, when the agreement was entered into, the parties all expected that the purchaser would provide the

17 [2022] EWHC 65 (Ch).
18 [2015] CSOH 29.
19 [2023] EWHC 990 (Ch).

evidence on time. But the drafter did not seem to have asked the question: What if that does not happen?[20]

What if the timetable slips?

13.8 From the examples so far considered, it is already clear that to ask the right 'What if?' questions, drafters need to challenge the assumptions they have (consciously or unconsciously) made. One assumption that has a way of undermining even sophisticated drafting is that anticipated events will play out over a particular period. A drafter may well cater for the question: what if the events assumed to take place do not happen at all? But the drafting may overlook the possibility that the events do happen, but later than it was assumed they would. Drafting that would have proved perfectly sensible on the original timetable may not fit the bill if the timetable slips, as experience shows is all too often the case.[21]

So when in 2006 a contract was drafted[22] awarding a bank a performance fee for finding an investor, the formula for determining the fee was based on the investee company's 2006 EBITDA. But the investor did not invest until December 2007, by which time the 2006 EBITDA was receding in the rear-view mirror. The drafter had not challenged the assumption, implicit in the drafting, that the 2006 EBITDA would still be an appropriate basis on which to calculate the fee when the transaction eventually happened.

In another case,[23] a solicitor's retainer provided for a fixed fee 'subject to the completion of the Matter by 31 May 2017'. The drafter was confident enough not to make clear what fee arrangements would apply if the timetable was missed. It was indeed missed, and the solicitors had to fight a disputed case in court to establish that any payment for their work was due at all.[24]

What if the existing legal structure changes?

13.9 A drafter may construct a contract that makes sense in the context of the legal relationships as they stand when the contract is prepared, but ceases to do so if those relationships change.

[20] The court rescued the drafting by finding that an *implied* term required the purchaser to provide evidence of a construction contract within a reasonable time after the longstop date, failing which the Council could take steps to bring the contract to an end. But as suggested elsewhere, drafting has failed if it has to rely on the court implying a term into it.

[21] It is rare for contracting parties to *over*estimate the amount of time needed to negotiate a contract: their error is usually the exact reverse.

[22] *ING Bank NV v Ros Roca SA* [2011] EWCA Civ 353.

[23] *Blacklion Law LLP v Amire Nature Foods* [2022] EWHC 1500 (Ch).

[24] See also *Petroplus Marketing AG v Shell Trading International Ltd* [2009] EWHC 1024 (contract for purchase of oil specifying assumed lifting dates later overtaken by events).

In *Rail for London Ltd v London Borough of Hackney*,[25] a lease of railway arches fixed the rent payable to the landlord council by reference to the rent received by the tenant T under a specific underlease. The commercial effect was to pass on an agreed proportion of the rents ultimately received from occupational tenants of the arches. This made sense while the underlease was in place. But when it was surrendered, no rent was thereafter payable *under that underlease* to T. T continued to benefit from the rents payable by the occupational tenants, but now received them directly rather than in the form of rent paid under the (now defunct) underlease.

The drafting on its face had failed: only the finding of an implied term saved the drafter's blushes.[26] What the drafter had done was to focus too closely on the existing legal structure, and had not asked the question: what if the underlease is surrendered? The drafter would have done better to stand back from the existing legal structure; recognised that the commercial objective was the pass-through of occupational rents, in whatever form T received them; and drafted in more general terms to achieve this.

What if assets change hands?

13.10 It is in the nature of assets that different people can own them at different times.

In *Attorney General for Belize v Belize Telecom Ltd*,[27] the document at issue was the articles of association of a privatisation company, whose share capital included a special share and a class of C shares. The holder of the special share (the Belize government) also held C shares and was therefore, the articles provided, entitled to appoint some 'C directors'. The government did so. The drafter of the articles had also thought to include a provision entitling the holder of the special share to *remove* the C directors, again provided the holder of the special share held enough C shares.

The drafter's assumption was that the special share and the C shares would always remain in the same ownership. This was doubtless the plan, but by the time the question arose, the ownership of the special share and the C shares had become separated because of a default on a loan and the enforcement of security. So the 'removal of C directors' article did not work.

The case is chiefly known to lawyers these days as one of the leading authorities on when implied terms can be read into an agreement. But a logically prior question throws an unflattering light on the quality of the drafting. If a party

[25] [2022] EWHC 2929.

[26] Only that finding rescued the council: a negligence claim brought against its solicitors would have been time-barred: ibid at [53].

[27] [2009] UKPC 10.

has to argue that a term should be implied, the drafting has failed.[28] Here the drafter's failure was to ask a 'What if?' question. The drafting assumed that the special share and the C shares would remain in the same hands. But what would happen if that assumption was wrong, and they became separated? The drafter did not think about this, with the result that the express terms of the articles made no sense as they stood.[29]

A similar fate awaited the drafting in *Farstad Supply A/S v Enviroco Limited.*[30] The drafter borrowed the definition of 'subsidiary' from the Companies Act 1985. The statutory definition depended on the legal ownership of shares as evidenced by the share register, which had been lost by the 'parent' because of the particular way in which the shares had been pledged to a bank. So the change in ownership of an asset caused a problem with the drafting. The drafter needed to have asked the 'What if?' question: what if the legal and beneficial ownership of the shares become detached from one another as part of the provision of security?

What if one of the parties becomes insolvent?

13.11 This circumstance is very often in contracting parties' minds, usually with an exclusive focus on the other party's position rather than their own. It is often dealt with by providing that the contract can be terminated by the solvent party, but the 'What if?' questions can be wider. For example, in a reinsurance contract, the insolvency of the reinsured party may lead to that party not paying out the insured under the original contract of insurance. In such circumstances, should the reinsurer be obliged to pay out under the reinsurance contract, even though the reinsured party has not met its liability to the original insured? The point has arisen in more than one case,[31] with drafting that did not go far enough to determine the outcome clearly. The drafting would have avoided the need for litigation if it had addressed separately the 'What if?' question: what should happen if the reinsured becomes insolvent?

28 See **1.4** above.

29 The drafter also failed to contemplate the possibility that the special share, which was redeemable, might be redeemed. This did not happen, but could have. And if it had, the drafting would, again, not have worked. This illustrates vividly a common characteristic of poor drafting, namely that it is not merely that the only possible circumstance that could have derailed the drafting has occurred: in truth the drafting is riddled with potential difficulties, and what has actually happened is just one of a great many possible triggers for a problem.

30 [2011] UKSC 56.

31 In *Charter Reinsurance v Fagan* [1997] AC 313 the phrase 'actually paid' was discussed in this context, and was held to mean something different from its meaning in the context of the more extensive drafting of 'shall have become liable to pay and shall actually have paid', the language in *Firma C-Trade SA v Newcastle Protection and Indemnity Association (The Fanti)* [1991] 2 AC 1: see **11.2** above.

Anthracite Rated Investments (Jersey) Limited v Lehman Brothers Finance SA (in liquidation)[32] throws light on the same problem in a different context. In a transaction devised by a Lehman group company, it was arguable on the drafting that Lehman enjoyed a right to a substantial compensation payment on an early termination of the arrangements, including in a circumstance where the reason for the early termination was Lehman's *own* default. This can surely not, if the parties had been asked the question at the outset, have been their commercial intention. But the drafter had not asked the question: what if the reason for an early termination is Lehman's own default?

The 'What if?' question discussed in this paragraph can naturally crop up alongside the question identified in the previous one (assets changing hands). This may arise when a contracting party which is a company runs into financial difficulties, leading to the appointment of administrators who then sell the company's assets in the course of administration. An example of this type of unfortunate combination is *Stichd Sportmerchandising BV v Rowley and Baker*,[33] in which administrators of a company that owned a Formula One team sold off the business of operating the team, leaving a company that had contracted to supply 'Team Uniforms' in the unfortunate position of having no team to supply them to.

What if a transaction's objectives are achieved, but not in the way expected?

13.12 Drafting should not presuppose that an objective will be achieved in a particular way, if other ways are possible. Drafting that (for example) rewards one party if method X is used to achieve a contractual objective may unfairly leave the party unrewarded if the objective is accomplished by method Y instead.

Contra Holdings Ltd v Bamford[34] in volved an agreement providing for a fee to an adviser if a transaction referred to as 'Project Crakemarsh' was carried out. Project Crakemarsh was defined to mean the sale of a particular company. In the adviser's mind, the sale was but one method of achieving an overall objective – that of regularising the respective interests of the family members who were the beneficiaries of the trusts that held the company's shares. But an argument that the fee was payable when other arrangements achieved that same objective was defeated in court.

A similar underlying problem bedevilled the drafting in *EMFC Loan Syndications LLP v Resort Group Plc*.[35] A debt adviser agreed to help a client

32 [2011] EWHC 1822 (Ch).
33 [2022] EWHC 933.
34 [2022] EWHC 1857 (Comm); confirmed on appeal at [2023] EWCA Civ 374.
35 [2021] EWCA Civ 844.

and its bank raise borrowings in the debt markets. The adviser's fee was to be based on the amount raised. Because of disagreements about the best markets to tap, the client decided to use its bank and not the adviser to pursue the raising of finance. The debt adviser's services were accordingly not called on to implement the client's borrowing. But the drafter had not thought to make it a condition of the adviser's entitlement to its fee that the adviser's efforts actually led to the fund-raising goal being accomplished. So the adviser, no doubt to the chagrin of the client, was held entitled to the fee.

What if something goes wrong between the parties?

13.13 Parties do not enter into an agreement expecting it to turn out badly for them. If that is what they expected, they would not sign it. It follows that one of the most basic 'What if?' questions – and one that does not receive enough attention – is: what happens if something goes wrong and the parties fall into dispute? Perhaps lawyers, who are trained to look at questions of risk, have a particular responsibility to think about this basic risk and to draft appropriately for it through an appropriate dispute resolution clause (and to persuade the parties to pay attention to it).[36]

A jurisdiction clause needs to make it clear whether the territory whose courts are stated to have jurisdiction over a dispute should have 'exclusive' jurisdiction or 'non-exclusive' jurisdiction. If exclusive jurisdiction is intended to be confined to, say, the English courts, it is best to say so explicitly. This reduces the scope of uncertainty under the 'What if?' question: what if a party tries to secure a tactical advantage by initiating proceedings in another territory? If a drafter does not answer this 'What if?' question (which can be done simply by use of the words 'exclusive' or 'non-exclusive'), further uncertainty is created: see, for example, *Hin-Pro International Logistics Ltd v Compania Sud America de Vapores SA*.[37]

More generally, parties may underestimate the need to draft in detail the provisions that will regulate their relationship if they do not see eye to eye. In an agreement designed to record the basis of sharing merchandising income generated by the character Paddington Bear, a provision for audit of records was succinct:

[36] Including in particular the stipulation as to which courts should have jurisdiction to determine a dispute: in *Sebastian Holdings Inc v Deutsche Bank AG* [2010] EWCA Civ 998, Thomas LJ said at [57], citing in support an article by Richard Fentiman in *International Commercial Litigation* (2010): 'Jurisdiction clauses are rarely the subject of detailed negotiation and there is nothing to suggest that in these transactions any detailed attention was paid in the negotiations to the jurisdiction clauses.' But a well-drawn jurisdiction clause is essential to answer the 'What if?' question: what if one of the parties wants to enforce the contract in the courts? In which territory's courts should the dispute be heard?

[37] [2015] EWCA Civ 401; also *Al Mana Lifestyle Trading LLC v United Fidelity Insurance Company PSC* [2022] EWHC 2049 (Comm). In neither case did the words 'exclusive' or 'non-exclusive' feature.

> During the term of this Agreement a third party auditor may, upon prior written notice to Paddington and not more than once per every two year period, inspect the agreements and any other business records of Paddington with respect to the relevant records or associated matters during normal working hours to verify Paddington's compliance with this Agreement.

But it gave rise to no fewer than ten different issues which a judge had to determine.[38]

If the relationship between the parties comes under pressure, any contractual mechanism which they agreed at the outset can become snagged, and break down. If, for example, payments between the parties depend on the mechanism working smoothly, a party expecting payment may be left unsatisfied. In *Aston Martin MENA Ltd v Aston Martin Lagonda Ltd*,[39] a distributor of luxury cars was entitled to payments described in the contract as 'Manager Committed Minimum Profit' or MCMP, based on a business plan to be agreed annually. But when relations deteriorated and no business plan was agreed for a particular year, it was held that no MCMP fell to be paid for that year. The disappointed distributor had no protection. The distributor would have wished for the contract to deal with the question: 'what if no business plan is agreed for a year?'

What if the general financial environment changes?

13.14 In *Re Sigma Corporation*,[40] a security trustee was appointed to protect the interests of secured creditors of Sigma, a special purpose vehicle that acquired financial assets. The role of the trustee was to hold and if necessary enforce security over Sigma's assets. The drafter of the security trust deed provided in detail how, if the security fell to be enforced, the trustee would realise Sigma's assets, marshal the proceeds and use them to pay out the various classes of Sigma's secured creditors.

One provision directed the trustee to use funds thrown off by the realisation during a 60-day 'Realisation Period' to pay as they fell due obligations owed to a particular class of secured creditors, those holding what were termed 'Short Term Liabilities'.

The drafter did not qualify that direction at all, having apparently assumed that funnelling available funds towards the holders of Short Term Liabilities in that period should not affect the rights of other secured bondholders, who would be paid in due course what they were owed by Sigma. But in the catastrophic financial crash of late 2008, it turned out that if the security

38 *Pixdene Ltd v Paddington and Company Ltd* [2022] EWHC 2765 (IPEC).
39 [2023] EWHC 3285 (Comm).
40 [2009] UKSC 2.

trustee had obeyed the direction to satisfy holders of Short Term Liabilities during the Realisation Period, there would be nothing left over for the other secured noteholders *at all*. The Supreme Court concluded that the provisions were

> all drafted on the assumption of a situation in which Sigma has enough assets to cover at least its secured creditors.[41]

So the drafter, in providing for an unqualified direction in relation to the Realisation Period, made an assumption that, however safe it seemed at the time, proved totally wrong; and pitched the parties into litigation.

What if exchange rates fluctuate?

13.15 In a world where exchange rates fluctuate, contracting parties will always need to consider whether they are exposed to unwelcome currency movements, and to hedge against them. Of course, a party can choose to do this on its own account by entering into an external hedge. But the parties need also to consider whether and how to address the possibility of currency fluctuation within the four corners of the contract.

A case where the parties apparently failed to address this question (or thought they had addressed it but failed) is *The Procter & Gamble Company v Svenska Cellulosa Aktiebolaget SCA*.[42] A contract for the supply of paper products by Procter & Gamble to Svenska was apparently intended, because of the circumstances in which it was entered into, to reflect P&G's costs of manufacture. But these costs were mostly in sterling. The contract fixed a purchase price for the products in euros, the amount of which had been established by projecting the sterling costs at a fixed forward sterling/euro exchange rate. When sterling weakened against the euro by more than the forward rate inherently assumed, Svenska turned out to be paying P&G more than P&G's actual costs. But that was a risk that had not been squared away in the contract, and Svenska had to shoulder the full costs. Moore-Bick LJ observed:[43]

> No one perhaps anticipated that there would be such a material change in the £/€ rate within the next year from that which the parties had adopted for the purpose of calculating their agreed prices. If so, that would reflect a lacuna in the contract…contract calculations are frequently capable of being disappointed by unforeseen exchange rate fluctuations.

41 ibid at [13] (Lord Mance). If Lord Mance was right about what the drafter had assumed, the assumption could scarcely have been more wrong: the aggregate amount owed to the secured creditors was around $6.2 billion, the amount of the proceeds of its assets around $450 million (only around one-fifteenth as much).
42 [2012] EWCA Civ 1413.
43 ibid at [37].

In other words, Svenska had not asked: what if the actual exchange rates differ materially from the forward rate assumed when fixing the price?

What if an externally-provided benchmark changes?

13.16 Parties may rely on information derived from a third party to determine (say) the level of payments required under their contract. But the drafter should ask: what if that information ceases to be available, either at all or in its current form?

This caused a dispute in *Regal Seas Maritime SA v Oldendorff Carriers GmbH and Co KG*,[44] which involved the charter of a vessel weighing around 180,000 tons. The charter payments were set by adjusting rates published by the Baltic Exchange, which at the time of the charter related to vessels of 172,000 tons. So the charter provided for a 4% adjustment to the Baltic Exchange published rate to find the contractual charterhire. But the drafter did not address what contractual consequence would follow from the change of the weight used by the Baltic Exchange as the basis for the figures it published. Accordingly, when the Baltic Exchange stopped publishing rates for a 172,000 ton vessel in favour of a different tonnage, the contract did not provide any fallback for establishing the contractual charterhire. A court case duly ensued.

OTHER 'WHAT IF?' QUESTIONS

While the 'What if?' questions identified below are less obvious than those discussed above, the drafter would ideally have asked them in the cases discussed. Had that happened, a great deal of cost and anxiety might have been avoided.

What if the legal or regulatory environment changes?

13.17 The legal and regulatory environment is likely to be subject to changes over which the parties have no control, and any changes could have an unpredictable outcome on the parties' position. Changes of this type tend therefore to be more difficult to draft for than questions of a party's insolvency, whose effect may be drastic but is at least easy to envisage.

An example of how hard it is to draft effectively in this area is *BNY Mellon Corporate Trustee Services Limited v LBG Capital No 1 Plc*,[45] in which the drafters had to try and craft terms and conditions for a note issue that made sense in

44 [2021] EWHC 566.
45 [2016] UKSC 29.

the context of a regulatory landscape that was fluid. The aim was to allow an issuing company in the Lloyds Bank group to redeem the notes if they ceased to confer the regulatory capital benefit that had caused them to be issued in the first place. All this was occurring against a regulatory capital background that was expected to change, given the turmoil in the financial markets in 2009 when the notes were issued.

The drafters did their best. They managed to foresee that the regulator itself might be replaced, so the definition of the regulator extended to any successor regulator.[46] But they were less successful when they provided that redemption would be triggered if the notes

> cease to be taken into account … for the purposes of any stress test applied by the [regulator] in respect of the Consolidated Core Tier I Ratio.

This ratio was crucial when the notes were issued. But later regulatory changes made that particular ratio beside the point. At a practical level, the notes no longer did the job that Lloyds had issued them to do. Lloyds managed in the end to persuade the courts that it deserved to be able to redeem the notes. But the regulatory landscape had changed in such a way that the test as drafted, referring to a defunct ratio, did not really meet the underlying purpose.[47] Whilst nobody could really criticise the drafters in the extreme circumstances at play in this case, it does emphasise that drafters' 'What if?' questions need to address the legal and regulatory framework of the contract, and try to address what should happen if that changes in a way that can realistically be envisaged.

What if a third party proves uncooperative?

13.18 A drafter may well draft provisions that rely on a third party performing some role in the contractual mechanism. Though of course the third party is not bound by a contract which it has not itself signed, it may look reasonable to rely on the third party doing what is expected, particularly if it is a professional organisation with an existing relationship with one of the contracting parties. But what if, after the contract has been signed, the third party proves unwilling to play the role envisaged for it? In *Asher v Jaywing plc*,[48] that is exactly what happened. The mechanism for calculating an earn-out

[46] Sure enough, by the time the relevant term had to be tested, the Financial Services Authority had been replaced by the Prudential Regulation Authority. Regulatory authorities tend to come and go with a regularity depressing to the drafter. For example, the Independent Broadcasting Authority or IBA, responsible for regulating the independent television network in 1990 when the contracts in *Excelsior Group Productions Ltd v Yorkshire Television Ltd* ([2009] EWHC 1751 (Comm)) were put in place, had been dissolved and replaced by the Independent Television Commission by the time the contracts fell to be litigated.

[47] With the benefit of hindsight, the drafters might perhaps have been better to draft in terms of a broader principle of the type of regulatory capital benefit that the notes had to continue to deliver in order to be spared from redemption.

[48] [2022] EWHC 893 (Ch).

payment on sale of a company contemplated that the purchaser's auditors would prepare a statement calculating the earn-out payment. But the auditors, presumably fearing a conflict of interest, declined to do so.[49] The drafting did not cater for this happening: only the finding of an implied term saved the drafter's blushes. If the drafter had identified the 'What if?' question at the drafting stage, the problem could have been addressed.

Looked at a different way, the case serves to reinforce a recommendation made at **13.3** above: that the drafter should verify whatever can be verified before the contract date. Presumably, if the auditors had been asked before the contract was signed: 'will you be prepared to draw up a statement calculating the earn-out amount?' they would have said that they would or might decline to do so. That would surely have prompted the drafter to plug the gap in the drafting.

What if a new scientific development renders the drafting obsolete?

13.19 A failure of to ask this type of 'What if?' question undermined the drafting at issue in *BAI (Run Off) Limited (in scheme of arrangement) v Durham.*[50] Insurance policies designed to protect employers against claims from employees suffering injury at work either applied or did not apply depending on whether the injury was 'sustained' or a disease 'contracted' during the year covered by the policy. In a straightforward case (where a worker say fell from a ladder) there would be no difficulty in establishing the year this happened. But for industrial diseases like mesothelioma, the disease might manifest itself only several years after the worker was exposed to the hazard that eventually manifested itself when the worker became obviously ill. This might not have mattered too much if an employer had always used the same insurer. But if an employer did change insurer, the question as to which year the injury or disease was sustained or contracted became critical.

The drafter's failure was to fail to ask the quasi-scientific 'What if' question: what if it is not clear, with a disease of long gestation, when it can be said to have been 'contracted'? The failure was to use language that was not sophisticated enough to deal with a case when a disease developed over a number of years rather than as an immediate result of a single accident.

A similar example of nature confounding drafters' expectations can be seen in one of the many pieces of litigation relating to business interruption cover following the Covid-19 pandemic, *Financial Conduct Authority v Arch Insurance (UK) Ltd.*[51] The cover in some policies related to losses covered by

49 ibid at [235].
50 [2012] UKSC 14.
51 [2021] UKSC 1.

the 'occurrence' of a notifiable disease within a stated radius of the insured's business premises. But an 'occurrence' suggested a particular event occurring at a particular time and place, and in a particular way. As the Supreme Court pointed out:[52]

> a disease that spreads is not something that occurs at a particular time and place and in a particular way: it occurs at a multiplicity of different times and places.

The language in the policies was not well-fitted to capture the events that happened.

Technological advances can easily outstrip the drafter's expectations. In a 1990 contract designed to reward a television production company for the broadcast of some of its productions, the drafter used the concept of broadcast

> from all the transmitters of the IBA[53] serving ITV or Channel Four

to describe the type of broadcast that would attract a higher royalty rate than other types of broadcast. At the time, all the transmitters were analogue transmitters. Satellite and cable transmission was in its infancy, and digital transmission of terrestrial television lay in the future. So the broadcast of the programmes on digital transmitters could, to the disappointment of the production company, command only the lower royalty rate.[54]

The drafter here was faced with the problem that contracts fall to be interpreted as at the time they were made. So to deal explicitly with the question: what if technology permits different modes of broadcast? The drafter would have had to draft something like

> transmission in any manner, whether through transmitters of the type currently used for the purpose or through other methods of transmission of any type in use at any future date.

What if one of the parties tries to exploit shortcomings in the drafting?

13.20 If the objective is to *prevent* an event taking place, the drafter's question should be directed at identifying all the ways in which it could take place, not merely the most obvious one. This is particularly the case if the outcome to be prevented is one that one of the contracting parties may actively want to achieve.

52 ibid at [69].
53 The Independent Broadcasting Authority, the then regulator set up under the Broadcasting Act 1981.
54 *Excelsior Group Productions Ltd v Yorkshire Television Ltd* [2009] EWHC 1751 (Comm).

In *McKillen v Misland (Cyprus) Investments Ltd*,[55] the drafting of a shareholders' agreement imposed detailed pre-emption provisions relating to the shares of a company (Coroin) set up to acquire control of four landmark London hotels. But the drafting bit only at the level of shares in Coroin itself. The agreement did therefore apply to prevent any one shareholder group acquiring control of the hotels by acquiring shares in Coroin without going through the pre-emption mechanism. But they did not inhibit a shareholder group acquiring control by doing so *indirectly* – by acquiring from another group all the shares in a company that *itself* held shares in Coroin.

Assuming that the drafter would have wanted to prevent control being acquired by such a manoeuvre, the drafting failure was to concentrate single-mindedly on the most obvious way of acquiring control of Coroin, at the expense of thinking about other strategies that a determined and inventive shareholder might resort to. The drafting could perhaps have proceeded by a statement of *objectives* or *principles* rather than *mechanics.* An alternative would have been a recital of the intended objective of the pre-emption, together with an operative provision requiring the parties not to take any steps that would frustrate that objective. The expression 'directly or indirectly' would also have helped.

A similar issue arose in *Aberdeen City Council v Stewart Milne Group Ltd.*[56] A seller of land was entitled to an uplifted in the sales price if the purchaser on-sold the land. But the drafting assumed that any sale would be at a full price. The purchaser, however, tried to exploit the naiveté of the drafting by selling to an associated company at an undervalue. The drafter did not ask the question: what if the assumption that any sale will be at full value proves false?[57]

What if the contract deals with existing events of a particular type, but future instances also occur?

13.21 Sometimes – particularly with a settlement or compromise agreement – the drafter fails to ask: what if the events I know about are not the only ones that have occurred or may occur? This may lead to uncertainty over whether the agreement deals only with already existing or already identified events, or is meant to embrace future examples that have either not happened yet, or have happened but not yet been identified. For example, does a 'full and final settlement of all or any claims' include future claims, or just claims already made?[58]

55 [2012] EWCA Civ 179.

56 [2011] UKSC 56.

57 The Supreme Court managed to spare the drafter's blushes by creatively finding an implied term to achieve the result the express drafting had not on its face succeeded in achieving (ibid at [20] (Lord Hope)).

58 The question that arose in *Bank of Credit and Commerce International SA (in liquidation) v Ali (no. 1)* [2001] UKHL 8: held (Lord Hoffmann dissenting) that the drafter, despite the redundant doubles (see **11.9** above) had not gone far enough to embrace future claims.

For an example of a drafter who went just far enough to preclude future claims leading to liability, see *Point West London Ltd v Mivan Ltd* [2012] EWHC 1223 (TCC).[59] And for drafting that was admirably effective to embrace release of all possible claims, see *Adare Finance DAC v Yellowstone Capital Management SA*.[60]

What if the parties do not discharge their contractual obligations?

13.22 Many drafters would assume that one issue that their drafting does not need to address is the consequence if one party fails to fulfil the obligations it has assumed under the contract itself. If pressed as to why, the drafter might respond by observing that the failure by one party to observe the terms of the contract will necessarily amount to a breach, giving the innocent party at least a remedy in damages, and possibly also the right to terminate the contract if the breach is serious enough.

It is understandable that this 'What if?' question is not uppermost in drafters' minds. But they should not ignore it. In particular, it cannot be assumed that the common law applied to a contract will always lead to a clear answer. And if the contract does not make the consequences clear, the consequence can be a dispute which the parties will not thank the drafter for landing them in.

For example, in *Griffon Shipping LLC v Firodi Shipping Ltd*,[61] a ship was sold under the terms of a contract heavily based on a standard form (the 'Norwegian Saleform'). This standard form was in common use,[62] and provided for a purchaser of a vessel to pay a deposit within a specified period. The standard form did not stipulate all the consequences that would flow if the purchaser failed to pay the deposit. The seller could clearly cancel the agreement. But the contract was silent as to whether the seller could also recover the unpaid deposit.

The answer turned out to be that the seller could indeed recover the deposit. But the contract's silence forced the seller to resort to law: the parties would have been clearer about the position if the contract had been explicit and comprehensive about the consequences of the purchaser failing to meet its contractual obligations.

59 The drafter, not apparently a lawyer, crucially included the words 'together with any and all outstanding matters': this was enough to signify that future potential liabilities of a sub-contractor were within the scope of the settlement, though not so clearly that the contractor did not feel it was worth bringing a case to argue the contrary.

60 [2020] EWHC 2776 (release of 'all obligations, undertakings, duties, responsibilities and liabilities of any kind (past, present, future, actual or contingent or otherwise)': the judge commented on the 'breadth and all-embracing nature' of the language (at [113]).

61 [2013] EWCA Civ 1567.

62 Tomlinson LJ described it (ibid at [1]) as 'the most commonly used form of contract for the sale and purchase of second hand tonnage'. A version of this form of contract also featured in *King Crude Carriers SA v Ridgebury November LLC* [2023] EWHC 3220 (Comm): see **13.5** above.

What if developments in the future reverse direction (if 'prices go down as well as up')?

13.23 Inadequate 'What if?' reasoning can cause difficulties if the drafter does not think through what should happen if a change of circumstances occurs but the status quo is subsequently reinstated. This is akin to failing to distinguish between trigger conditions and state-of-affairs conditions (see **9.29** above).

For example, where a seller of a private company breaches a warranty, drafters often acknowledge in their drafting that the breach may be 'remedied' or 'cured', with the consequence that the pre-breach status quo deserves to be reinstated. The drafting may accordingly allow a grace period. If the breach is remedied or cured within the grace period, the purchaser's right to damages for the temporary breach is cancelled: the raison d'être for a claim has disappeared. In other words, the breach is treated as a state-of-affairs condition.

With financial covenants in loan arrangements, the drafting usually requires the borrower's financial position to be assessed at regular specific dates rather than continuously. Particular care is needed to make sure these tests are described so as to work coherently; otherwise, drafting that treats the covenants as trigger conditions risks collapsing a perfectly viable financing structure.[63] A similar concept underlies language in loan documentation that allows a lender to accelerate repayments if the borrower has committed a default only if the breach 'is continuing'.

It is easy to overlook, if a contractual provision requires an outcome to be determined by the movement of a price or market index, that fluctuations are unpredictable. For example, the level of market rents can go up or go down over a period, and the direction in any period may well be different from that in the previous one. The drafter of a lease therefore needs to ask: what if rents go up in one rent review period but down in the next? The failure to ask that question can cause a rental adjustment clause to be unclear in its effect.[64]

A similar issue arises if a contractual payment depending on a formula is expected to flow in one direction, from party A to party B, but in the events that happen the formula unexpectedly throws up a negative number. Can that lead to B having to pay A? The answer was held to be no in *Westminster City Council v Sports and Leisure Management Ltd*,[65] but the court only reached

63 As nearly happened in *LB Re Financing No. 3 Ltd v Excalibur Funding No 1 Plc* [2011] EWHC 2111, where a glitch in the drafting caused one of the financial tests to be failed on a 'Determination Date', even though cash would clearly become available three days later.

64 As in *Scottish Widows Fund & Life Assurance Society v BGC International* [2012] EWCA Civ 607 (see also **5.7** above).

65 [2021] EWHC 98 (TCC).

this answer by clues derived from the context. It would have been better if the drafter had made it explicit that the formula could not result in what must have seemed to one of the parties as water flowing uphill.

What if individual events too small to have a particular contractual effect combine to cause a more serious issue?

13.24 Parties to a contract may often agree to ignore minor breaches. This reflects common sense. The remedy for a minor breach of contract is likely to be a trivial sum by way of damages, which it is not worth the innocent party's while to enforce.

Similarly, it is incongruous for a party who does not want a contract to survive to be able to bring it to an end on the pretext of a breach by the other party that, looked at objectively, is of minor importance. For that reason, modern English judges will resist allowing a party to bring a contract to an end simply because the other party has breached a term of a contract labelled as a 'condition'.[66] Instead, if the consequences of a breach are not specified in the contract itself, a court is more likely to look to see whether the consequences of the breach are objectively serious enough to warrant termination, whatever the breached term is called, or whether the innocent party should have a right only to damages.[67]

In some contracts, drafters are used to reflecting this type of hierarchy of breach. For example, in a sale and purchase agreement under which the seller gives the buyer warranties about the company being sold, the drafting of the clause may state expressly that a breach which would give rise to a claim falling below a particular monetary threshold is to be ignored.

Individual minor breaches, however, may in combination amount to a problem that is too significant to be ignored. In the context of breaches of warranty, that issue is often addressed by providing that, if the cumulative total of damages for breaches minor in themselves exceeds a specified threshold, the buyer can make a claim for the aggregate amount.

That type of concept is easier to draft for in cases where (as in a share sale) the relationship between the parties is otherwise complete, and no longer depends on cooperation. It is harder to deal with when a contract is ongoing. And difficulties can arise if the contract purports to distinguish between categories of breach, some less important and some more important, qualitatively rather by reference to value. What if the breaches that occur are of themselves in the

66 *Schuler (LG) AG v Wickman Machine Tools Sales Ltd* [1974] 1 AC 235.
67 *Hongkong Fir Shipping Co Ltd v Kawasaki Kisen Kaisha Ltd* [1962] 2 QB 26.

minor category, but occur in a combination that causes a major difficulty for the other party?[68]

Reasonableness as a way of fudging 'What if?' questions

13.25 Drafters may reasonably acknowledge that there is a limit to being able to predict what the future might bring, and that an unknowable set of circumstances may cause drafting prepared today to look a mistake tomorrow. They may therefore sensibly qualify an obligation or a contractual threshold by stipulating that it is to be undertaken or applies only if it is 'reasonable'.[69] Reasonableness is an objective test that the courts can evaluate, so there should be no risk of the uncertainty over what will turn out to be reasonable rendering the contract, or part of it, void for uncertainty.

But there is no guarantee that a 'reasonableness' override will eliminate difficulties in the future, as parties that have divergent interests may very well have divergent views on what is reasonable.

In *Porton Capital Technology Funds v 3M UK Holdings Ltd*[70] the sellers of a biomedical company were entitled to an earn-out payment dependent on the post-sale revenues from certain products. The business could not be closed down following the sale without the consent of the sellers, 'which shall not be unreasonably withheld'. Following the sale, the purchasers asserted that the business was uneconomic and shut it down, despite the sellers refusing to consent.

The drafting point here is that providing for the consent not to be 'unreasonably withheld' may have seemed, at the time of drafting the contract, an uncontroversial piece of drafting which was likely to reduce the chances of a dispute. But it did not, and the dispute that arose was hard-fought and doubtless costly.[71]

To put the same point a different way, the drafter had creditably identified, in the context of the transaction, the 'What if' question: what if the purchasers want to shut the business down? But the contractual answer 'they can do so only if the sellers give consent, which they must do unless it is reasonable for them to withhold it' succeeded only in postponing the problem, not lancing the boil. The criterion of reasonableness is objective, but not as objective as

[68] In *GB Gas Holdings Ltd v Accenture (UK) Ltd* [2010] EWCA Civ 912, the contract drew a distinction between 'Material Defects' (adverse effect on the business of British Gas) and 'Fundamental Defects' (severe adverse effect on that business). But the contract was unclear as to whether individual breaches of warranty, each of would not cause a 'Fundamental Defect' in itself, could be aggregated so as to amount to one.

[69] See also the discussion of 'reasonable endeavours' clauses in **3.16**.

[70] [2011] EWHC 2895 (Comm).

[71] It is apparent from the report of the case (ibid) that the parties spent 23 days in court arguing about this and other points.

hard numbers would have been. If the drafter had spent a single day drafting a set of numerical criteria – sales figures or profit figures which would represent a threshold below which the purchasers would be entitled to shut the business down, perhaps – that might have saved the 23 days in court later on. The reasonableness criterion in this case, therefore, turned out to have been an expensive fudge.

Index

[*All references are to paragraph numbers*]